ORDER OF
CHRISTIAN FUNERALS

APPROVED FOR USE IN THE DIOCESES OF THE UNITED STATES OF AMERICA BY THE
NATIONAL CONFERENCE OF CATHOLIC BISHOPS AND CONFIRMED BY THE APOSTOLIC SEE

Prepared by
International Commission on English in the Liturgy
A Joint Commission of Catholic Bishops' Conferences

Concordat cum originali: Ronald F. Krisman, Executive Director
Bishops' Committee on the Liturgy
National Conference of Catholic Bishops

Approved by the National Conference of Catholic Bishops for use
in the dioceses of the United States of America, 14 November 1985.
Confirmed by decree of the Congregation for Divine Worship,
29 April 1987 (Prot. No. CD 1550/85).

Published by authority of the Bishops' Committee on the Liturgy,
National Conference of Catholic Bishops.

ACKNOWLEDGMENTS

The English translation, original texts, general introduction, pastoral notes, arrangement,
and design of *Order of Christian Funerals* © 1989, 1985, International Committee on English
in the Liturgy, Inc. (ICEL); excerpts from the English translation of *The Roman Missal*
© 1973, ICEL; excerpts from the English translation of *Holy Communion and Worship of
the Eucharist outside Mass* © 1974, ICEL; excerpts from the English translation of *The Liturgy
of the Hours* © 1974, ICEL; excerpts from *Pastoral Care of the Sick: Rites of Anointing and Viaticum* © 1982, ICEL. All rights reserved.

The Scripture readings are taken from *The New American Bible with Revised New Testament*,
copyright © 1986, Confraternity of Christian Doctrine, Washington D.C. Used by license
of copyright owner. All rights reserved.

Psalm texts from *The Psalms: A New Translation* © The Grail (England) 1963. The complete psalms first published in 1963 by and available through Wm. Collins, Sons & Company, Ltd. In North America through the Paulist Press, Inc. and Collins + World. Used
by permission.

Prayer texts of committal, "In sure and certain hope . . ." and "Into your hands, O merciful Savior, . . .," used by permission, from the *Book of Common Prayer*, 1979, published by
The Church Pension Fund.

ISBN 0-930467-68-X

Cover art, Steve Erspamer.

Printed and bound in the United States of America.

Copyright © 1990, Archdiocese of Chicago. All rights reserved.

Liturgy Training Publications, 1800 North Hermitage Avenue, Chicago, Illinois 60622-1101;
312/486-7008.

DECREE

In accord with the norms established by decree of the Sacred Congregation of Rites *Cum, nostra aetate* (27 January 1966), the *Order of Christian Funerals* is declared to be the vernacular typical edition of the *Ordo Exsequiarum* for the dioceses of the United States of America, and may be published by authority of the National Conference of Catholic Bishops.

The *Order of Christian Funerals* was canonically approved by the National Conference of Catholic Bishops in plenary assembly on 14 November 1985 and was subsequently confirmed by the Apostolic See by decree of the Congregation for Divine Worship on 29 April 1987 (Prot. N. CD 1550/85).

On 1 October 1989 the *Order of Christian Funerals* may be published and used in funeral celebrations. From All Souls Day, 2 November 1989, its use is mandatory in the dioceses of the United States of America. From that date forward no other English version of these rites may be used.

Given at the General Secretariat of the National Conference of Catholic Bishops, Washington, D.C., on 15 August 1989, the Solemnity of the Assumption.

℣ John L. May
Archbishop of Saint Louis
President
National Conference of Catholic Bishops

Robert N. Lynch
General Secretary

CONTENTS

EDITORIAL NOTE

Beginning with the General Introduction, the numbering system in this book diverges from the Latin edition of *Ordo Exsequiarum*. The new numbering system appears at the left-hand side of the page. The corresponding number from the Latin edition appears in the right-hand margin. A text having a number on the left but no reference number in the right-hand margin is either newly composed or is a text from *The Roman Missal*, *Holy Communion and Worship of the Eucharist outside Mass*, *The Liturgy of the Hours*, or *Pastoral Care of the Sick: Rites of Anointing and Viaticum*.

"Funeral rites" is a general designation used of all the liturgical celebrations in this book. "Funeral liturgy" is a more particular designation applied to the two forms of liturgical celebration presented under the headings "Funeral Mass" and "Funeral Liturgy outside Mass."

Part IV presents morning prayer and evening prayer of the office for the dead from *The Liturgy of the Hours*.

Part V contains "Holy Communion outside Mass," which is an excerpt from *Holy Communion and Worship of the Eucharist outside Mass*.

CONGREGATION FOR DIVINE WORSHIP

Prot. no. 720/69

DECREE

By means of the funeral rites it has been the practice of the Church, as a tender mother, not simply to commend the dead to God but also to raise high the hope of its children and to give witness to its own faith in the future resurrection of the baptized with Christ.

Vatican Council II accordingly directed in the Constitution on the Liturgy that the funeral rites be revised in such a way that they would more clearly express the paschal character of the Christian's death and also that the rites for the burial of children would have a proper Mass (art. 81-82).

The Consilium prepared the desired rites and put them into trial use in different parts of the world. Now Pope Paul VI by his apostolic authority has approved and ordered the publication of these rites as henceforth obligatory for all those using the Roman Ritual.

Also by order of Pope Paul this Congregation for Divine Worship promulgates the *Order of Funerals*, stipulating that its effective date is 1 June 1970.

The Congregation further establishes that until 1 June 1970, when Latin is used in celebrating funerals there is an option to use either the present rite or the rite now in the Roman Ritual; after 1 June 1970 only this new *Order of Funerals* is to be used.

Once the individual conferences of bishops have prepared a vernacular version of the rite and received its confirmation from this Congregation, they have authorization to fix any other, feasible effective date prior to 1 June 1970 for use of the *Order of Funerals*.

All things to the contrary notwithstanding.

Congregation for Divine Worship, 15 August 1969, the solemnity of the Assumption.

Benno Cardinal Gut
Prefect

A. Bugnini
Secretary

ORDER OF
CHRISTIAN FUNERALS

Why do you search for the Living One among the dead?

ORDER OF CHRISTIAN FUNERALS

GENERAL INTRODUCTION

1   In the face of death, the Church confidently proclaims that God has created each person for eternal life and that Jesus, the Son of God, by his death and resurrection, has broken the chains of sin and death that bound humanity. Christ "achieved his task of redeeming humanity and giving perfect glory to God, principally by the paschal mystery of his blessed passion, resurrection from the dead, and glorious ascension."[1]

2   The proclamation of Jesus Christ "who was put to death for our sins and raised to life to justify us" (Romans 4:25) is at the center of the Church's life. The mystery of the Lord's death and resurrection gives power to all of the Church's activity. "For it was from the side of Christ as he slept the sleep of death upon the cross that there came forth the sublime sacrament of the whole Church."[2] The Church's liturgical and sacramental life and proclamation of the Gospel make this mystery present in the life of the faithful. Through the sacraments of baptism, confirmation, and eucharist, men and women are initiated into this mystery. "You have been taught that when we were baptized in Christ Jesus we were baptized into his death; in other words when we were baptized we went into the tomb with him and joined him in death, so that as Christ was raised from the dead by the Father's glory, we too might live a new life. If in union with Christ we have imitated his death, we shall also imitate him in his resurrection" (Romans 6:3-5).

3   In the eucharistic sacrifice, the Church's celebration of Christ's Passover from death to life, the faith of the baptized in the paschal mystery is renewed and nourished. Their union with Christ and with each other is strengthened: "Because there is one bread, we who are many, are one body, for we all partake of the one bread" (1 Corinthians 10:17).

4   At the death of a Christian, whose life of faith was begun in the waters of baptism and strengthened at the eucharistic table, the Church intercedes on behalf of the deceased because of its confident belief that death is not the end nor does it break the bonds forged in life. The Church also ministers to the sorrowing and consoles them in the funeral rites with the comforting word of God and the sacrament of the eucharist.

---

[1] Vatican Council II, Constitution on the Liturgy *Sacrosanctum Concilium*, art. 5.

[2] Ibid.

5   Christians celebrate the funeral rites to offer worship, praise, and thanksgiving to God for the gift of a life which has now been returned to God, the author of life and the hope of the just. The Mass, the memorial of Christ's death and resurrection, is the principal celebration of the Christian funeral.

6   The Church through its funeral rites commends the dead to God's merciful love and pleads for the forgiveness of their sins. At the funeral rites, especially at the celebration of the eucharistic sacrifice, the Christian community affirms and expresses the union of the Church on earth with the Church in heaven in the one great communion of saints. Though separated from the living, the dead are still at one with the community of believers on earth and benefit from their prayers and intercession. At the rite of final commendation and farewell, the community acknowledges the reality of separation and commends the deceased to God. In this way it recognizes the spiritual bond that still exists between the living and the dead and proclaims its belief that all the faithful will be raised up and reunited in the new heavens and a new earth, where death will be no more.

7   The celebration of the Christian funeral brings hope and consolation to the living. While proclaiming the Gospel of Jesus Christ and witnessing to Christian hope in the resurrection, the funeral rites also recall to all who take part in them God's mercy and judgment and meet the human need to turn always to God in times of crisis.

MINISTRY AND PARTICIPATION

8   "If one member suffers in the body of Christ which is the Church, all the members suffer with that member" (1 Corinthians 12:26). For this reason, those who are baptized into Christ and nourished at the same table of the Lord are responsible for one another. When Christians are sick, their brothers and sisters share a ministry of mutual charity and "do all that they can to help the sick return to health, by showing love for the sick, and by celebrating the sacraments with them."[3] So too when a member of Christ's Body dies, the faithful are called to a ministry of consolation to those who have suffered the loss of one whom they love. Christian consolation is rooted in that hope that comes from faith in the saving death and resurrection of the Lord Jesus Christ. Christian hope faces the reality of death and the anguish of grief but trusts confidently that the power of sin and death has been vanquished by the risen Lord. The Church calls each member of Christ's Body—priest, deacon, layperson—to participate

---

[3] See Roman Ritual, *Pastoral Care of the Sick: Rites of Anointing and Viaticum*, General Introduction, no. 33.

in the ministry of consolation: to care for the dying, to pray for the dead, to comfort those who mourn.

COMMUNITY

9   The responsibility for the ministry of consolation rests with the believing community, which heeds the words and example of the Lord Jesus: "Blessed are they who mourn; they shall be consoled" (Matthew 5:3). Each Christian shares in this ministry according to the various gifts and offices in the Church. As part of the pastoral ministry, pastors, associate pastors, and other ministers should instruct the parish community on the Christian meaning of death and on the purpose and significance of the Church's liturgical rites for the dead. Information on how the parish community assists families in preparing for funerals should also be provided.

By giving instruction, pastors and associate pastors should lead the community to a deeper appreciation of its role in the ministry of consolation and to a fuller understanding of the significance of the death of a fellow Christian. Often the community must respond to the anguish voiced by Martha, the sister of Lazarus: "Lord, if you had been here, my brother would never have died" (John 11:21) and must console those who mourn, as Jesus himself consoled Martha: "Your brother will rise again. . . . I am the resurrection and the life: those who believe in me, though they should die, will come to life; and those who are alive and believe in me will never die" (John 11:25-26). The faith of the Christian community in the resurrection of the dead brings support and strength to those who suffer the loss of those whom they love.

10   Members of the community should console the mourners with words of faith and support and with acts of kindness, for example, assisting them with some of the routine tasks of daily living. Such assistance may allow members of the family to devote time to planning the funeral rites with the priest and other ministers and may also give the family time for prayer and mutual comfort.

11   The community's principal involvement in the ministry of consolation is expressed in its active participation in the celebration of the funeral rites, particularly the vigil for the deceased, the funeral liturgy, and the rite of committal. For this reason these rites should be scheduled at times that permit as many of the community as possible to be present. The assembly's participation can be assisted by the preparation of booklets that contain an outline of the rite, the texts and songs belonging to the people, and directions for posture, gesture, and movement.

12   At the vigil for the deceased or on another occasion before the eucharistic celebration, the presiding minister should invite all to be present at the funeral liturgy and to take an active part in it. The minister may

also describe the funeral liturgy and explain why the community gathers to hear the word of God proclaimed and to celebrate the eucharist when one of the faithful dies.

Pastors, associate pastors, and other ministers should also be mindful of those persons who are not members of the Catholic Church, or Catholics who are not involved in the life of the Church.

13   As a minister of reconciliation, the priest should be especially sensitive to the possible needs for reconciliation felt by the family and others. Funerals can begin the process of reconciling differences and supporting those ties that can help the bereaved adjust to the loss brought about by death. With attentiveness to each situation, the priest can help to begin the process of reconciliation when needed. In some cases this process may find expression in the celebration of the sacrament of penance, either before the funeral liturgy or at a later time.

LITURGICAL MINISTERS

Presiding Minister

14   Priests, as teachers of faith and ministers of comfort, preside at the funeral rites, especially the Mass; the celebration of the funeral liturgy is especially entrusted to pastors and associate pastors. When no priest is available, deacons, as ministers of the word, of the altar, and of charity, preside at funeral rites. When no priest or deacon is available for the vigil and related rites or the rite of committal, a layperson presides.

Other Liturgical Ministers

15   In the celebration of the funeral rites laymen and laywomen may serve as readers, musicians, ushers, pallbearers, and, according to existing norms, as special ministers of the eucharist. Pastors and other priests should instill in these ministers an appreciation of how much the reverent exercise of their ministries contributes to the celebration of the funeral rites. Family members should be encouraged to take an active part in these ministries, but they should not be asked to assume any role that their grief or sense of loss may make too burdensome.

MINISTRY FOR THE MOURNERS AND THE DECEASED

FAMILY AND FRIENDS

16   In planning and carrying out the funeral rites the pastor and all other ministers should keep in mind the life of the deceased and the circumstances of death. They should also take into consideration the spiritual and psychological needs of the family and friends of the deceased to express grief

and their sense of loss, to accept the reality of death, and to comfort one another.

17 Whenever possible, ministers should involve the family in planning the funeral rites: in the choice of texts and rites provided in the ritual, in the selection of music for the rites, and in the designation of liturgical ministers.

Planning of the funeral rites may take place during the visit of the pastor or other minister at some appropriate time after the death and before the vigil service. Ministers should explain to the family the meaning and significance of each of the funeral rites, especially the vigil, the funeral liturgy, and the rite of committal.

If pastoral and personal considerations allow, the period before death may be an appropriate time to plan the funeral rites with the family and even with the family member who is dying. Although planning the funeral before death should be approached with sensitivity and care, it can have the effect of helping the one who is dying and the family face the reality of death with Christian hope. It can also help relieve the family of numerous details after the death and may allow them to benefit more fully from the celebration of the funeral rites.

Deceased

18 Through the celebration of the funeral rites, the Church manifests its care for the dead, both baptized members and catechumens. In keeping with the provisions of *Codex Iuris Canonici*, can. 1183, the Church's funeral rites may be celebrated for a child who died before baptism and whose parents intended to have the child baptized.

At the discretion of the local Ordinary, the Church's funeral rites may be celebrated for a baptized member of another Church or ecclesial community provided this would not be contrary to the wishes of the deceased person and provided the minister of the Church or ecclesial community in which the deceased person was a regular member or communicant is unavailable.

19 Since in baptism the body was marked with the seal of the Trinity and became the temple of the Holy Spirit, Christians respect and honor the bodies of the dead and the places where they rest. Any customs associated with the preparation of the body of the deceased should always be marked with dignity and reverence and never with the despair of those who have no hope. Preparation of the body should include prayer, especially at those intimate moments reserved for family members. For the final disposition of the body, it is the ancient Christian custom to bury or entomb the bodies of the dead; cremation is permitted, unless it is evident that cremation was chosen for anti-Christian motives.

20 In countries or regions where an undertaker, and not the family or community, carries out the preparation and transfer of the body, the

pastor and other ministers are to ensure that the undertakers appreciate the values and beliefs of the Christian community.

The family and friends of the deceased should not be excluded from taking part in the services sometimes provided by undertakers, for example, the preparation and laying out of the body.

LITURGICAL ELEMENTS

21   Since liturgical celebration involves the whole person, it requires attentiveness to all that affects the senses. The readings and prayers, psalms and songs should be proclaimed or sung with understanding, conviction, and reverence. Music for the assembly should be truly expressive of the texts and at the same time simple and easily sung. The ritual gestures, processions, and postures should express and foster an attitude of reverence and reflectiveness in those taking part in the funeral rites. The funeral rites should be celebrated in an atmosphere of simple beauty, in a setting that encourages participation. Liturgical signs and symbols affirming Christian belief and hope in the paschal mystery are abundant in the celebration of the funeral rites, but their undue multiplication or repetition should be avoided. Care must be taken that the choice and use of signs and symbols are in accord with the culture of the people.

THE WORD OF GOD

Readings

22   In every celebration for the dead, the Church attaches great importance to the reading of the word of God. The readings proclaim to the assembly the paschal mystery, teach remembrance of the dead, convey the hope of being gathered together again in God's kingdom, and encourage the witness of Christian life. Above all, the readings tell of God's designs for a world in which suffering and death will relinquish their hold on all whom God has called his own. A careful selection and use of readings from Scripture for the funeral rites will provide the family and the community with an opportunity to hear God speak to them in their needs, sorrows, fears, and hopes.

23   In the celebration of the liturgy of the word at the funeral liturgy, the biblical readings may not be replaced by nonbiblical readings. But during prayer services with the family nonbiblical readings may be used in addition to readings from Scripture.

24   Liturgical tradition assigns the proclamation of the readings in the celebration of the liturgy of the word to readers and the deacon. The presiding minister proclaims the readings only when there are no assisting

ministers present. Those designated to proclaim the word of God should prepare themselves to exercise this ministry.[5]

Psalmody

25   The psalms are rich in imagery, feeling, and symbolism. They power-fully express the suffering and pain, the hope and trust of people of every age and culture. Above all the psalms sing of faith in God, of revelation and redemption. They enable the assembly to pray in the words that Jesus himself used during his life on earth. Jesus, who knew anguish and the fear of death, "offered up prayer and entreaty, aloud and in silent tears, to the one who had the power to save him out of death. . . . Although he was Son, he learned to obey through suffering; but having been made per-fect, he became for all who obey him the source of eternal salvation . . ." (Hebrews 5:7-9). In the psalms the members of the assembly pray in the voice of Christ, who intercedes on their behalf before the Father.[6] The Church, like Christ, turns again and again to the psalms as a genuine ex-pression of grief and of praise and as a sure source of trust and hope in times of trial. Pastors and other ministers are, therefore, to make an ear-nest effort through an effective catechesis to lead their communities to a clearer and deeper grasp of at least some of the psalms provided for the funeral rites.

26   The psalms are designated for use in many places in the funeral rites (for example, as responses to the readings, for the processions, for use at the vigil for the deceased). Since the psalms are songs, whenever possible, they should be sung.

Homily

27   A brief homily based on the readings is always given after the gospel reading at the funeral liturgy and may also be given after the readings at the vigil service; but there is never to be a eulogy. Attentive to the grief of those present, the homilist should dwell on God's compassionate love and on the paschal mystery of the Lord, as proclaimed in the Scripture readings. The homilist should also help the members of the assembly to understand that the mystery of God's love and the mystery of Jesus' vic-torious death and resurrection were present in the life and death of the deceased and that these mysteries are active in their own lives as well. Through the homily members of the family and community should re-ceive consolation and strength to face the death of one of their members with a hope nourished by the saving word of God. Laypersons who pre-side at the funeral rites give an instruction on the readings.

---

[5] See *Lectionary for Mass* (2nd *editio typica*, 1981), General Introduction, nos. 49, 52, and 55.

[6] See General Instruction of the Liturgy of the Hours, no. 109.

Prayers and Intercessions

28   In the presidential prayers of the funeral rites the presiding minister addresses God on behalf of the deceased and the mourners in the name of the entire Church. From the variety of prayers provided the minister in consultation with the family should carefully select texts that truly capture the unspoken prayers and hopes of the assembly and also respond to the needs of the mourners.

29   Having heard the word of God proclaimed and preached, the assembly responds at the vigil and at the funeral liturgy with prayers of intercession for the deceased and all the dead, for the family and all who mourn, and for all in the assembly. The holy people of God, confident in their belief in the communion of saints, exercise their royal priesthood by joining together in this prayer for all those who have died.[7]
    Several models of intercessions are provided within the rites for adaptation to the circumstances.

Music

30   Music is integral to the funeral rites. It allows the community to express convictions and feelings that words alone may fail to convey. It has the power to console and uplift the mourners and to strengthen the unity of the assembly in faith and love. The texts of the songs chosen for a particular celebration should express the paschal mystery of the Lord's suffering, death, and triumph over death and should be related to the readings from Scripture.

31   Since music can evoke strong feelings, the music for the celebration of the funeral rites should be chosen with great care. The music at funerals should support, console, and uplift the participants and should help to create in them a spirit of hope in Christ's victory over death and in the Christian's share in that victory.

32   Music should be provided for the vigil and funeral liturgy and, whenever possible, for the funeral processions and the rite of committal. The specific notes that precede each of these rites suggest places in the rites where music is appropriate. Many musical settings used by the parish community during the liturgical year may be suitable for use at funerals. Efforts should be made to develop and expand the parish's repertoire for use at funerals.

33   An organist or other instrumentalist, a cantor, and, whenever possible, even a choir should assist the assembly's full participation in singing the songs, responses, and acclamations of these rites.

---

[7] See *De Oratione communi seu fidelium* (2nd ed., Vatican Polyglot Press, 1966), chapter 1, no. 3, p. 7: tr., *Documents on the Liturgy* (The Liturgical Press, 1982), no. 1893.

SILENCE

34   Prayerful silence is an element important to the celebration of the funeral rites. Intervals of silence should be observed, for example, after each reading and during the final commendation and farewell, to permit the assembly to reflect upon the word of God and the meaning of the celebration.

SYMBOLS

Easter Candle and Other Candles

35   The Easter candle reminds the faithful of Christ's undying presence among them, of his victory over sin and death, and of their share in that victory by virtue of their initiation. It recalls the Easter Vigil, the night when the Church awaits the Lord's resurrection and when new light for the living and the dead is kindled. During the funeral liturgy and also during the vigil service, when celebrated in the church, the Easter candle may be placed beforehand near the position the coffin will occupy at the conclusion of the procession.

According to local custom, other candles may also be placed near the coffin during the funeral liturgy as a sign of reverence and solemnity.

Holy Water

36   Blessed or holy water reminds the assembly of the saving waters of baptism. In the rite of reception of the body at the church, its use calls to mind the deceased's baptism and initiation into the community of faith. In the rite of final commendation the gesture of sprinkling may also signify farewell.

Incense

37   Incense is used during the funeral rites as a sign of honor to the body of the deceased, which through baptism became the temple of the Holy Spirit. Incense is also used as a sign of the community's prayers for the deceased rising to the throne of God and as a sign of farewell.

Other Symbols

38   If it is the custom in the local community, a pall may be placed over the coffin when it is received at the church. A reminder of the baptismal garment of the deceased, the pall is a sign of the Christian dignity of the person. The use of the pall also signifies that all are equal in the eyes of God (see James 2:1-9).

A Book of the Gospels or a Bible may be placed on the coffin as a sign that Christians live by the word of God and that fidelity to that word leads to eternal life.

A cross may be placed on the coffin as a reminder that the Christian is marked by the cross in baptism and through Jesus' suffering on the cross is brought to the victory of his resurrection.

Fresh flowers, used in moderation, can enhance the setting of the funeral rites.

Only Christian symbols may rest on or be placed near the coffin during the funeral liturgy. Any other symbols, for example, national flags, or flags or insignia of associations, have no place in the funeral liturgy (see no. 132).

Liturgical Color

39   The liturgical color chosen for funerals should express Christian hope but should not be offensive to human grief or sorrow. In the United States, white, violet, or black vestments may be worn at the funeral rites and at other offices and Masses for the dead.

RITUAL GESTURES AND MOVEMENT

40   The presiding minister or an assisting minister may quietly direct the assembly in the movements, gestures, and posture appropriate to the particular ritual moment or action.

41   Processions, especially when accompanied with music and singing, can strengthen the bond of communion in the assembly. For processions, ministers of music should give preference to settings of psalms and songs that are responsorial or litanic in style and that allow the people to respond to the verses with an invariable refrain. During the various processions, it is preferable that the pallbearers carry the coffin as a sign of reverence and respect for the deceased.

42   Processions continue to have special significance in funeral celebrations, as in Christian Rome where funeral rites consisted of three "stages" or "stations" joined by two processions. Christians accompanied the body on its last journey. From the home of the deceased the Christian community proceeded to the church singing psalms. When the service in the church concluded, the body was carried in solemn procession to the grave or tomb. During the final procession the congregation sang psalms praising the God of mercy and redemption and antiphons entrusting the deceased to the care of the angels and saints. The funeral liturgy mirrored the journey of human life, the Christian pilgrimage to the heavenly Jerusalem.

In many places and situations a solemn procession on foot to the church or to the place of committal may not be possible. Nevertheless at the conclusion of the funeral liturgy an antiphon or versicle and response may be sung as the body is taken to the entrance of the church. Psalms, hymns, or liturgical songs may also be sung when the participants gather at the place of committal.

SELECTION OF RITES FROM
THE ORDER OF CHRISTIAN FUNERALS

43   The *Order of Christian Funerals* makes provision for the minister, in consultation with the family, to choose those rites and texts that are most suitable to the situation: those that most closely apply to the needs of the mourners, the circumstances of the death, and the customs of the local Christian community. The minister and family may be assisted in the choice of a rite or rites by the reflections preceding each rite or group of rites.

44   Part I, "Funeral Rites," of the *Order of Christian Funerals* provides those rites that may be used in the funerals of Christians and is divided into three groups of rites that correspond in general to the three principal ritual moments in Christian funerals: "Vigil and Related Rites and Prayers," "Funeral Liturgy," and "Rite of Committal."

45   The section entitled "Vigil and Related Rites and Prayers" includes rites that may be celebrated between the time of death and the funeral liturgy or, should there be no funeral liturgy, before the rite of committal. The vigil is the principal celebration of the Christian community during the time before the funeral liturgy. It may take the form of a liturgy of the word (see nos. 54-97) or of some part of the office for the dead (see Part IV, nos. 348-395). Two vigil services are provided: "Vigil for the Deceased" and "Vigil for the Deceased with Reception at the Church." The second service is used when the vigil is celebrated in the church and the body is to be received at this time.

"Related Rites and Prayers" includes three brief rites that may be used on occasions of prayer with the family: "Prayers after Death," "Gathering in the Presence of the Body," and "Transfer of the Body to the Church or to the Place of Committal." These rites are examples or models of what can be done and should be adapted to the circumstances.

46   The section entitled "Funeral Liturgy" provides two forms of the funeral liturgy, the central celebration of the Christian community for the deceased: "Funeral Mass" and "Funeral Liturgy outside Mass." When one of its members dies, the Church especially encourages the celebration of the Mass. When Mass cannot be celebrated (see no. 178), the second form of the funeral liturgy may be used and a Mass for the deceased should be celebrated, if possible, at a later time.

47   The section entitled "Rite of Committal" includes two forms of the rite of committal, the concluding rite of the funeral: "Rite of Committal"

and "Rite of Committal with Final Commendation." The first form is used when the final commendation is celebrated as part of the conclusion of the funeral liturgy. The second form is used when the final commendation does not take place during the funeral liturgy or when no funeral liturgy precedes the committal.

48   Part II, "Funeral Rites for Children," provides an adaptation of the principal rites in Part I: "Vigil for a Deceased Child," "Funeral Liturgy," and "Rite of Committal." These rites may be used in the funerals of infants and young children, including those of early school age. The rites in Part II include texts for use in the case of a baptized child and in the case of a child who died before baptism.

In some instances, for example, the death of an infant, the vigil and funeral liturgy may not be appropriate. Only the rite of committal and perhaps one of the forms of prayer with the family as provided in "Related Rites and Prayers" may be desirable. Part II does not contain "Related Rites and Prayers," but the rites from Part I may be adapted.

49   Part III, "Texts from Sacred Scripture," includes the Scripture readings and psalms for the celebration of the funeral rites. Part IV, "Office for the Dead," includes "Morning Prayer," "Evening Prayer," and "Additional Hymns." Part V, "Additional Texts," contains "Prayers and Texts in Particular Circumstances" and "Holy Communion outside Mass." The texts that appear in the various rites in Parts I, II, and IV may be replaced by corresponding readings and psalms given in Part III and by corresponding prayers and texts given in Part V.

PART I
FUNERAL RITES

God is not the God of the dead but of the living;
for in him all are alive

PART I
FUNERAL RITES

50   Part I of the *Order of Christian Funerals* is divided into three groups of rites that correspond in general to the three principal ritual moments in the funerals of Christians: "Vigil and Related Rites and Prayers," "Funeral Liturgy," and "Rite of Committal." The minister, in consultation with those concerned, chooses from within these three groups of rites those that best correspond to the particular needs and customs of the mourners. This choice may be assisted by the reflections given in the General Introduction and in the introduction to each rite or group of rites.

VIGIL
AND RELATED RITES
AND PRAYERS

Do not let your hearts be troubled; trust in God still

VIGIL
AND RELATED RITES
AND PRAYERS

51   The rites provided here may be celebrated between the time of death and the funeral liturgy or, should there be no funeral liturgy, before the rite of committal. Two forms of the vigil are presented here: "Vigil for the Deceased," and "Vigil for the Deceased with Reception at the Church," for convenient use in accord with the circumstances.

"Related Rites and Prayers" includes three brief rites that may be used on occasions of prayer with the family: "Prayers after Death," "Gathering in the Presence of the Body," and "Transfer of the Body to the Church or to the Place of Committal." These rites are examples or models of what can be done and should be adapted to the circumstances.

52   The time immediately following death is often one of bewilderment and may involve shock or heartrending grief for the family and close friends. The ministry of the Church at this time is one of gently accompanying the mourners in their initial adjustment to the fact of death and to the sorrow this entails. Through a careful use of the rites contained in this section, the minister helps the mourners to express their sorrow and to find strength and consolation through faith in Christ and his resurrection to eternal life. The members of the Christian community offer support to the mourners, especially by praying that the one they have lost may have eternal life.

53   Ministers should be aware that the experience of death can bring about in the mourners possible needs for reconciliation. With attentiveness to each situation, the minister can help to begin the process of reconciliation. In some cases this process may find expression in the celebration of the sacrament of penance, either before the funeral liturgy or at a later time.

1 VIGIL FOR THE DECEASED

Happy now are the dead who die in the Lord;
they shall find rest from their labors

54 The vigil for the deceased is the principal rite celebrated by the Christian community in the time following death and before the funeral liturgy, or if there is no funeral liturgy, before the rite of committal. It may take the form either of a liturgy of the word (nos. 69-81, 82-97) or of some part of the office for the dead (see Part IV, p. 296). Two vigil services are provided: "Vigil for the Deceased" and "Vigil for the Deceased with Reception at the Church." The second service is used when the vigil is celebrated in the church and begins with the reception of the body.

55 The vigil may be celebrated in the home of the deceased, in the funeral home, parlor or chapel of rest, or in some other suitable place. It may also be celebrated in the church, but at a time well before the funeral liturgy, so that the funeral liturgy will not be lengthy and the liturgy of the word repetitious. Adaptations of the vigil will often be suggested by the place in which the celebration occurs. A celebration in the home of the deceased, for example, may be simplified and shortened.

If the reception of the body at church is celebrated apart from the vigil or the funeral liturgy, the "Vigil for the Deceased with Reception at the Church" may be used and simplified.

56 At the vigil the Christian community keeps watch with the family in prayer to the God of mercy and finds strength in Christ's presence. It is the first occasion among the funeral rites for the solemn reading of the word of God. In this time of loss the family and community turn to God's word as the source of faith and hope, as light and life in the face of darkness and death. Consoled by the redeeming word of God and by the abiding presence of Christ and his Spirit, the assembly at the vigil calls upon the Father of mercy to receive the deceased into the kingdom of light and peace.

STRUCTURE AND CONTENT OF THE VIGIL

57 The vigil in the form of the liturgy of the word consists of the introductory rites, the liturgy of the word, the prayer of intercession, and a concluding rite.

INTRODUCTORY RITES

58 The introductory rites gather the faithful together to form a community and to prepare all to listen to God's word. The introductory rites of

the vigil for the deceased include the greeting, an opening song, an invitation to prayer, a pause for silent prayer, and an opening prayer.

In the vigil for the deceased with reception at the church, the rite of reception forms the introductory rites (nos. 82-86). In this case the family and others who have accompanied the body are greeted at the entrance of the church. The body is then sprinkled with holy water and, if it is the custom, the pall is placed on the coffin by family members, friends, or the minister. The entrance procession follows, during which a hymn or psalm is sung. At the conclusion of the procession a symbol of the Christian life may be placed on the coffin. Then the invitation to prayer, a pause for silent prayer, and an opening prayer conclude the introductory rites.

The opening song or entrance song should be a profound expression of belief in eternal life and the resurrection of the dead, as well as a prayer of intercession for the dead.

LITURGY OF THE WORD

59 The proclamation of the word of God is the high point and central focus of the vigil. The liturgy of the word usually includes a first reading, responsorial psalm, gospel reading, and homily. A reader proclaims the first reading. The responsorial psalm should be sung, whenever possible. If an assisting deacon is present, he proclaims the gospel reading. Otherwise the presiding minister proclaims the gospel reading.

60 The purpose of the readings at the vigil is to proclaim the paschal mystery, teach remembrance of the dead, convey the hope of being gathered together in God's kingdom, and encourage the witness of Christian life. Above all, the readings tell of God's designs for a world in which suffering and death will relinquish their hold on all whom God has called his own. The responsorial psalm enables the community to respond in faith to the reading and to express its grief and its praise of God. In the selection of readings the needs of the mourners and the circumstances of the death should be kept in mind.

61 A homily based on the readings is given at the vigil to help those present find strength and hope in God's saving word.

PRAYER OF INTERCESSION

62 In the prayer of intercession the community calls upon God to comfort the mourners and to show mercy to the deceased. The prayer of intercession takes the form of a litany, the Lord's Prayer, and a concluding prayer.

After this prayer and before the blessing or at some other suitable time during the vigil, a member of the family or a friend of the deceased may speak in remembrance of the deceased.

CONCLUDING RITE

63 The vigil concludes with a blessing, which may be followed by a liturgical song or a few moments of silent prayer or both.

MINISTRY AND PARTICIPATION

64 Members of the local parish community should be encouraged to participate in the vigil as a sign of concern and support for the mourners. In many circumstances the vigil will be the first opportunity for friends, neighbors, and members of the local parish community to show their concern for the family of the deceased by gathering for prayer. The vigil may also serve as an opportunity for participation in the funeral by those who, because of work or other reasons, cannot be present for the funeral liturgy or the rite of committal.

65 The full participation by all present is to be encouraged. This is best achieved through careful planning of the celebration. Whenever possible, the family of the deceased should take part in the selection of texts and music and in the designation of liturgical ministers.

66 Besides the presiding minister, other available ministers (a reader, a cantor, an acolyte) should exercise their ministries. Family members may assume some of these liturgical roles, unless their grief prevents them from doing so.

The presiding minister and assisting ministers should vest for the vigil according to local custom. If the vigil is celebrated in the church, a priest or deacon who presides wears an alb or surplice with stole.

67 As needs require, and especially if the funeral liturgy or rite of committal is not to take place for a few days, the vigil may be celebrated more than once and should be adapted to each occasion.

68 Music is integral to any vigil, especially the vigil for the deceased. In the difficult circumstances following death, well-chosen music can touch the mourners and others present at levels of human need that words alone often fail to reach. Such music can enliven the faith of the community gathered to support the family and to affirm hope in the resurrection.

Whenever possible, an instrumentalist and a cantor or leader of song should assist the assembly's full participation in the singing.

In the choice of music for the vigil, preference should be given to the singing of the opening song and the responsorial psalm. The litany, the Lord's Prayer, and a closing song may also be sung.

OUTLINE OF THE RITE

INTRODUCTORY RITES

Greeting
Opening Song
Invitation to Prayer
Opening Prayer

LITURGY OF THE WORD

First Reading
Responsorial Psalm
Gospel
Homily

PRAYER OF INTERCESSION

Litany
The Lord's Prayer
Concluding Prayer

CONCLUDING RITE

Blessing

VIGIL FOR THE DECEASED

INTRODUCTORY RITES

GREETING

69   Using one of the following greetings, or in similar words, the minister greets those present.

A   May the God of hope give you the fullness of peace, and may the Lord of life be always with you.

R. And also with you.

B   The grace and peace of God our Father and the Lord Jesus Christ be with you.

R. And also with you.

C   The grace and peace of God our Father, who raised Jesus from the dead, be always with you.

R. And also with you.

D   May the Father of mercies, the God of all consolation, be with you.

R. And also with you.

OPENING SONG

70   The celebration continues with a song.

INVITATION TO PRAYER

71   In the following or similar words, the minister invites those present to pray.

My brothers and sisters, we believe that all the ties of friendship and affection which knit us as one throughout our lives do not unravel with death.

Confident that God always remembers the good we have done
and forgives our sins, let us pray, asking God to gather N. to
himself:

Pause for silent prayer.

Opening Prayer

72 The minister says one of the following prayers or one of
those provided in nos. 398-399, p. 333.

A   Lord our God,
the death of our brother/sister N.
recalls our human condition
and the brevity of our lives on earth.
But for those who believe in your love
death is not the end,
nor does it destroy the bonds
that you forge in our lives.
We share the faith of your Son's disciples
and the hope of the children of God.
Bring the light of Christ's resurrection
to this time of testing and pain
as we pray for N. and for those who love him/her,
through Christ our Lord.

R. Amen.

B   O God,   171
glory of believers and life of the just,
by the death and resurrection of your Son, we are redeemed:
have mercy on your servant N.,
and make him/her worthy to share the joys of paradise,
for he/she believed in the resurrection of the dead.

We ask this through Christ our Lord.

R. Amen.

LITURGY OF THE WORD

73 The celebration continues with the liturgy of the word. Other readings, psalms, and gospel readings are given in Part III, p. 207.

FIRST READING

74 A reader proclaims the first reading.

A reading from the second letter of Paul to the Corinthians   5:1, 6-10

We have an everlasting home in heaven.

We know that if our earthly dwelling, a tent, should be destroyed, we have a building from God, a dwelling not made with hands, eternal in heaven.

So we are always courageous, although we know that while we are at home in the body we are away from the Lord, for we walk by faith, not by sight. Yet we are courageous, and we would rather leave the body and go home to the Lord. Therefore, we aspire to please him, whether we are at home or away. For we must all appear before the judgment seat of Christ, so that each one may receive recompense, according to what he did in the body, whether good or evil.

This is the Word of the Lord.

RESPONSORIAL PSALM

75 The following psalm is sung or said or another psalm or song.

Psalm 27   110

R. The Lord is my light and my salvation.

Or:

R. I believe that I shall see the good things of the Lord in the land of the living.

The Lord is my light and my help;
whom shall I fear?
The Lord is the stronghold of my life;
before whom shall I shrink?

R. The Lord is my light and my salvation.

Or:

R. I believe that I shall see the good things of the Lord in the
land of the living.

There is one thing I ask of the Lord,
for this I long,
to live in the house of the Lord,
all the days of my life,
to savor the sweetness of the Lord,
to behold his temple. R.

O Lord, hear my voice when I call;
have mercy and answer.
It is your face, O Lord, that I seek;
hide not your face. R.

I am sure I shall see the Lord's goodness
in the land of the living.
Hope in him, hold firm and take heart.
Hope in the Lord! R.

GOSPEL

76   The gospel reading is then proclaimed.

A reading from the holy gospel according to Luke   12:35-40   134

Be prepared.

Jesus told his disciples:

"Gird your loins and light your lamps and be like servants who
await their master's return from a wedding, ready to open immediately when he comes and knocks. Blessed are those servants whom the master finds vigilant on his arrival. Amen, I

say to you, he will gird himself, have them recline at table, and proceed to wait on them. And should he come in the second or third watch and find them prepared in this way, blessed are those servants. Be sure of this: if the master of the house had known the hour when the thief was coming, he would not have let his house be broken into. You also must be prepared, for at an hour you do not expect, the Son of Man will come."

This is the Gospel of the Lord.

HOMILY

77 A brief homily on the readings is then given.

PRAYER OF INTERCESSION

LITANY

78 The minister leads those present in the following litany.

Let us turn to Christ Jesus with confidence and faith in the power of his cross and resurrection:

Assisting minister:
Risen Lord, pattern of our life for ever:
Lord, have mercy.

R. Lord, have mercy.

Assisting minister:
Promise and image of what we shall be:
Lord, have mercy.

R. Lord, have mercy.

Assisting minister:
Son of God who came to destroy sin and death:
Lord, have mercy.

R. Lord, have mercy.

Assisting minister:
Word of God who delivered us from the fear of death:
Lord, have mercy.

R. Lord, have mercy.

Assisting minister:
Crucified Lord, forsaken in death, raised in glory:
Lord, have mercy.

R. Lord, have mercy.

Assisting minister:
Lord Jesus, gentle Shepherd who bring rest to our souls, give peace to N. for ever:
Lord, have mercy.

R. Lord, have mercy.

Assisting minister:
Lord Jesus, you bless those who mourn and are in pain. Bless N.'s family and friends who gather around him/her today:
Lord, have mercy.

R. Lord, have mercy.

THE LORD'S PRAYER

79   Using one of the following invitations, or in similar words, the minister invites those present to pray the Lord's Prayer.

A   Friends [Brothers and sisters], our true home is heaven. Therefore let us pray to our heavenly Father as Jesus taught us:

B   With God there is mercy and fullness of redemption; let us pray as Jesus taught us:

C   Let us pray for the coming of the kingdom as Jesus taught us:

All:
Our Father . . .

CONCLUDING PRAYER

> 80 The minister says one of the following prayers or one of those provided in nos. 398-399, p. 333.

A Lord Jesus, our Redeemer,
you willingly gave yourself up to death,
so that all might be saved and pass from death to life.
We humbly ask you to comfort your servants in their grief
and to receive N. into the arms of your mercy.
You alone are the Holy One,
you are mercy itself;
by dying you unlocked the gates of life
    for those who believe in you.
Forgive N. his/her sins,
and grant him/her a place of happiness, light, and peace
in the kingdom of your glory for ever and ever.

R. Amen.

B Lord God,
you are attentive to the voice of our pleading.
Let us find in your Son
comfort in our sadness,
certainty in our doubt,
and courage to live through this hour.
Make our faith strong
through Christ our Lord.

R. Amen.

> A member or a friend of the family may speak in remembrance of the deceased.

CONCLUDING RITE

BLESSING

> 81 The minister says:

Blessed are those who have died in the Lord;
let them rest from their labors for their good deeds go with them.

A gesture, for example, signing the forehead of the deceased with the sign of the cross, may accompany the following words.

Eternal rest grant unto him/her, O Lord.

R. And let perpetual light shine upon him/her.

May he/she rest in peace.

R. Amen.

May his/her soul and the souls of all the faithful departed, through the mercy of God, rest in peace.

R. Amen.

A   A minister who is a priest or deacon says:

May the peace of God,
which is beyond all understanding,
keep your hearts and minds
in the knowledge and love of God
and of his Son, our Lord Jesus Christ.

R. Amen.

May almighty God bless you,
the Father, and the Son, ✠ and the Holy Spirit.

R. Amen.

B   A lay minister invokes God's blessing and signs himself or herself with the sign of the cross, saying:

May the love of God and the peace of the Lord Jesus Christ
bless and console us
and gently wipe every tear from our eyes:
in the name of the Father,
and of the Son, and of the Holy Spirit.

R. Amen.

The vigil may conclude with a song or a few moments of silent prayer or both.

OUTLINE OF THE RITE

INTRODUCTORY RITES

Greeting
Sprinkling with Holy Water
[Placing of the Pall]
Entrance Procession
[Placing of Christian Symbols]
Invitation to Prayer
Opening Prayer

LITURGY OF THE WORD

First Reading
Responsorial Psalm
Gospel
Homily

PRAYER OF INTERCESSION

Litany
The Lord's Prayer
Concluding Prayer

CONCLUDING RITE

Blessing

VIGIL FOR THE DECEASED
WITH RECEPTION AT THE CHURCH

INTRODUCTORY RITES

GREETING

> 82 The minister, with assisting ministers, goes to the door of the church and using one of the following greetings, or in similar words, greets those present.

A May the God of hope give you the fullness of peace, and may the Lord of life be always with you.

 R. And also with you.

B The grace and peace of God our Father and the Lord Jesus Christ be with you.

 R. And also with you.

C The grace and peace of God our Father, who raised Jesus from the dead, be always with you.

 R. And also with you.

D May the Father of mercies, the God of all consolation, be with you.

 R. And also with you.

SPRINKLING WITH HOLY WATER

> 83 The minister then sprinkles the coffin with holy water, saying:

In the waters of baptism
N. died with Christ and rose with him to new life.
May he/she now share with him eternal glory.

Placing of the Pall

84   If it is the custom in the local community, the pall is then placed on the coffin by family members, friends, or the minister.

Entrance Procession

85   The Easter candle may be placed beforehand near the position the coffin will occupy at the conclusion of the procession. The minister and assisting ministers precede the coffin and the mourners into the church. During the procession a psalm, song, or responsory is sung (see no. 403, p. 366).

Placing of Christian Symbols

86   A symbol of the Christian life, such as a Book of the Gospels, a Bible, or a cross, may be carried in procession, then placed on the coffin, either in silence or as a text from no. 400, p. 355, is said.

Invitation to Prayer

87   In the following or similar words, the minister invites those present to pray.

My brothers and sisters, we believe that all the ties of friendship and affection which knit us as one throughout our lives do not unravel with death.

Confident that God always remembers the good we have done and forgives our sins, let us pray, asking God to gather N. to himself:

Pause for silent prayer.

OPENING PRAYER

88 The minister says one of the following prayers or one of those provided in nos. 398-399, p. 333.

A Lord, in our grief we turn to you. 33
Are you not the God of love
who open your ears to all?

Listen to our prayers for your servant N.,
whom you have called out of this world:
lead him/her to your kingdom of light and peace
and count him/her among the saints in glory.

We ask this through Christ our Lord.

R. Amen.

B Lord Jesus, our Redeemer, 169
you willingly gave yourself up to death,
so that all might be saved and pass from death to life.
We humbly ask you to comfort your servants in their grief
and to receive N. into the arms of your mercy.
You alone are the Holy One,
you are mercy itself;
by dying you unlocked the gates of life
    for those who believe in you.
Forgive N. his/her sins,
and grant him/her a place of happiness, light, and peace
in the kingdom of your glory for ever and ever.

R. Amen.

LITURGY OF THE WORD

89 The celebration continues with the liturgy of the word. Other readings, psalms, and gospel readings are given in Part III, p. 207.

First Reading

90 A reader proclaims the first reading.

A reading from the first letter of John   3:1-2   103

We shall see God as he really is.

See what love the Father has bestowed on us that we may be
called the children of God. Yet so we are. The reason the world
does not know us is that it did not know him. Beloved, we are
God's children now; what we shall be has not yet been revealed.
We do know that when it is revealed we shall be like him, for
we shall see him as he is.

This is the Word of the Lord.

Responsorial Psalm

91 The following psalm is sung or said or another psalm or
song.

Psalm 103   11?

R. The Lord is kind and merciful.
Or:

R. The salvation of the just comes from the Lord.

The Lord is compassion and love,
slow to anger and rich in mercy.
He does not treat us according to our sins
nor repay us according to our faults. R.

As a father has compassion on his sons,
the Lord has pity on those who fear him;
for he knows of what we are made,
he remembers that we are dust. R.

As for man, his days are like grass;
he flowers like the flower of the field;
the wind blows and he is gone
and his place never sees him again. R.

But the love of the Lord is everlasting
upon those who hold him in fear;
his justice reaches out to children's children
when they keep his covenant in truth. R.

GOSPEL

92 The gospel reading is then proclaimed.

A reading from the holy gospel according to John   14:1-6   143

There are many rooms in my Father's house.

Jesus said to his disciples:

"Do not let your hearts be troubled. You have faith in God; have faith also in me. In my Father's house there are many dwelling places. If there were not, would I have told you that I am going to prepare a place for you? And if I go and prepare a place for you, I will come back again and take you to myself, so that where I am you also may be. Where I am going you know the way."

Thomas said to him, "Master, we do not know where you are going; how can we know the way?"

Jesus said to him, "I am the way and the truth and the life. No one comes to the Father except through me."

This is the Gospel of the Lord.

HOMILY

93 A brief homily on the readings is then given.

PRAYER OF INTERCESSION

LITANY

94 The minister leads those present in the following litany.

Let us turn to Christ Jesus with confidence and faith in the power of his cross and resurrection:

Assisting minister:
Risen Lord, pattern of our life for ever:
Lord, have mercy.
R. Lord, have mercy.

Assisting minister:
Promise and image of what we shall be:
Lord, have mercy.
R. Lord, have mercy.

Assisting minister:
Son of God who came to destroy sin and death:
Lord, have mercy.
R. Lord, have mercy.

Assisting minister:
Word of God who delivered us from the fear of death:
Lord, have mercy.
R. Lord, have mercy.

Assisting minister:
Crucified Lord, forsaken in death, raised in glory:
Lord, have mercy.
R. Lord, have mercy.

Assisting minister:
Lord Jesus, gentle Shepherd who bring rest to our souls, give peace to N. for ever:
Lord, have mercy.
R. Lord, have mercy.

Assisting minister:
Lord Jesus, you bless those who mourn and are in pain. Bless N.'s family and friends who gather around him/her today:
Lord, have mercy.
R. Lord, have mercy.

The Lord's Prayer

95 Using one of the following invitations, or in similar words,
the minister invites those present to pray the Lord's Prayer.

A   Friends [Brothers and sisters], our true home is heaven. Therefore let us pray to our heavenly Father as Jesus taught us:

B   With God there is mercy and fullness of redemption; let us pray
as Jesus taught us:

C   Let us pray for the coming of the kingdom as Jesus taught us:

All:
Our Father . . .

Concluding Prayer

96 The minister says one of the following prayers or one of those
provided in nos. 398-399, p. 333.

A   Lord God, in whom all find refuge,   175
we appeal to your boundless mercy:
grant to the soul of your servant N.
a kindly welcome,
cleansing of sin,
release from the chains of death,
and entry into everlasting life.
We ask this through Christ our Lord.
R. Amen.

B   Lord God,
you are attentive to the voice of our pleading.
Let us find in your Son
comfort in our sadness,
certainty in our doubt,
and courage to live through this hour.
Make our faith strong
through Christ our Lord.
R. Amen.

A member or a friend of the family may speak in remembrance
of the deceased.

CONCLUDING RITE

BLESSING

97   The minister says:

Blessed are those who have died in the Lord;
let them rest from their labors for their good deeds go with them.

A gesture, for example, signing the forehead of the deceased with
the sign of the cross, may accompany the following words.

Eternal rest grant unto him/her, O Lord.

R.   And let perpetual light shine upon him/her.

May he/she rest in peace.

R.   Amen.

May his/her soul and the souls of all the faithful departed,
through the mercy of God, rest in peace.

R.   Amen.

A   A minister who is a priest or deacon says:

May the peace of God,
which is beyond all understanding,
keep your hearts and minds
in the knowledge and love of God
and of his Son, our Lord Jesus Christ.

R.   Amen.

May almighty God bless you,
the Father, and the Son, ✠ and the Holy Spirit.

R.   Amen.

B   A lay minister invokes God's blessing and signs himself or herself with the sign of the cross, saying:

May the love of God and the peace of the Lord Jesus Christ
bless and console us
and gently wipe every tear from our eyes:
in the name of the Father,
and of the Son, and of the Holy Spirit.

R. Amen.

The vigil may conclude with a song or a few moments of silent
prayer or both.

2   RELATED RITES AND PRAYERS

If we have died with Christ, we believe we shall also live with him

98   The section entitled "Related Rites and Prayers" contains three brief rites, "Prayers after Death," "Gathering in the Presence of the Body," and "Transfer of the Body to the Church or to the Place of Committal." These rites are presented to help the minister and others pray with the family and close friends in the period soon after death. "Prayers after Death" may be used when the minister first meets with the family, "Gathering in the Presence of the Body," when the family first gathers together around the body of the deceased, and "Transfer of the Body to the Church or to the Place of Committal," when the family and friends prepare to accompany the body of the deceased in the procession to the church or to the place of committal.

99   These rites are signs of the concern of the Christian community for the family and close friends of the deceased. The compassionate presence of the minister and others and the familiar elements of these simple rites can have the effect of reassuring the mourners and of providing a consoling and hopeful situation in which to pray and to express their grief.

100   The circumstances for the celebration of these rites may vary from place to place and from culture to culture. The rites as given are only models, for adaptation by the minister according to the circumstances.

PRAYERS AFTER DEATH

Blessed are the sorrowing; they shall be consoled

101 This rite provides a model of prayer that may be used when the minister first meets with the family following death. The rite follows a common pattern of reading, response, prayer, and blessing and may be adapted according to the circumstances.

102 The presence of the minister and the calming effect of familiar prayers can comfort the mourners as they begin to face their loss. When the minister is present with the family at the time death occurs, this rite can be used as a quiet and prayerful response to the death. In other circumstances, for example, in the case of sudden or unexpected death, this form of prayer can be the principal part of the first pastoral visit of the minister.

103 The initial pastoral visit can be important as the first tangible expression of the community's support for the mourners. A minister unfamiliar with the family or the deceased person can learn a great deal on this occasion about the needs of the family and about the life of the deceased. The minister may also be able to form some preliminary judgments to help the family in planning the funeral rites. If circumstances allow, some first steps in the planning may take place at this time.

OUTLINE OF THE RITE

Invitation to Prayer
Reading
The Lord's Prayer
Concluding Prayers
Blessing

PRAYERS AFTER DEATH

INVITATION TO PRAYER

104 Using one of the following greetings, or in similar words, the minister greets those present.

A   In this moment of sorrow
the Lord is in our midst
and consoles us with his word:
Blessed are the sorrowful; they shall be comforted.

B   Praised be God, the Father of our Lord Jesus Christ,
the Father of mercies,
and the God of all consolation!
He comforts us in all our afflictions
and thus enables us to comfort those who grieve
with the same consolation
we have received from him.

The minister then invites those present to pray in silence.

READING

105 The minister or one of those present proclaims the reading. A reading from Part III, p. 207, or one of the following may be used.

A   Matthew 18:19-20

Jesus said: "If two of you agree on earth about anything for which they are to pray, it shall be granted to them by my heavenly Father. For where two or three are gathered together in my name, there am I in the midst of them."

B   John 11:21-24

Martha said to Jesus, "Lord, if you had been here, my brother would not have died. But even now I know that whatever you ask of God, God will give you." Jesus said to her, "Your brother will rise." Martha said to him, "I know he will rise, in the resurrection on the last day." Jesus told her, "I am the resurrection and the life; whoever believes in me, even if he dies, will live, and everyone who lives and believes in me will never die. Do you believe this?" She said to him, "Yes, Lord. I have come to believe that you are the Messiah, the Son of God, the one who is coming into the world."

C   Luke 20:35-38

Jesus said: "Those who are deemed worthy to attain to the coming age and to the resurrection of the dead neither marry nor are given in marriage. They can no longer die, for they are like angels; and they are the children of God because they are the ones who will rise. That the dead will rise even Moses made known in the passage about the bush, when he called 'Lord' the God of Abraham, the God of Isaac, and the God of Jacob; and he is not God of the dead, but of the living, for to him all are alive."

The Lord's Prayer

106 Using one of the following invitations, or in similar words, the minister invites those present to pray the Lord's Prayer.

A   With God there is mercy and fullness of redemption; let us pray as Jesus taught us:

B   Let us pray for the coming of the kingdom as Jesus taught us:

All:
Our Father . . .

Concluding Prayers

107 A prayer for the deceased person is then said. This prayer may be followed by a prayer for the mourners.

For the deceased person: The minister says the following prayer or one of those provided in no. 398, p. 333.

Holy Lord, almighty and eternal God,   167
hear our prayers for your servant N.,
whom you have summoned out of this world.
Forgive his/her sins and failings
and grant him/her a place of refreshment, light, and peace.
Let him/her pass unharmed through the gates of death
to dwell with the blessed in light,
as you promised to Abraham and his children for ever.
Accept N. into your safekeeping
and on the great day of judgment
raise him/her up with all the saints
to inherit your eternal kingdom.
We ask this through Christ our Lord.

R. Amen.

For the mourners: The minister may then say the following prayer or one of those provided in no. 399, p. 333.

Father of mercies and God of all consolation,   34
you pursue us with untiring love
and dispel the shadow of death
with the bright dawn of life.

[Comfort your family in their loss and sorrow.
Be our refuge and our strength, O Lord,
and lift us from the depths of grief
into the peace and light of your presence.]

Your Son, our Lord Jesus Christ,
by dying has destroyed our death,
and by rising, restored our life.
Enable us therefore to press on toward him,
so that, after our earthly course is run,
he may reunite us with those we love,
when every tear will be wiped away.
We ask this through Christ our Lord.

R. Amen.

Blessing

108 The minister says:

Blessed are those who have died in the Lord;
let them rest from their labors for their good deeds go with them.

A gesture, for example, signing the forehead of the deceased with the sign of the cross, may accompany the following words.

Eternal rest grant unto him/her, O Lord.

R. And let perpetual light shine upon him/her.

May he/she rest in peace.

R. Amen.

May his/her soul and the souls of all the faithful departed, through the mercy of God, rest in peace.

R. Amen.

A   *A minister who is a priest or deacon says:*

May the peace of God,
which is beyond all understanding,
keep your hearts and minds
in the knowledge and love of God
and of his Son, our Lord Jesus Christ.

R. Amen.

May almighty God bless you,
the Father, and the Son, ✠ and the Holy Spirit.

R. Amen.

B   *A lay minister invokes God's blessing and signs himself or her-self with the sign of the cross, saying:*

May the love of God and the peace of the Lord Jesus Christ
bless and console us
and gently wipe every tear from our eyes:
in the name of the Father,
and of the Son, and of the Holy Spirit.

R. Amen.

GATHERING IN THE PRESENCE OF THE BODY

If we have died with Christ, we believe we shall also live with him

109 This rite provides a model of prayer that may be used when the family first gathers in the presence of the body, when the body is to be prepared for burial, or after it has been prepared. The family members, in assembling in the presence of the body, confront in the most immediate way the fact of their loss and the mystery of death. Because cultural attitudes and practices on such occasions may vary, the minister should adapt the rite.

110 Through the presence of the minister and others and through the celebration of this brief rite, the community seeks to be with the mourners in their need and to provide an atmosphere of sensitive concern and confident faith. In prayer and gesture those present show reverence for the body of the deceased as a temple of the life-giving Spirit and ask, in that same Spirit, for the eternal life promised to the faithful.

111 The minister should try to be as attentive as possible to the particular needs of the mourners. The minister begins the rite at an opportune moment and, as much as possible, in an atmosphere of calm and recollection. The pause for silent prayer after the Scripture verse can be especially helpful in this regard.

OUTLINE OF THE RITE

Sign of the Cross
Scripture Verse
Sprinkling with Holy Water
Psalm
The Lord's Prayer
Concluding Prayer
Blessing

GATHERING IN THE PRESENCE OF THE BODY

SIGN OF THE CROSS

112 The minister and those present sign themselves with the sign of the cross as the minister says:

In the name of the Father, and of the Son, and of the Holy Spirit.

R. Amen.

SCRIPTURE VERSE

113 One of the following or another brief Scripture verse is read.

A   Matthew 11:28-30

My brothers and sisters, Jesus says:

"Come to me, all you who labor and are burdened, and I will give you rest. Take my yoke upon you and learn from me, for I am meek and humble of heart; and you will find rest for yourselves. For my yoke is easy, and my burden light."

B   John 14:1-3

My brothers and sisters, Jesus says:

"Do not let your hearts be troubled. You have faith in God; have faith also in me. In my Father's house there are many dwelling places. If there were not, would I have told you that I am going to prepare a place for you? And if I go and prepare a place for you, I will come back again and take you to myself, so that where I am you also may be."

Pause for silent prayer.

Sprinkling with Holy Water

114 Using one of the following formularies, the minister may sprinkle the body with holy water.

A   The Lord is our shepherd
and leads us to streams of living water.

B   Let this water call to mind our baptism into Christ,
who by his death and resurrection has redeemed us.

C   The Lord God lives in his holy temple yet abides in our midst.
Since in baptism N. became God's temple
and the Spirit of God lived in him/her,
with reverence we bless his/her mortal body.

Psalm

115 One of the following psalms is sung or said or another psalm provided in Part III, p. 207.

A   Psalm 130

R. I hope in the Lord, I trust in his word.

Out of the depths I cry to you, O Lord,
Lord, hear my voice!
O let your ears be attentive
to the voice of my pleading. R.

If you, O Lord, should mark our guilt,
Lord, who would survive?
But with you is found forgiveness:
for this we revere you. R.

My soul is waiting for the Lord,
I count on his word.
My soul is longing for the Lord
more than watchman for daybreak. R.

Because with the Lord there is mercy
and fullness of redemption,
Israel indeed he will redeem
from all its iniquity. R.

B   Psalm 115 and 116

R. I will walk in the presence of the Lord, in the land of the living.

How gracious is the Lord, and just;
our God has compassion.
The Lord protects the simple hearts;
I was helpless so he saved me. R.

I trusted, even when I said:
"I am sorely afflicted,"
and when I said in my alarm:
"No man can be trusted." R.

O precious in the eyes of the Lord
is the death of his faithful.
Your servant, Lord, your servant am I;
you have loosened my bonds. R.

THE LORD'S PRAYER

116 Using one of the following invitations, or in similar words, the minister invites those present to pray the Lord's Prayer.

A   With God there is mercy and fullness of redemption; let us pray as Jesus taught us:

B   Let us pray for the coming of the kingdom as Jesus taught us:

All:
Our Father . . .

CONCLUDING PRAYER

117 The minister says one of the following prayers or one of those provided in nos. 398-399, p. 333.

A   God of faithfulness, 30
   in your wisdom you have called your servant N.
     out of this world;
   release him/her from the bonds of sin,
   and welcome him/her into your presence,
   so that he/she may enjoy eternal light and peace
   and be raised up in glory with all your saints.

   We ask this through Christ our Lord.

   R. Amen.

B   Into your hands, O Lord, 168
   we humbly entrust our brother/sister N.
   In this life you embraced him/her with your tender love;
   deliver him/her now from every evil
   and bid him/her enter eternal rest.

   The old order has passed away:
   welcome him/her then into paradise,
   where there will be no sorrow, no weeping nor pain,
   but the fullness of peace and joy
   with your Son and the Holy Spirit
   for ever and ever.

   R. Amen.

BLESSING

118 The minister says:

Blessed are those who have died in the Lord;
let them rest from their labors for their good deeds go with them.

> A gesture, for example, signing the forehead of the deceased with
> the sign of the cross, may accompany the following words.

Eternal rest grant unto him/her, O Lord.

R. And let perpetual light shine upon him/her.

May he/she rest in peace.

R. Amen.

May his/her soul and the souls of all the faithful departed,
through the mercy of God, rest in peace.

R. Amen.

A A minister who is a priest or deacon says:

May the peace of God,
which is beyond all understanding,
keep your hearts and minds
in the knowledge and love of God
and of his Son, our Lord Jesus Christ.

R. Amen.

May almighty God bless you,
the Father, and the Son, ✠ and the Holy Spirit.

R. Amen.

B A lay minister invokes God's blessing and signs himself or herself with the sign of the cross, saying:

May the love of God and the peace of the Lord Jesus Christ
bless and console us
and gently wipe every tear from our eyes:
in the name of the Father,
and of the Son, and of the Holy Spirit.

R. Amen.

TRANSFER OF THE BODY TO THE CHURCH OR TO THE PLACE OF COMMITTAL

Your life is hidden now with Christ in God

119 This rite may be used for prayer with the family and close friends as they prepare to accompany the body of the deceased in the procession to the church or to the place of committal. It is a model, for adaptation by the minister according to the circumstances.

120 The procession to the church is a rite of initial separation of the mourners from the deceased; the procession to the place of committal is the journey to the place of final separation of the mourners from the deceased. Because the transfer of the body may be an occasion of great emotion for the mourners, the minister and other members of the community should make every effort to be present to support them. Reverent celebration of the rite can help reassure the mourners and create an atmosphere of calm preparation before the procession.

OUTLINE OF THE RITE

Invitation
Scripture Verse
Litany
The Lord's Prayer
Concluding Prayer
Invitation to the Procession
Procession to the Church
    or to the Place of Committal

TRANSFER OF THE BODY
TO THE CHURCH
OR TO THE PLACE OF COMMITTAL

INVITATION

121 In the following or similar words, the minister addresses those present.

Dear friends in Christ, in the name of Jesus and of his Church, we gather to pray for N., that God may bring him/her to everlasting peace and rest.

We share the pain of loss, but the promise of eternal life gives us hope. Let us comfort one another with these words:

SCRIPTURE VERSE

122 One of the following or another brief Scripture verse is read.

A   Colossians 3:3-4

You have died, and your life is hidden with Christ in God. When Christ your life appears, then you too will appear with him in glory.

B   Romans 6:8-9

If we have died with Christ, we believe that we shall also live with him. We know that Christ, raised from the dead, dies no more; death no longer has power over him.

LITANY

123 The minister leads those present in the following litany.

Dear friends, our Lord comes to raise the dead and comforts us with the solace of his love. Let us praise the Lord Jesus Christ.

Assisting minister:

Word of God, Creator of the earth to which N. now returns: in baptism you called him/her to eternal life to praise your Father for ever:
Lord, have mercy.
R. Lord, have mercy.

Assisting minister:

Son of God, you raise up the just and clothe them with the glory of your kingdom:
Lord, have mercy.
R. Lord, have mercy.

Assisting minister:

Crucified Lord, you protect the soul of N. by the power of your cross, and on the day of your coming you will show mercy to all the faithful departed:
Lord, have mercy.
R. Lord, have mercy.

Assisting minister:

Judge of the living and the dead, at your voice the tombs will open and all the just who sleep in your peace will rise and sing the glory of God:
Lord, have mercy.
R. Lord, have mercy.

Assisting minister:

All praise to you, Jesus our Savior, death is in your hands and all the living depend on you alone:
Lord, have mercy.
R. Lord, have mercy.

THE LORD'S PRAYER

124 In the following or similar words, the minister invites those present to pray the Lord's Prayer.

With faith and hope we pray to the Father in the words Jesus taught his disciples:

All:
Our Father . . .

CONCLUDING PRAYER

125 The minister says one of the following prayers or one of those provided in nos. 398-399, p. 333.

A   Lord,
N. is gone now from this earthly dwelling
and has left behind those who mourn his/her absence.
Grant that as we grieve for our brother/sister
we may hold his/her memory dear
and live in hope of the eternal kingdom
where you will bring us together again.

We ask this through Christ our Lord.

R. Amen.

B   Lord, in our grief we turn to you.   33
Are you not the God of love
who open your ears to all?

Listen to our prayers for your servant N.,
whom you have called out of this world:
lead him/her to your kingdom of light and peace
and count him/her among the saints in glory.

We ask this through Christ our Lord.

R. Amen.

C   God of all consolation,   176
open our hearts to your word,
so that, listening to it, we may comfort one another,
finding light in time of darkness
and faith in time of doubt.

We ask this through Christ our Lord.

R. Amen.

The minister invites those present to pray in silence while all
is made ready for the procession.

Invitation to the Procession

126 In the following or similar words, the minister invites those
present to join in the procession.

The Lord guards our coming in and our going out.
May God be with us today
as we make this last journey with our brother/sister.

Procession to the Church
or to the Place of Committal

127 During the procession, psalms and other suitable songs may
be sung. If this is not possible, a psalm is sung or recited either
before or after the procession. The following psalm and others
provided in Part III, p. 267, may be used.

Psalm 122   115

R. I rejoiced when I heard them say: let us go to the house
of the Lord.

Or:

R. Let us go rejoicing to the house of the Lord.

I rejoiced when I heard them say:
"Let us go to God's house."
And now our feet are standing
within your gates, O Jerusalem. R.

Jerusalem is built as a city
strongly compact.
It is there that the tribes go up,
the tribes of the Lord. R.

For Israel's law it is,
there to praise the Lord's name.
There were set the thrones of judgment
of the house of David. R.

For the peace of Jerusalem pray:
"Peace be to your homes!
May peace reign in your walls,
in your palaces, peace!" R.

For love of my brethren and friends
I say: "Peace upon you!"
For love of the house of the Lord
I will ask for your good. R.

> If the reception of the body at the church is celebrated apart from
> the vigil or the funeral liturgy, the "Vigil for the Deceased with
> Reception at the Church" (nos. 82-97) may be used and
> simplified.

FUNERAL LITURGY

All will be brought to life in Christ

FUNERAL LITURGY

128 The funeral liturgy is the central liturgical celebration of the Christian community for the deceased. Two forms of the funeral liturgy are presented here: "Funeral Mass" and "Funeral Liturgy outside Mass."

When one of its members dies, the Church encourages the celebration of the Mass. But when Mass cannot be celebrated (see no. 178), the second form of the funeral liturgy is used. When the funeral liturgy is celebrated outside Mass before the committal, a Mass for the deceased should be scheduled, if possible, for the family and friends at a convenient time after the funeral.

129 At the funeral liturgy the community gathers with the family and friends of the deceased to give praise and thanks to God for Christ's victory over sin and death, to commend the deceased to God's tender mercy and compassion, and to seek strength in the proclamation of the paschal mystery. Through the Holy Spirit the community is joined together in faith as one Body in Christ to reaffirm in sign and symbol, word and gesture that each believer through baptism shares in Christ's death and resurrection and can look to the day when all the elect will be raised up and united in the kingdom of light and peace.

STRUCTURE AND CONTENT
OF THE FUNERAL LITURGY

130 The funeral Mass includes the reception of the body, if this has not already occurred, the celebration of the liturgy of the word, the liturgy of the eucharist, and the final commendation and farewell. The funeral liturgy outside Mass includes all these elements except the liturgy of the eucharist. Both the funeral Mass and the funeral liturgy outside Mass may be followed by the procession to the place of committal.

RECEPTION AT THE CHURCH

131 Since the church is the place where the community of faith assembles for worship, the rite of reception of the body at the church has great significance. The church is the place where the Christian life is begotten in baptism, nourished in the eucharist, and where the community gathers to commend one of its deceased members to the Father. The church is at once a symbol of the community and of the heavenly liturgy that the celebration of the liturgy anticipates. In the act of receiving the body, the members of the community acknowledge the deceased as one of their own, as

one who was welcomed in baptism and who held a place in the assembly. Through the use of various baptismal symbols the community shows the reverence due to the body, the temple of the Spirit, and in this way prepares for the funeral liturgy in which it asks for a share in the heavenly banquet promised to the deceased and to all who have been washed in the waters of rebirth and marked with the sign of faith.

132 Any national flags or the flags or insignia of associations to which the deceased belonged are to be removed from the coffin at the entrance of the church. They may be replaced after the coffin has been taken from the church.

133 The rite of reception takes place at the beginning of the funeral liturgy, usually at the entrance of the church. It begins with a greeting of the family and others who have accompanied the coffin to the door of the church. The minister sprinkles the coffin with holy water in remembrance of the deceased person's initiation and first acceptance into the community of faith. If it is the custom in the local community, a funeral pall, a reminder of the garment given at baptism, and therefore signifying life in Christ, may then be placed on the coffin by family members, friends, or the minister. The entrance procession follows. The minister precedes the coffin and the mourners into the church. If the Easter candle is used on this occasion, it may be placed beforehand near the position the coffin will occupy at the conclusion of the procession.

134 If in this rite a symbol of the Christian life is to be placed on the coffin, it is carried in the procession and is placed on the coffin by a family member, friend, or the minister at the conclusion of the procession.

135 To draw the community together in prayer at the beginning of the funeral liturgy, the procession should be accompanied, whenever possible, by the singing of the entrance song. This song ought to be a profound expression of belief in eternal life and the resurrection of the dead as well as a prayer of intercession for the deceased (see, for example, no. 403).

136 If the rite of reception has already taken place, the funeral Mass begins in the usual way and the funeral liturgy outside Mass begins with the entrance song, followed by the greeting and an invitation to prayer.

LITURGY OF THE WORD

137 The reading of the word of God is an essential element of the celebration of the funeral liturgy. The readings proclaim the paschal mystery, teach remembrance of the dead, convey the hope of being gathered together again in God's kingdom, and encourage the witness of Christian life. Above all, the readings tell of God's design for a world in which suffering and death will relinquish their hold on all whom God has called his own.

138 Depending on pastoral circumstances, there may be either one or two readings before the gospel reading. When there is a first and second reading before the gospel reading, it is preferable to have a different reader for each.

139 The responsorial psalm enables the community to respond in faith to the first reading. Through the psalms the community expresses its grief and praise, and acknowledges its Creator and Redeemer as the sure source of trust and hope in times of trial. Since the responsorial psalm is a song, whenever possible, it should be sung. Psalms may be sung responsorially, with the response sung by the assembly and all the verses by the cantor or choir, or directly, with no response and all the verses sung by all or by the cantor or choir. When not sung, the responsorial psalm after the reading should be recited in a manner conducive to meditation on the word of God.[1]

140 In the *alleluia*, or the gospel acclamation, the community welcomes the Lord who is about to speak to it. If the *alleluia* is not sung, it is omitted. The cantor or choir sings the *alleluia* or Lenten acclamation first and the people repeat it. The verse is then sung by the cantor or choir and the *alleluia* or Lenten acclamation is then sung once more by all.

141 A brief homily based on the readings should always be given at the funeral liturgy, but never any kind of eulogy. The homilist should dwell on God's compassionate love and on the paschal mystery of the Lord as proclaimed in the Scripture readings. Through the homily, the community should receive the consolation and strength to face the death of one of its members with a hope that has been nourished by the proclamation of the saving word of God.

142 In the intercessions the community responds to the proclamation of the word of God by prayer for the deceased and all the dead, for the bereaved and all who mourn, and for all in the assembly. The intercessions provided may be used or adapted to the circumstances, or new intercessions may be composed.

Liturgy of the Eucharist

143 At the funeral Mass, the community, having been spiritually renewed at the table of God's word, turns for spiritual nourishment to the table of the eucharist. The community with the priest offers to the Father the sacrifice of the New Covenant and shares in the one bread and the one cup. In partaking of the body of Christ, all are given a foretaste of eternal life in Christ and are united with Christ, with each other, and with all the faith-

---

[1] See *Lectionary for Mass* (2nd *editio typica*, 1981), General Introduction, no. 22.

ful, living and dead: "Because there is one bread, we who are many are one body, for we all partake of the one bread" (1 Corinthians 10:17).

144 The liturgy of the eucharist takes place in the usual manner at the funeral Mass. Members of the family or friends of the deceased should bring the gifts to the altar. Instrumental music or a song (for example, Psalm 18:1-6, Psalm 63, Psalm 66:13-20, or Psalm 138) may accompany the procession with the gifts. Before the priest washes his hands, he may incense the gifts and the altar. Afterward the deacon or other minister may incense the priest and the congregation.

Eucharistic Prayer II and Eucharistic Prayer III are especially appropriate for use at the funeral Mass, because they provide special texts of intercession for the dead. Since music gives greater solemnity to a ritual action, the singing of the people's parts of the eucharistic prayer should be encouraged, that is, the responses of the preface dialogue, the Sanctus, the memorial acclamation, and the Great Amen.

To reinforce and to express more fully the unity of the congregation during the communion rite, the people may sing the Lord's Prayer, the doxology, the Lamb of God, and a song for the communion procession (for example, Psalm 23, Psalm 27, Psalm 34, Psalm 63, or Psalm 121).

FINAL COMMENDATION AND FAREWELL

145 At the conclusion of the funeral liturgy, the rite of final commendation and farewell is celebrated, unless it is to be celebrated later at the place of committal.

146 The final commendation is a final farewell by the members of the community, an act of respect for one of their members, whom they entrust to the tender and merciful embrace of God. This act of last farewell also acknowledges the reality of separation and affirms that the community and the deceased, baptized into the one Body, share the same destiny, resurrection on the last day. On that day the one Shepherd will call each by name and gather the faithful together in the new and eternal Jerusalem.

147 The rite begins with the minister's opening words and a few moments of silent prayer. The opening words serve as a brief explanation of the rite and as an invitation to pray in silence for the deceased. The pause for silence allows the bereaved and all present to relate their own feelings of loss and grief to the mystery of Christian hope in God's abundant mercy and his promise of eternal life.

Where this is customary, the body may then be sprinkled with holy water and incensed, or this may be done during or after the song of farewell. The sprinkling is a reminder that through baptism the person was marked for eternal life and the incensation signifies respect for the body as the temple of the Holy Spirit.

The song of farewell, which should affirm hope and trust in the paschal mystery, is the climax of the rite of final commendation. It should be sung to a melody simple enough for all to sing. It may take the form of a responsory or even a hymn. When singing is not possible, invocations may be recited by the assembly.

A prayer of commendation concludes the rite. In this prayer the community calls upon God's mercy, commends the deceased into God's hands, and affirms its belief that those who have died in Christ will share in Christ's victory over death.

PROCESSION TO THE PLACE OF COMMITTAL

148 At the conclusion of the funeral liturgy, the procession is formed and the body is accompanied to the place of committal. This final procession of the funeral rite mirrors the journey of human life as a pilgrimage to God's kingdom of peace and light, the new and eternal Jerusalem.

149 Especially when accompanied with music and singing, the procession can help to reinforce the bond of communion between the participants. Whenever possible, psalms or songs may accompany the entire procession from the church to the place of committal. In situations where a solemn procession on foot from the church to the place of committal is not possible, an antiphon or song may be sung as the body is being taken to the entrance of the church. Psalms, hymns, or liturgical songs may also be sung by the participants as they gather at the place of committal.

MINISTRY AND PARTICIPATION

150 Because the funeral liturgy is the central celebration for the deceased, it should be scheduled for a time that permits as many of the Christian community as possible to be present. The full and active participation of the assembly affirms the value of praying for the dead, gives strength and support to the bereaved, and is a sure sign of faith and hope in the paschal mystery. Every effort, therefore, should be made by the various liturgical ministers to encourage the active participation of the family and of the entire assembly.

151 The priest is the ordinary presiding minister of the funeral liturgy. Except for Mass, a deacon may conduct the funeral liturgy. If pastoral need requires, the conference of bishops, with the permission of the Apostolic See, may decide that laypersons also preside at the funeral liturgy outside Mass.

152 Whenever possible, ministers should involve the family in the planning of the funeral liturgy: in the choice of readings, prayers, and music for the liturgy and in the designation of ushers, pallbearers, readers, aco-

lytes, special ministers of the eucharist, when needed, and musicians. The family should also be given the opportunity to designate persons who will place the pall or other Christian symbols on the coffin during the rite of reception of the body at the church and who will bring the gifts to the altar at Mass.

153 An organist or other instrumentalist, a cantor, and, whenever possible, a choir should be present to assist the congregation in singing the songs, responses, and acclamations of the funeral liturgy.

3   FUNERAL MASS

Until the Lord comes, you are proclaiming his death

154 When one of its members dies, the Church encourages the celebration of the Mass. In the proclamation of the Scriptures, the saving word of God through the power of the Spirit becomes living and active in the minds and hearts of the community. Having been strengthened at the table of God's word, the community calls to mind God's saving deeds and offers the Father in the Spirit the eucharistic sacrifice of Christ's Passover from death to life, a living sacrifice of praise and thanksgiving, of reconciliation and atonement. Communion nourishes the community and expresses its unity. In communion, the participants have a foretaste of the heavenly banquet that awaits them and are reminded of Christ's own words: "Whoever eats my flesh and drinks my blood shall live for ever" (John 6:55). Confident in Jesus' presence among them in the living word, the living sacrifice, the living meal, those present in union with the whole Church offer prayers and petitions for the deceased, whom they entrust to God's merciful love.

155 The funeral Mass is ordinarily celebrated in the parish church.

156 The Mass texts are those of the Roman Missal and the Lectionary for Mass, "Masses for the Dead." The intercessions should be adapted to the circumstances. Models are given in place and in Part V, p. 356, no. 401.

157 In the choice of music for the funeral Mass, preference should be given to the singing of the acclamations, the responsorial psalm, the entrance and communion songs, and especially the song of farewell at the final commendation.

OUTLINE OF THE RITE

INTRODUCTORY RITES

Greeting
Sprinkling with Holy Water
[Placing of the Pall]
Entrance Procession
[Placing of Christian Symbols]
Opening Prayer

LITURGY OF THE WORD

Readings
Homily
General Intercessions

LITURGY OF THE EUCHARIST

FINAL COMMENDATION

Invitation to Prayer
Silence
[Signs of Farewell]
Song of Farewell
Prayer of Commendation

PROCESSION TO
THE PLACE OF COMMITTAL

FUNERAL MASS

158 If the rite of reception of the body takes place at the beginning of the funeral Mass, the introductory rites are those given here and the usual introductory rites for Mass, including the penitential rite, are omitted. If the rite of reception of the body has already taken place, the Mass begins in the usual way.

INTRODUCTORY RITES

GREETING

159 The priest, with assisting ministers, goes to the door of the church and using one of the following greetings, or in similar words, greets those present.

A   The grace of our Lord Jesus Christ and the love of God and the fellowship of the Holy Spirit be with you all.

R. And also with you.

B   The grace and peace of God our Father and the Lord Jesus Christ be with you.

R. And also with you.

C   The grace and peace of God our Father, who raised Jesus from the dead, be always with you.

R. And also with you.

D   May the Father of mercies, the God of all consolation, be with you.

R. And also with you.

SPRINKLING WITH HOLY WATER

160 The priest then sprinkles the coffin with holy water, saying:

In the waters of baptism
N. died with Christ and rose with him to new life.
May he/she now share with him eternal glory.

Placing of the Pall

161 If it is the custom in the local community, the pall is then placed on the coffin by family members, friends, or the priest.

Entrance Procession

162 The Easter candle may be placed beforehand near the position the coffin will occupy at the conclusion of the procession. The priest and assisting ministers precede the coffin and the mourners into the church. During the procession a psalm, song, or responsory is sung (see no. 403, p. 366).

Placing of Christian Symbols

163 A symbol of the Christian life, such as a Book of the Gospels, a Bible, or a cross, may be carried in procession, then placed on the coffin, either in silence or as a text from no. 400, p. 355, is said.

On reaching the altar, the priest, with the assisting ministers, makes the customary reverence, kisses the altar, and (if incense is used) incenses it. Then he goes to the chair.

Opening Prayer

164 When all have reached their places, the priest invites the assembly to pray.

Let us pray.

After a brief period of silent prayer, the priest sings or says one of the following prayers or one of those provided in no. 398, p. 333.

A

Almighty God and Father,
it is our certain faith
that your Son, who died on the cross, was raised from the dead,
the firstfruits of all who have fallen asleep.
Grant that through this mystery
your servant N., who has gone to his/her rest in Christ,
may share in the joy of his resurrection.

We ask this through our Lord Jesus Christ, your Son,
who lives and reigns with you and the Holy Spirit,
one God, for ever and ever.

R. Amen.

B   Outside the Easter season

O God,
to whom mercy and forgiveness belong,
hear our prayers on behalf of your servant N.,
whom you have called out of this world;
and because he/she put his/her hope and trust in you,
command that he/she be carried safely home to heaven
and come to enjoy your eternal reward.

We ask this through our Lord Jesus Christ, your Son,
who lives and reigns with you and the Holy Spirit,
one God, for ever and ever.

R. Amen.

C   Outside the Easter season

O God,
in whom sinners find mercy and the saints find joy,
we pray to you for our brother/sister N.,
whose body we honor with Christian burial,
that he/she may be delivered from the bonds of death.
Admit him/her to the joyful company of your saints
and raise him/her on the last day
to rejoice in your presence for ever.

We ask this through our Lord Jesus Christ, your Son,
who lives and reigns with you and the Holy Spirit,
one God, for ever and ever.

R. Amen.

God of loving kindness,
listen favorably to our prayers:
strengthen our belief that your Son has risen from the dead
and our hope that your servant N. will also rise again.

We ask this through our Lord Jesus Christ, your Son,
who lives and reigns with you and the Holy Spirit,
one God, for ever and ever.

R. Amen.

LITURGY OF THE WORD

READINGS

165 After the introductory rites, the liturgy of the word is celebrated. Depending upon pastoral circumstances, either one or
two readings may be read before the gospel reading.

HOMILY

166 A brief homily is given after the gospel reading.

GENERAL INTERCESSIONS

167 One of the following intercessions or those given in no. 401,
p. 356, may be used or adapted to the circumstances, or new
intercessions may be composed.

A   The priest begins:

Brothers and sisters, Jesus Christ is risen from the dead and
sits at the right hand of the Father, where he intercedes for his
Church. Confident that God hears the voices of those who trust
in the Lord Jesus, we join our prayers to his:

Assisting minister:

In baptism N. received the light of Christ. Scatter the darkness now and lead him/her over the waters of death.
Lord, in your mercy:

R. Hear our prayer.

Assisting minister:

Our brother/sister N. was nourished at the table of the Savior. Welcome him/her into the halls of the heavenly banquet.
Lord, in your mercy:

R. Hear our prayer.

Assisting minister:

[For a religious: Our brother/sister N. spent his/her life following Jesus, poor, chaste, and obedient. Count him/her among all holy men and women who sing in your courts.
Lord, in your mercy:

R. Hear our prayer.]

Assisting minister:

[For a bishop or priest: Our brother N. shared in the priesthood of Jesus Christ, leading God's people in prayer and worship. Bring him into your presence where he will take his place in the heavenly liturgy.
Lord, in your mercy:

R. Hear our prayer.]

Assisting minister:

[For a deacon: Our brother N. served God's people as a deacon of the Church. Prepare a place for him in the kingdom whose coming he proclaimed.
Lord, in your mercy:

R. Hear our prayer.]

Assisting minister:

Many friends and members of our families have gone before us and await the kingdom. Grant them an everlasting home with your Son.
Lord, in your mercy:

R. Hear our prayer.

Assisting minister:

Many people die by violence, war, and famine each day. Show your mercy to those who suffer so unjustly these sins against your love, and gather them to the eternal kingdom of peace.
Lord, in your mercy:

R. Hear our prayer.

Assisting minister:

Those who trusted in the Lord now sleep in the Lord. Give refreshment, rest, and peace to all whose faith is known to you alone.
Lord, in your mercy:

R. Hear our prayer.

. Assisting minister:

[For the mourners: The family and friends of N. seek comfort and consolation. Heal their pain and dispel the darkness and doubt that come from grief.
Lord, in your mercy:

R. Hear our prayer.]

Assisting minister:

We are assembled here in faith and confidence to pray for our brother/sister N. Strengthen our hope so that we may live in the expectation of your Son's coming.
Lord, in your mercy:

R. Hear our prayer.

The priest then concludes:

Lord God,
giver of peace and healer of souls,
hear the prayers of the Redeemer, Jesus Christ,
and the voices of your people,
whose lives were purchased by the blood of the Lamb.
Forgive the sins of all who sleep in Christ
and grant them a place in the kingdom.

We ask this through Christ our Lord.

R. Amen.

B   The priest begins:

God, the almighty Father, raised Christ his Son from the dead;   200
with confidence we ask him to save all his people, living and
dead:

> Assisting minister:

For N. who in baptism was given the pledge of eternal life, that
he/she may now be admitted to the company of the saints.
We pray to the Lord.

R. Lord, hear our prayer.

> Assisting minister:

For our brother/sister who ate the body of Christ, the bread
of life, that he/she may be raised up on the last day.
We pray to the Lord.

R. Lord, hear our prayer.

> Assisting minister:

[For a deacon: For our brother N., who proclaimed the Good
News of Jesus Christ and served the needs of the poor, that he
may be welcomed into the sanctuary of heaven.
We pray to the Lord.

R. Lord, hear our prayer.]

> Assisting minister:

[For a bishop or priest: For our brother N., who served the Church
as a priest, that he may be given a place in the liturgy of heaven.
We pray to the Lord.

R. Lord, hear our prayer.]

> Assisting minister:

For our deceased relatives and friends and for all who have
helped us, that they may have the reward of their goodness.
We pray to the Lord.

R. Lord, hear our prayer.

> Assisting minister:

For those who have fallen asleep in the hope of rising again,
that they may see God face to face.
We pray to the Lord.

R. Lord, hear our prayer.

Assisting minister:

[For the mourners: For the family and friends of our brother/
sister N., that they may be consoled in their grief by the Lord,
who wept at the death of his friend Lazarus.
We pray to the Lord.

R. Lord, hear our prayer.]

Assisting minister:

For all of us assembled here to worship in faith, that we may
be gathered together again in God's kingdom.
We pray to the Lord.

R. Lord, hear our prayer.

The priest then concludes:

God, our shelter and our strength,
you listen in love to the cry of your people:
hear the prayers we offer for our departed brothers and sisters.
Cleanse them of their sins
and grant them the fullness of redemption.

We ask this through Christ our Lord.

R. Amen.

LITURGY OF THE EUCHARIST

168 The liturgy of the eucharist is celebrated in the usual
manner.

169 If the final commendation is to be celebrated at the place
of committal, the procession to the place of committal (no. 176)
begins following the prayer after communion.

FINAL COMMENDATION

170 Following the prayer after communion, the priest goes to a place near the coffin. The assisting ministers carry the censer and holy water, if these are to be used.

A member or a friend of the family may speak in remembrance of the deceased before the final commendation begins.

INVITATION TO PRAYER

171 Using one of the following invitations, or one of those provided in no. 402, p. 365, or in similar words, the priest faces the people and begins the final commendation.

A   Before we go our separate ways, let us take leave of our brother/ sister. May our farewell express our affection for him/her; may it ease our sadness and strengthen our hope. One day we shall joyfully greet him/her again when the love of Christ, which conquers all things, destroys even death itself.   185

B   Trusting in God, we have prayed together for N. and now we come to the last farewell. There is sadness in parting, but we take comfort in the hope that one day we shall see N. again and enjoy his/her friendship. Although this congregation will disperse in sorrow, the mercy of God will gather us together again in the joy of his kingdom. Therefore let us console one another in the faith of Jesus Christ.   186

SILENCE

172 All pray in silence.

SIGNS OF FAREWELL

173 The coffin may now be sprinkled with holy water and incensed, or this may take place during or after the song of farewell. If the body was sprinkled with holy water during the rite of reception at the beginning of Mass, the sprinkling is ordinarily omitted in the rite of final commendation.

SONG OF FAREWELL

> 174 The song of farewell is then sung. The following or other responsories chosen from no. 403, p. 366, may be used or some other song may be sung.

Saints of God, come to his/her aid!   47
Hasten to meet him/her, angels of the Lord!   66

R. Receive his/her soul and present him/her to God the Most High.

May Christ, who called you, take you to himself;
may angels lead you to the bosom of Abraham. R.

Eternal rest grant unto him/her, O Lord,
and let perpetual light shine upon him/her. R.

PRAYER OF COMMENDATION

> 175 The priest then says one of the following prayers.

A   Into your hands, Father of mercies,   48
we commend our brother/sister N.
in the sure and certain hope
that, together with all who have died in Christ,
he/she will rise with him on the last day.

[We give you thanks for the blessings
which you bestowed upon N. in this life:
they are signs to us of your goodness
and of our fellowship with the saints in Christ.]

Merciful Lord,
turn toward us and listen to our prayers:
open the gates of paradise to your servant
and help us who remain
to comfort one another with assurances of faith,
until we all meet in Christ
and are with you and with our brother/sister for ever.

We ask this through Christ our Lord.

R. Amen.

B   To you, O Lord, we commend the soul of N. your servant; 192
in the sight of this world he/she is now dead;
in your sight may he/she live for ever.
Forgive whatever sins he/she committed through human
  weakness
and in your goodness grant him/her everlasting peace.
We ask this through Christ our Lord.
R. Amen.

PROCESSION TO THE PLACE OF COMMITTAL

176 The deacon or, in the absence of a deacon, the priest says:

In peace let us take our brother/sister to his/her place of rest.

If a symbol of the Christian life has been placed on the coffin,
it should be removed at this time.

The procession then begins: the priest and assisting ministers
precede the coffin; the family and mourners follow.

One or more of the following texts or other suitable songs may
be sung during the procession to the entrance of the church. The
singing may continue during the journey to the place of committal.

A   The following antiphon may be sung with verses from Psalm 25,
p. 268, or separately. A metrical version of this text is given on
p. 330, no. 396, E.

May the angels lead you into paradise; 50
may the martyrs come to welcome you
and take you to the holy city,
the new and eternal Jerusalem.

B   The following antiphon may be sung with verses from Psalm 116,
p. 274, or separately.

May choirs of angels welcome you 50
and lead you to the bosom of Abraham;
and where Lazarus is poor no longer
may you find eternal rest.

C   Whoever believes in me,
even though that person die, shall live.

R. I am the resurrection and the life.

Whoever lives and believes in me shall never die. R.

D   The following psalms may also be used.

Psalm 118, p. 275; Psalm 42, p. 269; Psalm 93, p. 272; Psalm 25, p. 268; Psalm 119, p. 277.

4 FUNERAL LITURGY OUTSIDE MASS

I am the resurrection and the life; whoever believes in me shall never die

177 In the funeral liturgy outside Mass the community gathers to hear the message of Easter hope proclaimed in the liturgy of the word and to commend the deceased to God.

178 This rite may be used for various reasons:
1. when the funeral Mass is not permitted, namely, on solemnities of obligation, on Holy Thursday and the Easter Triduum, and on the Sundays of Advent, Lent, and the Easter Season;[1]
2. when in some places or circumstances it is not possible to celebrate the funeral Mass before the committal, for example, if a priest is not available;
3. when for pastoral reasons the pastor and the family judge that the funeral liturgy outside Mass is a more suitable form of celebration.

179 The funeral liturgy outside Mass is ordinarily celebrated in the parish church, but may also be celebrated in the home of the deceased, a funeral home, parlor, chapel of rest, or cemetery chapel.

180 The readings are those of the Lectionary for Mass, "Masses for the Dead." The intercessions should be adapted to the circumstances. Models are given in place and in Part V, p. 356, no. 401. The celebration may also include holy communion.

181 In the choice of music for the funeral liturgy, preference should be given to the singing of the entrance song, the responsorial psalm, the gospel acclamation, and especially the song of farewell at the final commendation.

182 The minister who is a priest or deacon wears an alb with stole (a cope may be used, if desired); a layperson who presides wears the liturgical vestments approved for the region.

---

[1] See General Instruction of the Roman Missal, no. 336.

OUTLINE OF THE RITE

INTRODUCTORY RITES

Greeting
Sprinkling with Holy Water
[Placing of the Pall]
Entrance Procession
[Placing of Christian Symbols]
Invitation to Prayer
Opening Prayer

LITURGY OF THE WORD

Readings
Homily
General Intercessions
The Lord's Prayer

FINAL COMMENDATION

Invitation to Prayer
Silence
[Signs of Farewell]
Song of Farewell
Prayer of Commendation

PROCESSION TO THE PLACE OF COMMITTAL

FUNERAL LITURGY OUTSIDE MASS

183 If the rite of reception of the body takes place at the beginning of the funeral liturgy, the introductory rites are those given here. If the rite of reception of the body has already taken place, the liturgy begins with an entrance song and the greeting (no. 184), followed by the invitation to prayer (no. 189).

INTRODUCTORY RITES

GREETING

184 The presiding minister, with assisting ministers, goes to the door of the church and using one of the following greetings, or in similar words, greets those present.

A The grace of our Lord Jesus Christ and the love of God and the fellowship of the Holy Spirit be with you all.

R. And also with you.

B The grace and peace of God our Father and the Lord Jesus Christ be with you.

R. And also with you.

C The grace and peace of God our Father, who raised Jesus from the dead, be always with you.

R. And also with you.

D May the Father of mercies, the God of all consolation, be with you.

R. And also with you.

SPRINKLING WITH HOLY WATER

185 The presiding minister then sprinkles the coffin with holy water, saying:

In the waters of baptism
N. died with Christ and rose with him to new life.
May he/she now share with him eternal glory.

Placing of the Pall

186 If it is the custom in the local community, the pall is then placed on the coffin by family members, friends, or the minister.

Entrance Procession

187 The Easter candle may be placed beforehand near the position the coffin will occupy at the conclusion of the procession. The presiding minister and assisting ministers precede the coffin and the mourners into the church. During the procession a psalm, song, or responsory is sung (see no. 403, p. 366).

Placing of Christian Symbols

188 A symbol of the Christian life, such as a Book of the Gospels, a Bible, or a cross, may be carried in procession, then placed on the coffin, either in silence or as a text from no. 400, p. 355, is said.

On reaching the altar, the presiding minister, with the assisting ministers, makes the customary reverence and goes to the chair.

Invitation to Prayer

189 When all have reached their places, the presiding minister, using the following or similar words, invites the assembly to pray.

My brothers and sisters,
we have come together to renew our trust in Christ
who, by dying on the cross, has freed us from eternal death
and, by rising, has opened for us the gates of heaven.

Let us pray for our brother/sister,
that he/she may share in Christ's victory,
and let us pray for ourselves,
that the Lord may grant us
the gift of his loving consolation.

Opening Prayer

190 After a brief period of silent prayer, the presiding minister sings or says one of the following prayers or one of those provided in no. 398, p. 333.

A   Outside the Easter season   170

Almighty God and Father,
it is our certain faith
that your Son, who died on the cross, was raised from the dead,
the firstfruits of all who have fallen asleep.
Grant that through this mystery
your servant N., who has gone to his/her rest in Christ,
may share in the joy of his resurrection.

We ask this through our Lord Jesus Christ, your Son,
who lives and reigns with you and the Holy Spirit,
one God, for ever and ever.

R. Amen.

B   Outside the Easter season

O God,
to whom mercy and forgiveness belong,
hear our prayers on behalf of your servant N.,
whom you have called out of this world;
and because he/she put his/her hope and trust in you,
command that he/she be carried safely home to heaven
and come to enjoy your eternal reward.

We ask this through our Lord Jesus Christ, your Son,
who lives and reigns with you and the Holy Spirit,
one God, for ever and ever.

R. Amen.

C   Outside the Easter season

O God,
in whom sinners find mercy and the saints find joy,
we pray to you for our brother/sister N.,
whose body we honor with Christian burial,
that he/she may be delivered from the bonds of death.
Admit him/her to the joyful company of your saints
and raise him/her on the last day
to rejoice in your presence for ever.

We ask this through our Lord Jesus Christ, your Son,
who lives and reigns with you and the Holy Spirit,
one God, for ever and ever.

R. Amen.

D   During the Easter season   173

God of loving kindness,
listen favorably to our prayers:
strengthen our belief that your Son has risen from the dead
and our hope that your servant N. will also rise again.

We ask this through our Lord Jesus Christ, your Son,
who lives and reigns with you and the Holy Spirit,
one God, for ever and ever.

R. Amen.

LITURGY OF THE WORD

READINGS

191 After the introductory rites, the liturgy of the word is celebrated. Depending upon pastoral circumstances, either one or
two readings may be read before the gospel reading.

HOMILY

192 A brief homily should be given after the gospel reading.

GENERAL INTERCESSIONS

193 One of the following intercessions or those given in no. 401, p. 356, may be used or adapted to the circumstances, or new intercessions may be composed.

A   The presiding minister begins:

God, the almighty Father, raised Christ his Son from the dead;   200 with confidence we ask him to save all his people, living and dead:

Assisting minister:

For N. who in baptism was given the pledge of eternal life, that he/she may now be admitted to the company of the saints. We pray to the Lord.

R. Lord, hear our prayer.

Assisting minister:

For our brother/sister who ate the body of Christ, the bread of life, that he/she may be raised up on the last day. We pray to the Lord.

R. Lord, hear our prayer.

Assisting minister:

[For a deacon: For our brother N., who proclaimed the Good News of Jesus Christ and served the needs of the poor, that he may be welcomed into the sanctuary of heaven. We pray to the Lord.

R. Lord, hear our prayer.]

Assisting minister:

[For a bishop or priest: For our brother N., who served the Church as a priest, that he may be given a place in the liturgy of heaven. We pray to the Lord.

R. Lord, hear our prayer.]

For our deceased relatives and friends and for all who have helped us, that they may have the reward of their goodness. We pray to the Lord.

R. Lord, hear our prayer.

Assisting minister:

For those who have fallen asleep in the hope of rising again, that they may see God face to face. We pray to the Lord.

R. Lord, hear our prayer.

Assisting minister:

[For the mourners: For the family and friends of our brother/ sister N., that they may be consoled in their grief by the Lord, who wept at the death of his friend Lazarus. We pray to the Lord.

R. Lord, hear our prayer.]

Assisting minister:

For all of us assembled here to worship in faith, that we may be gathered together again in God's kingdom. We pray to the Lord.

R. Lord, hear our prayer.

The presiding minister then concludes:

God, our shelter and our strength,
you listen in love to the cry of your people:
hear the prayers we offer for our departed brothers and sisters.
Cleanse them of their sins
and grant them the fullness of redemption.

We ask this through Christ our Lord.

R. Amen.

B   The presiding minister begins:

Brothers and sisters, Jesus Christ is risen from the dead and sits at the right hand of the Father, where he intercedes for his Church. Confident that God hears the voices of those who trust in the Lord Jesus, we join our prayers to his:

Assisting minister:

In baptism N. received the light of Christ. Scatter the darkness now and lead him/her over the waters of death.
Lord, in your mercy:

R. Hear our prayer.

Assisting minister:

Our brother/sister N. was nourished at the table of the Savior. Welcome him/her into the halls of the heavenly banquet.
Lord, in your mercy:

R. Hear our prayer.

Assisting minister:

[For a religious: Our brother/sister N. spent his/her life following Jesus, poor, chaste, and obedient. Count him/her among all holy men and women who sing in your courts.
Lord, in your mercy:

R. Hear our prayer.]

Assisting minister:

[For a bishop or priest: Our brother N. shared in the priesthood of Jesus Christ, leading God's people in prayer and worship. Bring him into your presence where he will take his place in the heavenly liturgy.
Lord, in your mercy:

R. Hear our prayer.]

Assisting minister:

[For a deacon: Our brother N. served God's people as a deacon of the Church. Prepare a place for him in the kingdom whose coming he proclaimed.
Lord, in your mercy:

R. Hear our prayer.]

Assisting minister:

Many friends and members of our families have gone before us and await the kingdom. Grant them an everlasting home with your Son.
Lord, in your mercy:

R. Hear our prayer.

Assisting minister:

Many people die by violence, war, and famine each day. Show your mercy to those who suffer so unjustly these sins against your love, and gather them to the eternal kingdom of peace. Lord, in your mercy:

R. Hear our prayer.

Assisting minister:

Those who trusted in the Lord now sleep in the Lord. Give refreshment, rest, and peace to all whose faith is known to you alone.
Lord, in your mercy:

R. Hear our prayer.

Assisting minister:

[For the mourners: The family and friends of N. seek comfort and consolation. Heal their pain and dispel the darkness and doubt that come from grief.
Lord, in your mercy:

R. Hear our prayer.]

Assisting minister:

We are assembled here in faith and confidence to pray for our brother/sister N. Strengthen our hope so that we may live in the expectation of your Son's coming.
Lord, in your mercy:

R. Hear our prayer.

The presiding minister then concludes:

Lord God,
giver of peace and healer of souls,
hear the prayers of the Redeemer, Jesus Christ,
and the voices of your people,
whose lives were purchased by the blood of the Lamb.
Forgive the sins of all who sleep in Christ
and grant them a place in the kingdom.

We ask this through Christ our Lord.

R. Amen.

The Lord's Prayer

194 Using one of the following invitations, or in similar words, the minister invites those present to pray the Lord's Prayer.

A   Now let us pray as Christ the Lord has taught us:

B   With longing for the coming of God's kingdom, let us offer our prayer to the Father:

All say:
Our Father . . .

---

195 The celebration may include holy communion (Part V, p. 377, nos. 409-410).

---

196 If the final commendation is to be celebrated at the place of committal, the procession to the place of committal (no. 203) begins following the Lord's Prayer or the prayer after communion.

FINAL COMMENDATION

197 Following the Lord's Prayer (or the prayer after communion), the presiding minister goes to a place near the coffin. The assisting ministers carry the censer and holy water, if these are to be used.

A member or a friend of the family may speak in remembrance of the deceased before the final commendation begins.

Invitation to Prayer

198 Using one of the following invitations, or one of those provided in no. 402, p. 365, or in similar words, the presiding minister faces the people and begins the final commendation.

A   Before we go our separate ways, let us take leave of our brother/ 185
     sister. May our farewell express our affection for him/her; may
     it ease our sadness and strengthen our hope. One day we shall
     joyfully greet him/her again when the love of Christ, which con-
     quers all things, destroys even death itself.

B   Trusting in God, we have prayed together for N. and now we 186
     come to the last farewell. There is sadness in parting, but we
     take comfort in the hope that one day we shall see N. again
     and enjoy his/her friendship. Although this congregation will
     disperse in sorrow, the mercy of God will gather us together
     again in the joy of his kingdom. Therefore let us console one
     another in the faith of Jesus Christ.

SILENCE

199 All pray in silence.

SIGNS OF FAREWELL

200 The coffin may now be sprinkled with holy water and incensed, or this may take place during or after the song of farewell. If the body was sprinkled with holy water during the rite
of reception at the beginning of the funeral liturgy, the sprinkling is ordinarily omitted in the rite of final commendation.

SONG OF FAREWELL

201 The song of farewell is then sung. The following or other
responsories chosen from no. 403, p. 366, may be used or some
other song may be sung.

Saints of God, come to his/her aid! 47
Hasten to meet him/her, angels of the Lord!

R. Receive his/her soul and present him/her to God the
Most High.

May Christ, who called you, take you to himself;
may angels lead you to the bosom of Abraham. R.

Eternal rest grant unto him/her, O Lord,
and let perpetual light shine upon him/her. R.

PRAYER OF COMMENDATION

202 The presiding minister then says one of the following prayers.

A   Into your hands, Father of mercies,   48
      we commend our brother/sister N.   67
      in the sure and certain hope
      that, together with all who have died in Christ,
      he/she will rise with him on the last day.

      [We give you thanks for the blessings
      which you bestowed upon N. in this life:
      they are signs to us of your goodness
      and of our fellowship with the saints in Christ.]

      Merciful Lord,
      turn toward us and listen to our prayers:
      open the gates of paradise to your servant
      and help us who remain
      to comfort one another with assurances of faith,
      until we all meet in Christ
      and are with you and with our brother/sister for ever.

      We ask this through Christ our Lord.

      R. Amen.

B   To you, O Lord, we commend the soul of N. your servant;   192
      in the sight of this world he/she is now dead;
      in your sight may he/she live for ever.

      Forgive whatever sins he/she committed
         through human weakness
      and in your goodness grant him/her everlasting peace.

      We ask this through Christ our Lord.

      R. Amen.

PROCESSION TO THE
PLACE OF COMMITTAL

203 An assisting minister, or in the absence of an assisting minister, the presiding minister says:

In peace let us take our brother/sister to his/her place of rest.

If a symbol of the Christian life has been placed on the coffin, it should be removed at this time.

The procession then begins: the presiding minister and assisting ministers precede the coffin; the family and mourners follow.

One or more of the following texts or other suitable songs may be sung during the procession to the entrance of the church. The singing may continue during the journey to the place of committal.

A   The following antiphon may be sung with verses from Psalm 25, p. 268, or separately. A metrical version of this text is given on p. 330, no. 396, E.

May the angels lead you into paradise;
may the martyrs come to welcome you
and take you to the holy city,
the new and eternal Jerusalem.

B   The following antiphon may be sung with verses from Psalm 116, p. 274, or separately.

May choirs of angels welcome you
and lead you to the bosom of Abraham;
and where Lazarus is poor no longer
may you find eternal rest.

C   Whoever believes in me,
even though that person die, shall live.

R. I am the resurrection and the life.

Whoever lives and believes in me shall never die. R.

D   The following psalms may also be used.
Psalm 118, p. 275; Psalm 42, p. 269; Psalm 93, p. 272; Psalm 25, p. 268; Psalm 119, p. 277.

RITE OF COMMITTAL

Joseph took Jesus down from the cross,
wrapped him in a shroud,
and laid him in a tomb

RITE OF COMMITTAL

204 The rite of committal, the conclusion of the funeral rites, is the final act of the community of faith in caring for the body of its deceased member. It may be celebrated at the grave, tomb, or crematorium and may be used for burial at sea. Whenever possible, the rite of committal is to be celebrated at the site of committal, that is, beside the open grave or place of interment, rather than at a cemetery chapel.

205 Two forms of the rite of committal are provided here: "Rite of Committal" and "Rite of Committal with Final Commendation." The first form is used when the final commendation is celebrated as part of the conclusion of the funeral liturgy. The second form is used when the final commendation does not take place during the funeral liturgy or when no funeral liturgy precedes the committal rite.

206 In committing the body to its resting place, the community expresses the hope that, with all those who have gone before marked with the sign of faith, the deceased awaits the glory of the resurrection. The rite of committal is an expression of the communion that exists between the Church on earth and the Church in heaven: the deceased passes with the farewell prayers of the community of believers into the welcoming company of those who need faith no longer but see God face to face.

STRUCTURE AND CONTENT
OF THE RITE OF COMMITTAL

207 Both forms of the committal rite begin with an invitation, Scripture verse, and a prayer over the place of committal. The several alternatives for the prayer over the place of committal take into account whether the grave, tomb, or resting place has already been blessed and situations in which the final disposition of the body will actually take place at a later time (for example, when the body is to be cremated or will remain in a cemetery chapel until burial at a later time).

208 The rite of committal continues with the words of committal, the intercessions, and the Lord's Prayer.
   The rite of committal with final commendation continues with an invitation to prayer, a pause for silent prayer, the sprinkling and incensing of the body, where this is customary, the song of farewell, and the prayer of commendation (see nos. 227-231).

209 The act of committal takes place after the words of committal (in the rite of committal with final commendation, after the prayer of commen-

dation) or at the conclusion of the rite. The act of committal expresses the full significance of this rite. Through this act the community of faith proclaims that the grave or place of interment, once a sign of futility and despair, has been transformed by means of Christ's own death and resurrection into a sign of hope and promise.

210 Both forms of the rite conclude with a prayer over the people, which includes the verse *Eternal rest*, and a blessing. Depending on local custom, a song may then be sung and a gesture of final leave-taking may be made, for example, placing flowers or soil on the coffin.

ADAPTATION

211 If there is pastoral need for a longer committal rite than those provided here, for example, when the funeral liturgy has been celebrated on a previous day or in a different community, the minister may use the appropriate form of the committal rite and adapt it, for example, by adding a greeting, song, one or more readings, a psalm, and a brief homily. When there has been no funeral liturgy prior to the committal rite, the "Rite of Committal with Final Commendation" may be used and similarly adapted.

212 The rite of committal may be celebrated in circumstances in which the final disposition of the body will not take place for some time, for example, when winter delays burial or when ashes are to be interred at some time after cremation. The rite of committal may then be repeated on the later occasion when the actual burial or interment takes place. On the second occasion the rite may include a longer Scripture reading as well as a homily.

In the case of a body donated to science, the rite of committal may be celebrated whenever interment takes place.

MINISTRY AND PARTICIPATION

213 The community continues to show its concern for the mourners by participating in the rite of committal. The rite marks the separation in this life of the mourners from the deceased, and through it the community assists them as they complete their care for the deceased and lay the body to rest. The act of committal is a stark and powerful expression of this separation. When carried out in the midst of the community of faith, the committal can help the mourners to face the end of one relationship with the deceased and to begin a new one based on prayerful remembrance, gratitude, and the hope of resurrection and reunion.

By their presence and prayer members of the community signify their intention to continue to support the mourners in the time following the funeral.

214 The singing of well-chosen music at the rite of committal can help the mourners as they face the reality of the separation. At the rite of committal with final commendation, whenever possible, the song of farewell should be sung. In either form of the committal rite, a hymn or liturgical song that affirms hope in God's mercy and in the resurrection of the dead is desirable at the conclusion of the rite.

215 In the absence of a parish minister, a friend or member of the family should lead those present in the rite of committal.

The minister should vest according to local custom.

OUTLINE OF THE RITE

Invitation
Scripture Verse
Prayer over the Place of Committal

Committal
Intercessions
The Lord's Prayer
Concluding Prayer

Prayer over the People

5 RITE OF COMMITTAL

Invitation

> 216 When the funeral procession arrives at the place of committal, the minister says the following or a similar invitation.

Our brother/sister N. has gone to his/her rest in the peace of Christ. May the Lord now welcome him/her to the table of God's children in heaven. With faith and hope in eternal life, let us assist him/her with our prayers.

Let us pray to the Lord also for ourselves. May we who mourn be reunited one day with our brother/sister; together may we meet Christ Jesus when he who is our life appears in glory.

Scripture Verse

> 217 One of the following verses or another brief Scripture verse is read. The minister first says:

We read in sacred Scripture:

A   Matthew 25:34   119

Come, you who are blessed by my Father, says the Lord,
inherit the kingdom prepared for you from the foundation
of the world.

B   John 6:39   121

This is the will of the one who sent me, says the Lord,
that I should not lose anything of what he gave me,
but that I should raise it on the last day.

C   Philippians 3:20   124

Our citizenship is in heaven,
and from it we also await a savior,
the Lord Jesus Christ.

D   Revelation 1:5-6   126

Jesus Christ is the firstborn of the dead;
to him be glory and power forever and ever. Amen.

Prayer over the Place of Committal

218 The minister says one of the following prayers or one of those provided in no. 405, p. 370.

A   If the place of committal is to be blessed:

Lord Jesus Christ,   53
by your own three days in the tomb,
you hallowed the graves of all who believe in you
and so made the grave a sign of hope
that promises resurrection
even as it claims our mortal bodies.

Grant that our brother/sister may sleep here in peace
until you awaken him/her to glory,
for you are the resurrection and the life.
Then he/she will see you face to face
and in your light will see light
and know the splendor of God,
for you live and reign for ever and ever.

R. Amen.

B   If the place of committal has already been blessed:

All praise to you, Lord of all creation.
Praise to you, holy and living God.
We praise and bless you for your mercy,
we praise and bless you for your kindness.
Blessed is the Lord, our God.

R. Blessed is the Lord, our God.

You sanctify the homes of the living
and make holy the places of the dead.
You alone open the gates of righteousness
and lead us to the dwellings of the saints.
Blessed is the Lord, our God.

R. Blessed is the Lord, our God.

We praise you, our refuge and strength.
We bless you, our God and Redeemer.
Your praise is always in our hearts and on our lips.
We remember the mighty deeds of the covenant.
Blessed is the Lord, our God.

R. Blessed is the Lord, our God.

Almighty and ever-living God,
remember the mercy with which you graced your servant N.
  in life.
Receive him/her, we pray, into the mansions of the saints.
As we make ready our brother's/sister's resting place,
look also with favor on those who mourn
and comfort them in their loss.

Grant this through Christ our Lord.

R. Amen.

C　　When the final disposition of the body is to take place at a later
　　time:

Almighty and ever-living God,
in you we place our trust and hope,
in you the dead, whose bodies were temples of the Spirit,
  find everlasting peace.

As we take leave of our brother/sister,
give our hearts peace in the firm hope
that one day N. will live
in the mansion you have prepared for him/her in heaven.

We ask this through Christ our Lord.

R. Amen.

COMMITTAL

219　The minister then says the words of committal. One of the
following formularies or one provided in no. 406, p. 372, may
be used.

A　Because God has chosen to call our brother/sister N.　　　55
　　from this life to himself,
we commit his/her body to the earth
  [or the deep or the elements or its resting place],
for we are dust and unto dust we shall return.

But the Lord Jesus Christ will change our mortal bodies
  to be like his in glory,
for he is risen, the firstborn from the dead.

So let us commend our brother/sister to the Lord,
that the Lord may embrace him/her in peace
and raise up his/her body on the last day.

B   In sure and certain hope of the resurrection to eternal life
       through our Lord Jesus Christ,
     we commend to Almighty God our brother/sister N.,
     and we commit his/her body to the ground
       [*or* the deep *or* the elements *or* its resting place]:
     earth to earth, ashes to ashes, dust to dust.

     The Lord bless him/her and keep him/her,
     the Lord make his face to shine upon him/her
       and be gracious to him/her,
     the Lord lift up his countenance upon him/her
       and give him/her peace.

         The committal takes place at this time or at the conclusion of
         the rite.

INTERCESSIONS

         220 One of the following intercessions or those given in no. 407,
         p. 374, may be used or adapted to the circumstances, or new
         intercessions may be composed.

A   The minister begins:

     For our brother/sister, N., let us pray to our Lord Jesus Christ,
     who said, "I am the resurrection and the life. Whoever believes
     in me shall live even in death and whoever lives and believes
     in me shall never die."

         Assisting minister:

     Lord, you consoled Martha and Mary in their distress; draw
     near to us who mourn for N., and dry the tears of those who
     weep.
     We pray to the Lord:

     R. Lord, have mercy.

         Assisting minister:

     You wept at the grave of Lazarus, your friend; comfort us in
     our sorrow.
     We pray to the Lord:

     R. Lord, have mercy.

Assisting minister:

You raised the dead to life; give to our brother/sister eternal life.
We pray to the Lord:

R. Lord, have mercy.

Assisting minister:

You promised paradise to the repentant thief; bring N. to the joys of heaven.
We pray to the Lord:

R. Lord, have mercy.

Assisting minister:

Our brother/sister was washed in baptism and anointed with the Holy Spirit; give him/her fellowship with all your saints.
We pray to the Lord:

R. Lord, have mercy.

Assisting minister:

He/she was nourished with your body and blood; grant him/her a place at the table in your heavenly kingdom.
We pray to the Lord:

R. Lord, have mercy.

Assisting minister:

Comfort us in our sorrow at the death of N.; let our faith be our consolation, and eternal life our hope.
We pray to the Lord:

R. Lord, have mercy.

B   The minister begins:

Dear friends, in reverence let us pray to God, the source of all   202
mercies.

Assisting minister:

Gracious Lord, forgive the sins of those who have died in Christ.
Lord, in your mercy:

R. Hear our prayer.

Assisting minister:

Remember all the good they have done.
Lord, in your mercy:

R. Hear our prayer.

Assisting minister:

Welcome them into eternal life.
Lord, in your mercy:

R. Hear our prayer.

Assisting minister:

Let us pray for those who mourn.
Comfort them in their grief.
Lord, in your mercy:

R. Hear our prayer.

Assisting minister:

Lighten their sense of loss with your presence.
Lord, in your mercy:

R. Hear our prayer.

Assisting minister:

Increase their faith and strengthen their hope.
Lord, in your mercy:

R. Hear our prayer.

Assisting minister:

Let us pray also for ourselves on our pilgrimage through life.
Keep us faithful in your service.
Lord, in your mercy:

R. Hear our prayer.

Assisting minister:

Kindle in our hearts a longing for heaven.
Lord, in your mercy:

R. Hear our prayer.

The Lord's Prayer

221 In the following or similar words, the minister invites those present to pray the Lord's Prayer.

With longing for the coming of God's kingdom, let us pray:

All say:

Our Father . . .

Concluding Prayer

222 The minister says one of the following prayers or one of those provided in no. 408, p. 376.

A God of holiness and power, 56
accept our prayers on behalf of your servant N.;
do not count his/her deeds against him/her,
for in his/her heart he/she desired to do your will.
As his/her faith united him/her to your people on earth,
so may your mercy join him/her to the angels in heaven.

We ask this through Christ our Lord.

R. Amen.

B Almighty God, 199
through the death of your Son on the cross
you destroyed our death;
through his rest in the tomb
you hallowed the graves of all who believe in you;
and through his rising again
you restored us to eternal life.

God of the living and the dead,
accept our prayers
for those who have died in Christ
and are buried with him in the hope of rising again.
Since they were true to your name on earth,
let them praise you for ever in the joy of heaven.

We ask this through Christ our Lord.

R. Amen.

Prayer over the People

223 The assisting minister says:

Bow your heads and pray for God's blessing.

All pray silently. The minister, with hands outstretched, prays over the people:

Merciful Lord,
you know the anguish of the sorrowful,
you are attentive to the prayers of the humble.
Hear your people
who cry out to you in their need,
and strengthen their hope in your lasting goodness.
We ask this through Christ our Lord.

R. Amen.

The minister then says the following:

Eternal rest grant unto him/her, O Lord.

R. And let perpetual light shine upon him/her.

May he/she rest in peace.

R. Amen.

May his/her soul and the souls of all the faithful departed,
through the mercy of God, rest in peace.

R. Amen.

A   A minister who is a priest or deacon says:

May the peace of God,
which is beyond all understanding,
keep your hearts and minds
in the knowledge and love of God
and of his Son, our Lord Jesus Christ.

R. Amen.

May almighty God bless you,
the Father, and the Son, ✠ and the Holy Spirit.

R. Amen.

A lay minister invokes God's blessing and signs himself or herself with the sign of the cross, saying:

May the love of God and the peace of the Lord Jesus Christ
bless and console us
and gently wipe every tear from our eyes:
in the name of the Father,
and of the Son, and of the Holy Spirit.

R. Amen.

The minister then concludes:

Go in the peace of Christ.

R. Thanks be to God.

A song may conclude the rite. Where it is the custom, some sign or gesture of leave-taking may be made.

OUTLINE OF THE RITE

Invitation
Scripture Verse
Prayer over the Place of Committal

Invitation to Prayer
Silence
[Signs of Farewell]
Song of Farewell
Prayer of Commendation
Committal

Prayer over the People

6   RITE OF COMMITTAL
WITH FINAL COMMENDATION

Invitation

224 When the funeral procession arrives at the place of committal, the minister says one of the following or a similar invitation.

A   We gather here to commend our brother/sister N. to God our Father and to commit his/her body to the earth/elements. In the spirit of faith in the resurrection of Jesus Christ from the dead, let us [raise our voices in song and] offer our prayers for N.

B   As we gather to commend our brother/sister N. to God our Father and to commit his/her body to the earth/elements, let us express in [song and] prayer our common faith in the resurrection. As Jesus Christ was raised from the dead, we too are called to follow him through death to the glory where God will be all in all.

Scripture Verse

225 One of the following verses or another brief Scripture verse is read. The minister first says:

We read in sacred Scripture:

A   Matthew 25:34   119

Come, you who are blessed by my Father, says the Lord,
inherit the kingdom prepared for you from the foundation
   of the world.

B   John 6:39   121

This is the will of the one who sent me, says the Lord,
that I should not lose anything of what he gave me,
but that I should raise it on the last day.

C   Philippians 3:20   124

Our citizenship is in heaven,
and from it we also await a savior,
the Lord Jesus Christ.

D   Revelation 1:5-6   124

Jesus Christ is the firstborn of the dead;
to him be glory and power forever and ever. Amen.

PRAYER OVER THE PLACE OF COMMITTAL

226 The minister says one of the following prayers or one of those
provided in no. 405, p. 370.

A   If the place of committal is to be blessed: 53

Lord Jesus Christ,
by your own three days in the tomb,
you hallowed the graves of all who believe in you
and so made the grave a sign of hope
that promises resurrection
even as it claims our mortal bodies.

Grant that our brother/sister may sleep here in peace
until you awaken him/her to glory,
for you are the resurrection and the life.
Then he/she will see you face to face
and in your light will see light
and know the splendor of God,
for you live and reign for ever and ever.

R. Amen.

B   If the place of committal has already been blessed:

All praise to you, Lord of all creation.
Praise to you, holy and living God.
We praise and bless you for your mercy,
we praise and bless you for your kindness.
Blessed is the Lord, our God.

R. Blessed is the Lord, our God.

You sanctify the homes of the living
and make holy the places of the dead.
You alone open the gates of righteousness
and lead us to the dwellings of the saints.
Blessed is the Lord, our God.

R. Blessed is the Lord, our God.

We praise you, our refuge and strength.
We bless you, our God and Redeemer.
Your praise is always in our hearts and on our lips.
We remember the mighty deeds of the covenant.
Blessed is the Lord, our God.

R. Blessed is the Lord, our God.

Almighty and ever-living God,
remember the mercy with which you graced your servant N.
   in life.
Receive him/her, we pray, into the mansions of the saints.
As we make ready our brother's/sister's resting place,
look also with favor on those who mourn
and comfort them in their loss.

Grant this through Christ our Lord.

R. Amen.

C   When the final disposition of the body is to take place at a later
        time:

Almighty and ever-living God,
in you we place our trust and hope,
in you the dead, whose bodies were temples of the Spirit,
   find everlasting peace.

As we take leave of our brother/sister,
give our hearts peace in the firm hope
that one day N. will live
in the mansion you have prepared for him/her in heaven.

We ask this through Christ our Lord.

R. Amen.

Invitation to Prayer

227 Using one of the following invitations, or one of those provided in no. 402, p. 365, or in similar words, the minister faces the people and begins the final commendation.

A   Before we go our separate ways, let us take leave of our brother/ sister. May our farewell express our affection for him/her; may it ease our sadness and strengthen our hope. One day we shall joyfully greet him/her again when the love of Christ, which conquers all things, destroys even death itself.   185

B   Trusting in God, we have prayed together for N. and now we come to the last farewell. There is sadness in parting, but we take comfort in the hope that one day we shall see N. again and enjoy his/her friendship. Although this congregation will disperse in sorrow, the mercy of God will gather us together again in the joy of his kingdom. Therefore let us console one another in the faith of Jesus Christ.   186

Silence

228 All pray in silence.

Signs of Farewell

229 The coffin may now be sprinkled with holy water and incensed, or this may take place during or after the song of farewell.

Song of Farewell

230 The song of farewell is then sung. The following or other responsories chosen from no. 403, p. 366, may be used or some other song may be sung.

Saints of God, come to his/her aid!   47
Hasten to meet him/her, angels of the Lord!

R. Receive his/her soul and present him/her to God the Most High.

May Christ, who called you, take you to himself;
may angels lead you to the bosom of Abraham. R.

Eternal rest grant unto him/her, O Lord,
and let perpetual light shine upon him/her. R.

PRAYER OF COMMENDATION

231 The minister then says one of the following prayers.

A   Into your hands, Father of mercies,   48
we commend our brother/sister N.   67
in the sure and certain hope
that, together with all who have died in Christ,
he/she will rise with him on the last day.

[We give you thanks for the blessings
which you bestowed upon N. in this life:
they are signs to us of your goodness
and of our fellowship with the saints in Christ.]

Merciful Lord,
turn toward us and listen to our prayers:
open the gates of paradise to your servant
and help us who remain
to comfort one another with assurances of faith,
until we all meet in Christ
and are with you and with our brother/sister for ever.

We ask this through Christ our Lord.

R. Amen.

B   To you, O Lord, we commend the soul of N. your servant;   192
in the sight of this world he/she is now dead;
in your sight may he/she live for ever.

Forgive whatever sins he/she committed through human
    weakness
and in your goodness grant him/her everlasting peace.

We ask this through Christ our Lord.

R. Amen.

COMMITTAL

232 The act of committal takes place at this time or at the conclusion of the rite.

PRAYER OVER THE PEOPLE

233 The assisting minister says:

Bow your heads and pray for God's blessing.

All pray silently. The minister, with hands extended, prays over the people:

Merciful Lord,
you know the anguish of the sorrowful,
you are attentive to the prayers of the humble.
Hear your people
who cry out to you in their need,
and strengthen their hope in your lasting goodness.
We ask this through Christ our Lord.

R. Amen.

The minister then says the following:

Eternal rest grant unto him/her, O Lord.

R. And let perpetual light shine upon him/her.

May he/she rest in peace.

R. Amen.

May his/her soul and the souls of all the faithful departed, through the mercy of God, rest in peace.

R. Amen.

A   A minister who is a priest or deacon says:

May the peace of God,
which is beyond all understanding,
keep your hearts and minds
in the knowledge and love of God
and of his Son, our Lord Jesus Christ.

R. Amen.

May almighty God bless you,
the Father, and the Son, ✠ and the Holy Spirit.

R. Amen.

B   A lay minister invokes God's blessing and signs himself or her-
     self with the sign of the cross, saying:

May the love of God and the peace of the Lord Jesus Christ
bless and console us
and gently wipe every tear from our eyes:
in the name of the Father,
and of the Son, and of the Holy Spirit.

R. Amen.

The minister then concludes:

Go in the peace of Christ.

R. Thanks be to God.

A song may conclude the rite. Where it is the custom, some sign
or gesture of leave-taking may be made.

Part II
FUNERAL RITES
FOR CHILDREN

Let the little children come to me;
it is to such as these that the kingdom of God belongs

Part II
FUNERAL RITES
FOR CHILDREN

234 Part II of the *Order of Christian Funerals* provides rites that are used in the funerals of infants and young children, including those of early school age. It includes "Vigil for a Deceased Child," "Funeral Liturgy," and "Rite of Committal."

Part II does not contain "Related Rites and Prayers," nos. 98-127, which are brief rites for prayer with the family and friends before the funeral liturgy. The rites as they are presented in Part I are models and should be adapted by the minister to the circumstances of the funeral for a child.

235 The minister, in consultation with those concerned, chooses those rites that best correspond to the particular needs and customs of the mourners. In some instances, for example, the death of an infant, only the rite of committal and perhaps one of the forms of prayer with the family may be desirable.

236 In the celebration of the funeral of a child the Church offers worship to God, the author of life, commends the child to God's love, and prays for the consolation of the family and close friends.

237 Funeral rites may be celebrated for children whose parents intended them to be baptized but who died before baptism.[1] In these celebrations the Christian community entrusts the child to God's all-embracing love and finds strength in this love and in Jesus' affirmation that the kingdom of God belongs to little children (see Matthew 19:14).

238 In its pastoral ministry to the bereaved the Christian community is challenged in a particular way by the death of an infant or child. The bewilderment and pain that death causes can be overwhelming in this situation, especially for the parents and the brothers and sisters of the deceased child. The community seeks to offer support and consolation to the family during and after the time of the funeral rites.

239 Through prayer and words of comfort the minister and others can help the mourners to understand that their child has gone before them into the kingdom of the Lord and that one day they will all be reunited there in joy. The participation of the community in the funeral rites is a sign

---

[1] In the general catechesis of the faithful, pastors and other ministers should explain that the celebration of the funeral rites for children who die before baptism is not intended to weaken the Church's teaching on the necessity of baptism.

of the compassionate presence of Christ, who embraced little children, wept at the death of a friend, and endured the pain and separation of death in order to render it powerless over those he loves. Christ still sorrows with those who sorrow and longs with them for the fulfillment of the Father's plan in a new creation where tears and death will have no place.

240 The minister should invite members of the community to use their individual gifts in this ministry of consolation. Those who have lost children of their own may be able in a special way to help the family as they struggle to accept the death of the child.

241 Those involved in planning the funeral rites for a deceased child should take into account the age of the child, the circumstances of death, the grief of the family, and the needs and customs of those taking part in the rites. In choosing the texts and elements of celebration, the minister should bear in mind whether the child was baptized or died before baptism.

242 Special consideration should be given to any sisters, brothers, friends, or classmates of the deceased child who may be present at the funeral rites. Children will be better able to take part in the celebration if the various elements are planned and selected with them in mind: texts, readings, music, gesture, processions, silence. The minister may wish to offer brief remarks for the children's benefit at suitable points during the celebration.

If children will be present at the funeral rites, those with requisite ability should be asked to exercise some of the liturgical roles. During the funeral Mass, for example, children may serve as readers, acolytes, or musicians, or assist in the reading of the general intercessions and in the procession with the gifts. Depending upon the age and number of children taking part, adaptations recommended in the *Directory for Masses with Children* may be appropriate.

VIGIL

It is good to wait in silence for the Lord

7 VIGIL FOR A DECEASED CHILD

243 The vigil for the deceased is the principal celebration of the Christian community during the time before the funeral liturgy or, if there is no funeral liturgy, before the rite of committal. The vigil may take the form of a liturgy of the word, as described in Part I, nos. 57-68, or of some part of the office for the dead (see Part IV, p. 296).

244 The vigil may be celebrated at a convenient time in the home of the deceased child, in the funeral home, parlor or chapel of rest, or in some other suitable place. The vigil may also be celebrated in the church, but at a time well before the funeral liturgy, so that the funeral liturgy will not be lengthy and the liturgy of the word repetitious. When the body is brought to the church for the celebration of the vigil, the vigil begins with the rite of reception (see no. 58). Otherwise the vigil begins with a greeting, followed by an opening song, an invitation to prayer, and an opening prayer.

245 After the opening prayer, the vigil continues with the liturgy of the word, which usually includes a first reading, responsorial psalm, gospel reading, and homily. If there is to be only one reading, however, it should be the gospel reading. The prayer of intercession, which includes a litany, the Lord's Prayer, and a concluding prayer, then follows. Alternative concluding prayers are provided for use in the case of a baptized child or of a child who died before baptism. The vigil concludes with a blessing, which may be followed by a song or a few moments of silent prayer or both.

246 The minister should adapt the vigil to the circumstances. If, for example, a large number of children are present or if the vigil is held in the home of the deceased child, elements of the rite may be simplified or shortened and other elements or symbols that have special meaning for those taking part may be incorporated into the celebration. If custom and circumstances suggest, a member or a friend of the family may speak in remembrance of the deceased child.

OUTLINE OF THE RITE

INTRODUCTORY RITES

Greeting
Sprinkling with Holy Water
or Brief Address
[Placing of the Pall]
Entrance Procession
[Placing of Christian Symbols]
Invitation to Prayer
Opening Prayer

LITURGY OF THE WORD

First Reading
Responsorial Psalm
Gospel
Homily

PRAYER OF INTERCESSION

Litany
The Lord's Prayer
Concluding Prayer

CONCLUDING RITE

Blessing

VIGIL FOR A DECEASED CHILD

> 247 The vigil celebrated at the church may begin with the rite of reception (nos. 248-252) which then serves as the introductory rite. Otherwise the vigil may begin with an opening song followed by a greeting (no. 248) and the invitation to prayer (no. 253).

INTRODUCTORY RITES

GREETING

> 248 The minister, with assisting ministers, goes to the door of the church and using one of the following greetings, or in similar words, greets those present.

A   May Christ Jesus, who welcomed children and laid his hands in blessing upon them, comfort you with his peace and be always with you.

R. And also with you.

B   May the God of hope give you the fullness of peace, and may the Lord of life be always with you.

R. And also with you.

C   The grace and peace of God our Father, who raised Jesus from the dead, be always with you.

R. And also with you.

D   May the Father of mercies, the God of all consolation, be with you.

R. And also with you.

SPRINKLING WITH HOLY WATER OR BRIEF ADDRESS

> 249 If the child was baptized, the minister sprinkles the coffin with holy water (option A). If the child died before baptism, the sprinkling with holy water is omitted and a brief address is given (option B).

A SPRINKLING WITH HOLY WATER—If the child was baptized, the minister then sprinkles the coffin with holy water, saying:

In the waters of baptism
N. died with Christ and rose with him to new life.
May he/she now share with him eternal glory.

B BRIEF ADDRESS—If the child died before baptism, the minister may then address the mourners in the following or similar words.

My brothers and sisters, the Lord is a faithful God who created us all after his own image. All things are of his making, all creation awaits the day of salvation. We now entrust the soul of N. to the abundant mercy of God, that our beloved child may find a home in his kingdom.

PLACING OF THE PALL

250 If it is the custom in the local community and the child was baptized, the pall is then placed on the coffin by family members, friends, or the minister.

ENTRANCE PROCESSION

251 The Easter candle may be placed beforehand near the position the coffin will occupy at the conclusion of the procession. The minister and assisting ministers precede the coffin and the mourners into the church. During the procession a psalm, song, or responsory is sung (see no. 403, p. 366).

PLACING OF CHRISTIAN SYMBOLS

252 A symbol of the Christian life, such as a cross, may be carried in procession, then placed on the coffin, either in silence or as a text from no. 400, p. 355, is said.

Invitation to Prayer

253 In the following or similar words, the minister invites those present to pray.

Let us pray for this child and entrust him/her to the care of our loving God.

Pause for silent prayer.

Opening Prayer

254 The minister says one of the following prayers or one of those provided in nos. 398-399, p. 333.

A   A baptized child

To you, O Lord,   224
we humbly entrust this child,
so precious in your sight.
Take him/her into your arms
and welcome him/her into paradise,
where there will be no sorrow, no weeping nor pain,
but the fullness of peace and joy
with your Son and the Holy Spirit
for ever and ever.

R. Amen.

B   A baptized child

Lord, in our grief we call upon your mercy: 223
open your ears to our prayers,
and one day unite us again with N.,
who, we firmly trust,
already enjoys eternal life in your kingdom.

We ask this through Christ our Lord.

R. Amen.

C   A child who died before baptism

God of all consolation, 236
searcher of mind and heart,
the faith of these parents [N. and N.] is known to you.

Comfort them with the knowledge
that the child for whom they grieve
is entrusted now to your loving care.

We ask this through Christ our Lord.

R. Amen.

LITURGY OF THE WORD

255   The celebration continues with the liturgy of the word. Other readings, psalms, and gospel readings are given in Part III, pp. 247 and 261.

First Reading

256   A reader proclaims the first reading.

A reading from the first letter of John 3:1-2   10

We shall see God as he really is.

See what love the Father has bestowed on us that we may be called the children of God. Yet so we are. The reason the world does not know us is that it did not know him. Beloved, we are God's children now; what we shall be has not yet been revealed. We do know that when it is revealed we shall be like him, for we shall see him as he is.

This is the Word of the Lord.

Responsorial Psalm

257 The following psalm is sung or said or another psalm or song.

Psalm 23

R. The Lord is my shepherd; there is nothing I shall want.

The Lord is my shepherd;
there is nothing I shall want.
Fresh and green are the pastures
where he gives me repose.
Near restful waters he leads me,
to revive my drooping spirit. R.

He guides me along the right path;
he is true to his name.
If I should walk in the valley of darkness
no evil would I fear.
You are there with your crook and your staff;
with these you give me comfort. R.

You have prepared a banquet for me
in the sight of my foes.
My head you have anointed with oil;
my cup is overflowing. R.

Surely goodness and kindness shall follow me
all the days of my life.
In the Lord's own house shall I dwell
for ever and ever. R.

Gospel

258 The gospel reading is then proclaimed.

A reading from the holy gospel according to Mark   10:13-16

The kingdom of God belongs to little children.

People were bringing children to Jesus that he might touch them, but the disciples rebuked them. When Jesus saw this he became indignant and said to them, "Let the children come to me; do not prevent them, for the kingdom of God belongs to such as these. Amen, I say to you, whoever does not accept the kingdom of God like a child will not enter it." Then he embraced them and blessed them, placing his hands on them.

This is the Gospel of the Lord.

HOMILY

259 A brief homily on the readings is then given.

PRAYER OF INTERCESSION

LITANY

260 The minister leads those present in the following litany.

The Lord Jesus is the lover of his people and our only sure hope. Let us ask him to deepen our faith and sustain us in this dark hour.

Assisting minister:
You became a little child for our sake, sharing our human life. To you we pray:

R. Bless us and keep us, O Lord.

Assisting minister:
You grew in wisdom, age, and grace and learned obedience through suffering.
To you we pray:

R. Bless us and keep us, O Lord.

Assisting minister:
You welcomed children, promising them your kingdom. To you we pray:

R. Bless us and keep us, O Lord.

Assisting minister:

You comforted those who mourned the loss of children and friends.
To you we pray:

R. Bless us and keep us, O Lord.

Assisting minister:

You took upon yourself the suffering and death of us all.
To you we pray:

R. Bless us and keep us, O Lord.

Assisting minister:

You promised to raise up those who believe in you, just as you were raised up in glory by the Father.
To you we pray:

R. Bless us and keep us, O Lord.

THE LORD'S PRAYER

261 Using one of the following invitations, or in similar words, the minister invites those present to pray the Lord's Prayer.

A   Together let us pray for strength, for acceptance, and for the coming of the kingdom in the words our Savior taught us:

B   In love, God calls us his children, for that indeed is what we are. We ask for the strength we need by praying in the words Jesus gave us:

All say:

Our Father . . .

CONCLUDING PRAYER

262 The minister says one of the following prayers or one of those provided in nos. 398-399, p. 333.

A   A baptized child

Lord of all gentleness,   225
surround us with your care
and comfort us in our sorrow,
for we grieve at the loss of this [little] child.

As you washed N. in the waters of baptism
and welcomed him/her into the life of heaven,
so call us one day
to be united with him/her
and share for ever the joy of your kingdom.

We ask this through Christ our Lord.

R. Amen.

B   A child who died before baptism

Lord Jesus,
whose Mother stood grieving at the foot of the cross,
look kindly on these parents
who have suffered the loss of their child [N.].
Listen to the prayers of Mary on their behalf,
that their faith may be strong like hers
and find its promised reward,
for you live for ever and ever.

R. Amen.

CONCLUDING RITE

BLESSING

263 The minister says:

Jesus said: "Let the children come to me. Do not keep them
from me. The kingdom of God belongs to such as these."

A gesture, for example, signing the forehead of the deceased child
with the sign of the cross, may accompany the following words.

Eternal rest grant unto him/her, O Lord.

R. And let perpetual light shine upon him/her.

May he/she rest in peace.

R. Amen.

May his/her soul and the souls of all the faithful departed,
through the mercy of God, rest in peace.

R. Amen.

A   A minister who is a priest or deacon says:

May the peace of God,
which is beyond all understanding,
keep your hearts and minds
in the knowledge and love of God
and of his Son, our Lord Jesus Christ.

R. Amen.

May almighty God bless you,
the Father, and the Son, ✠ and the Holy Spirit.

R. Amen.

B   A lay minister invokes God's blessing and signs himself or herself with the sign of the cross, saying:

May the love of God and the peace of the Lord Jesus Christ
bless and console us
and gently wipe every tear from our eyes:
in the name of the Father,
and of the Son, and of the Holy Spirit.

R. Amen.

The vigil may conclude with a song or a few moments of silent
prayer or both.

FUNERAL LITURGY

The Lord will wipe away the tears from every cheek

FUNERAL LITURGY

264 The funeral liturgy, as described in nos. 128-153, is the central liturgical celebration of the Christian community for the deceased. Two forms of the funeral liturgy are provided: "Funeral Mass" and "Funeral Liturgy outside Mass." If the second form is used, Mass may be celebrated at a later date.

265 The funeral Mass includes the reception of the body, if this has not already occurred, the celebration of the liturgy of the word, the liturgy of the eucharist, and the final commendation and farewell. The funeral liturgy outside Mass includes all these elements except the liturgy of the eucharist. Both the funeral Mass and the funeral liturgy outside Mass may be followed by the procession to the place of committal.

266 The rite of reception of the body begins with a greeting of the family and others who have accompanied the body to the door of the church. The minister may give brief explanations of the symbols in this rite for the benefit of any children who may be present for the celebration. In the case of a baptized child, the minister sprinkles the coffin in remembrance of the deceased child's acceptance into the community of faith. If it is the custom in the local community, a funeral pall, a reminder of the garment given at baptism, and therefore signifying life in Christ, may then be placed on the coffin by family members, friends, or the minister. In the case of a child who died before baptism, the minister addresses the community with a few words. The entrance procession follows. The minister precedes the coffin and the mourners into the church, as all sing an entrance song. If the Easter candle is used on this occasion, it may be placed beforehand near the position the coffin will occupy at the conclusion of the procession.

If in this rite a symbol of the Christian life is to be placed on the coffin, it is carried in the procession and is placed on the coffin by a family member, friend, or the minister at the conclusion of the procession.

267 The rite of final commendation and farewell is celebrated at the conclusion of the funeral liturgy unless it is deferred for celebration at the place of committal. The rite begins with the invitation to prayer, followed by a pause for silent prayer. In the case of a baptized child, the body may then be sprinkled with holy water and incensed. Or this may be done during or after the song of farewell. The song of farewell is then sung and the rite concludes with the prayer of commendation.

Funeral Mass

268 The funeral Mass is ordinarily celebrated in the parish church.

269 The Mass texts are those of the Roman Missal and the Lectionary for Mass, "Masses for the Dead." The intercessions should be adapted to the circumstances; models are given in place and in Part V, p. 356, no. 401.

270 In the choice of music for the funeral Mass, preference should be given to the singing of the acclamations, the responsorial psalm, the entrance and communion songs, and especially the song of farewell at the final commendation.

Funeral Liturgy outside Mass

271 The funeral liturgy outside Mass may be celebrated for various reasons:
1. when the funeral Mass is not permitted, namely, on solemnities of obligation, on Holy Thursday and the Easter Triduum, and on the Sundays of Advent, Lent, and the Easter season;[1]
2. when in some places or circumstances it is not possible to celebrate the funeral Mass before the committal, for example, if a priest is not available;
3. when for pastoral reasons the pastor and the family decide that the funeral liturgy outside Mass is a more suitable form of celebration for the deceased child.

272 The funeral liturgy outside Mass is ordinarily celebrated in the parish church, but may also be celebrated in the home of the deceased, a funeral home, parlor, chapel of rest, or cemetery chapel.

273 The readings are those of the Lectionary for Mass, "Masses for the Dead." The intercessions should be adapted to the circumstances; models are given in place and in Part V, p. 356, no. 401. The celebration may include holy communion.

274 In the choice of music for the funeral liturgy, preference should be given to the singing of the entrance song, the responsorial psalm, the gospel acclamation, and especially the song of farewell at the final commendation.

275 The minister who is a priest or deacon wears an alb or surplice with stole (a cope may be used, if desired); a layperson who presides wears the liturgical vestments approved for the region.

---

[1] See General Instruction of the Roman Missal, no. 336.

OUTLINE OF THE RITE

INTRODUCTORY RITES

Greeting
Sprinkling with Holy Water
   or Brief Address
[Placing of the Pall]
Entrance Procession
[Placing of Christian Symbols]
Opening Prayer

LITURGY OF THE WORD

Readings
Homily
General Intercessions

LITURGY OF THE EUCHARIST

FINAL COMMENDATION

Invitation to Prayer
Silence
[Signs of Farewell]
Song of Farewell
Prayer of Commendation

PROCESSION TO
THE PLACE OF COMMITTAL

8 FUNERAL MASS

276 If the rite of reception of the body takes place at the beginning of the funeral Mass, the introductory rites are those given here and the usual introductory rites for Mass, including the penitential rite, are omitted. If the rite of reception of the body has already taken place, the Mass begins in the usual way.

INTRODUCTORY RITES

GREETING

277 The priest, with assisting ministers, goes to the door of the church and using one of the following greetings, or in similar words, greets those present.

A   The grace of our Lord Jesus Christ and the love of God and the fellowship of the Holy Spirit be with you all.

R. And also with you.

B   The grace and peace of God our Father and the Lord Jesus Christ be with you.

R. And also with you.

C   The grace and peace of God our Father, who raised Jesus from the dead, be always with you.

R. And also with you.

D   May the Father of mercies, the God of all consolation, be with you.

R. And also with you.

SPRINKLING WITH HOLY WATER OR BRIEF ADDRESS

278 If the child was baptized, the priest sprinkles the coffin with holy water (option A). If the child died before baptism, the sprinkling with holy water is omitted and a brief address is given (option B).

A   SPRINKLING WITH HOLY WATER—If the child was baptized, the priest then sprinkles the coffin with holy water, saying:

In the waters of baptism
N. died with Christ and rose with him to new life.
May he/she now share with him eternal glory.

B   BRIEF ADDRESS—If the child died before baptism, the priest may then address the mourners in the following or similar words.

My brothers and sisters, the Lord is a faithful God who created us all after his own image. All things are of his making, all creation awaits the day of salvation. We now entrust the soul of N. to the abundant mercy of God, that our beloved child may find a home in his kingdom.

PLACING OF THE PALL

279 If it is the custom in the local community and the child was baptized, the pall is then placed on the coffin by family members, friends, or the priest.

ENTRANCE PROCESSION

280 The Easter candle may be placed beforehand near the position the coffin will occupy at the conclusion of the procession. The priest and assisting ministers precede the coffin and the mourners into the church. During the procession a psalm, song, or responsory is sung (see no. 403, p. 366).

PLACING OF CHRISTIAN SYMBOLS

281 A symbol of the Christian life, such as a cross, may be carried in procession, then placed on the coffin, either in silence or as a text from no. 400, p. 355, is said.

On reaching the altar, the priest, with the assisting ministers, makes the customary reverence, kisses the altar, and (if incense is used) incenses it. Then he goes to the chair.

OPENING PRAYER

282 When all have reached their places, the priest invites the assembly to pray.

Let us pray.

After a brief period of silent prayer, the priest sings or says one of the following prayers or one of those provided in nos. 398-399, p. 333.

A   A baptized child

Merciful Lord,
whose wisdom is beyond human understanding,
you adopted N. as your own in baptism
and have taken him/her to yourself
even as he/she stood on the threshold of life.
Listen to our prayers and extend to us your grace,
that one day we may share eternal life with N.,
for we firmly believe that he/she now rests with you.

We ask this through our Lord Jesus Christ, your Son,
who lives and reigns with you and the Holy Spirit,
one God, for ever and ever.

R. Amen.

B   A baptized child

Lord God,
from whom human sadness is never hidden,
you know the burden of grief
that we feel at the loss of this child.

As we mourn his/her passing from this life,
comfort us with the knowledge
that N. lives now in your loving embrace.

We make our prayer through our Lord Jesus Christ, your Son,
who lives and reigns with you and the Holy Spirit,
one God, for ever and ever.

R. Amen.

C   A child who died before baptism 235

O Lord, whose ways are beyond understanding,
listen to the prayers of your faithful people:
that those weighed down by grief
    at the loss of this [little] child
may find reassurance in your infinite goodness.

We ask this through our Lord Jesus Christ, your Son,
who lives and reigns with you and the Holy Spirit,
one God, for ever and ever.

R. Amen.

D   A child who died before baptism 236

God of all consolation,
searcher of mind and heart,
the faith of these parents [N. and N.] is known to you.

Comfort them with the knowledge
that the child for whom they grieve
is entrusted now to your loving care.

We ask this through our Lord Jesus Christ, your Son,
who lives and reigns with you and the Holy Spirit,
one God, for ever and ever.

R. Amen.

LITURGY OF THE WORD

READINGS

283 After the introductory rites, the liturgy of the word is celebrated. Depending upon pastoral circumstances, either one or two readings may be read before the gospel reading.

HOMILY

284 A brief homily is given after the gospel reading.

GENERAL INTERCESSIONS

285 The following intercessions or those given in no. 401, p. 356, may be used or adapted to the circumstances, or new intercessions may be composed.

The priest begins:

Let us pray for N., his/her family and friends, and for all God's people.

Assisting minister:

For N., child of God [and heir to the kingdom], that he/she be held securely in God's loving embrace now and for all eternity. We pray to the Lord.

R. Lord, hear our prayer.

Assisting minister:

For N.'s family, especially his/her mother and father, [his/her brother(s) and sister(s)], that they feel the healing power of Christ in the midst of their pain and grief. We pray to the Lord.

R. Lord, hear our prayer.

Assisting minister:

For N.'s friends, those who played with him/her and those who cared for him/her, that they be consoled in their loss and strengthened in their love for one another. We pray to the Lord.

R. Lord, hear our prayer.

Assisting minister:

For all parents who grieve over the death of their children, that they be comforted in the knowledge that their children dwell with God. We pray to the Lord.

R. Lord, hear our prayer.

Assisting minister:

For children who have died of hunger and disease, that these little ones be seated close to the Lord at his heavenly table. We pray to the Lord.

R. Lord, hear our prayer.

Assisting minister:

For the whole Church, that we prepare worthily for the hour of our death, when God will call us by name to pass from this world to the next. We pray to the Lord.

R. Lord, hear our prayer.

The priest then concludes:

Lord God,
you entrusted N. to our care
and now you embrace him/her in your love.

Take N. into your keeping
together with all children who have died.

Comfort us, your sorrowing servants,
who seek to do your will
and to know your saving peace.

We ask this through Christ our Lord.

R. Amen.

LITURGY OF THE EUCHARIST

286 The liturgy of the eucharist is celebrated in the usual manner.

287 If the final commendation is to be celebrated at the place of committal, the procession to the place of committal (no. 294) begins following the prayer after communion.

FINAL COMMENDATION

288 Following the prayer after communion, the priest goes to a place near the coffin. The assisting ministers carry the censer and holy water, if these are to be used.

A member or a friend of the family may speak in remembrance of the deceased child before the final commendation begins.

Invitation to Prayer

289 Using one of the following invitations, or one of those provided in no. 402, p. 365, or in similar words, the priest faces the people and begins the final commendation.

A   A baptized child

God in his wisdom knows the span of our days; he has chosen   227
to call to himself this child, whom he adopted as his own in baptism. The body we must now bury will one day rise again to a new and radiant life that will never end.

Our firm belief is that N., because he/she was baptized, has already entered this new life; our firm hope is that we shall do the same. Let us ask God to comfort his/her family and friends and to increase our desire for the joys of heaven.

B   A baptized child

With faith in Jesus Christ, we must reverently bury the body   228
of N.

Let us pray with confidence to God, in whose sight all creation lives, that he will raise up in holiness and power the mortal body of this [little] child, for God has chosen to number his/her soul among the blessed.

C   A child who died before baptism

Let us commend this child to the Lord's merciful keeping; and   237
let us pray with all our hearts for N. and N. Even as they grieve at the loss of their [little] child, they entrust him/her to the loving embrace of God.

Silence

290 All pray in silence.

Signs of Farewell

291 The coffin of a baptized child may now be sprinkled with holy water and incensed, or this may take place during or after the song of farewell. If the body was sprinkled with holy water

during the rite of reception at the beginning of Mass, the sprinkling is ordinarily omitted in the rite of final commendation.

Song of Farewell

292 The song of farewell is then sung. The following or other responsories chosen from no. 403, p. 366, may be used or some other song may be sung.

A   I know that my Redeemer lives: 189
on the last day I shall rise again.

    R. And in my flesh I shall see God.

      Or:

    R. On the last day I shall rise again.

I shall see him myself, face to face;
and my own eyes shall behold my Savior. R.

Within my heart this hope I cherish:
that in my flesh I shall see God. R.

B   Saints of God, come to his/her aid!   47
Hasten to meet him/her, angels of the Lord!

    R. Receive his/her soul and present him/her to God the Most High.

May Christ, who called you, take you to himself;
may angels lead you to the bosom of Abraham. R.

Eternal rest grant unto him/her, O Lord,
and let perpetual light shine upon him/her. R.

Prayer of Commendation

293 The priest then says one of the following prayers or one of those provided in no. 404, p. 368.

A   A baptized child

You are the author and sustainer of our lives, O God.
You are our final home.
We commend to you N., our child.

In baptism he/she began his/her journey toward you.
Take him/her now to yourself
and give him/her the life
promised to those born again of water and the Spirit.

Turn also to us who have suffered this loss.
Strengthen the bonds of this family and our community.
Confirm us in faith, in hope, and in love,
so that we may bear your peace to one another
and one day stand together with all the saints
who praise you for your saving help.

We ask this in the name of your Son,
whom you raised from among the dead,
Jesus Christ, our Lord.

R. Amen.

B   A child who died before baptism

You are the author and sustainer of our lives, O God,
you are our final home.
We commend to you N., our child.

Trusting in your mercy
and in your all-embracing love,
we pray that you give him/her happiness for ever.

Turn also to us who have suffered this loss.
Strengthen the bonds of this family and our community.
Confirm us in faith, in hope, and in love,
so that we may bear your peace to one another
and one day stand together with all the saints
who praise you for your saving help.

We ask this in the name of your Son,
Jesus Christ, our Lord.

R. Amen.

PROCESSION TO THE PLACE OF COMMITTAL

294 The deacon or, in the absence of a deacon, the priest says:

In peace let us take N. to his/her place of rest.

If a symbol of the Christian life has been placed on the coffin, it should be removed at this time.

The procession then begins: the priest and assisting ministers precede the coffin; the family and mourners follow.

One or more of the following texts or other suitable songs may be sung during the procession to the entrance of the church. The singing may continue during the journey to the place of committal.

A   The following antiphon may be sung with verses from Psalm 25, p. 268, or separately. A metrical version of this text is given on p. 330, no. 396, E.

May the angels lead you into paradise;   50
may the martyrs come to welcome you
and take you to the holy city,
the new and eternal Jerusalem.

B   The following antiphon may be sung with verses from Psalm 116, p. 274, or separately.

May choirs of angels welcome you   50
and lead you to the bosom of Abraham;
and where Lazarus is poor no longer
may you find eternal rest.

C   Whoever believes in me,   166
even though that person die, shall live.

R. I am the resurrection and the life.

Whoever lives and believes in me shall never die. R.

D   The following psalms may also be used.

Psalm 118, p. 275; Psalm 42, p. 269; Psalm 93, p. 272; Psalm 25, p. 268; Psalm 119, p. 277.

OUTLINE OF THE RITE

INTRODUCTORY RITES

Greeting
Sprinkling with Holy Water
    or Brief Address
[Placing of the Pall]
Entrance Procession
[Placing of Christian Symbols]
Invitation to Prayer
Opening Prayer

LITURGY OF THE WORD

Readings
Homily
General Intercessions
The Lord's Prayer

FINAL COMMENDATION

Invitation to Prayer
Silence
[Signs of Farewell]
Song of Farewell
Prayer of Commendation

PROCESSION TO
THE PLACE OF COMMITTAL

9 FUNERAL LITURGY OUTSIDE MASS

295 If the rite of reception of the body takes place at the beginning of the funeral liturgy, the introductory rites are those given here. If the rite of reception of the body has already taken place, the liturgy begins with an entrance song and the greeting (no. 296), followed by the invitation to prayer (no. 301).

INTRODUCTORY RITES

GREETING

296 The presiding minister, with assisting ministers, goes to the door of the church and using one of the following greetings, or in similar words, greets those present.

A   The grace of our Lord Jesus Christ and the love of God and the fellowship of the Holy Spirit be with you all.

R. And also with you.

B   The grace and peace of God our Father and the Lord Jesus Christ be with you.

R. And also with you.

C   The grace and peace of God our Father, who raised Jesus from the dead, be always with you.

R. And also with you.

D   May the Father of mercies, the God of all consolation, be with you.

R. And also with you.

SPRINKLING WITH HOLY WATER OR BRIEF ADDRESS

297 If the child was baptized, the presiding minister sprinkles the coffin with holy water (option A). If the child died before baptism, the sprinkling with holy water is omitted and a brief address is given (option B).

A   SPRINKLING WITH HOLY WATER—If the child was baptized, the presiding minister then sprinkles the coffin with holy water, saying:

In the waters of baptism
N. died with Christ and rose with him to new life.
May he/she now share with him eternal glory.

B   BRIEF ADDRESS—If the child died before baptism, the presiding minister may then address the mourners in the following or similar words.

My brothers and sisters, the Lord is a faithful God who created us all after his own image. All things are of his making, all creation awaits the day of salvation. We now entrust the soul of N. to the abundant mercy of God, that our beloved child may find a home in his kingdom.

PLACING OF THE PALL

298 If it is the custom in the local community and the child was baptized, the pall is then placed on the coffin by family members, friends, or the minister.

ENTRANCE PROCESSION

299 The Easter candle may be placed beforehand near the position the coffin will occupy at the conclusion of the procession. The presiding minister and assisting ministers precede the coffin and the mourners into the church. During the procession a psalm, song, or responsory is sung (see no. 403. p. 366).

PLACING OF CHRISTIAN SYMBOLS

300 A symbol of the Christian life, such as a cross, may be carried in procession, then placed on the coffin, either in silence or as a text from no. 400, p. 355, is said.

On reaching the altar, the presiding minister, with the assisting ministers, makes the customary reverence and goes to the chair.

INVITATION TO PRAYER

301 When all have reached their places, the presiding minister, using the following or similar words, invites the assembly to pray.

My brothers and sisters,
we have come together to renew our trust in Christ
who, by dying on the cross, has freed us from eternal death
and, by rising, has opened for us the gates of heaven.
Let us pray that the Lord may grant us
the gift of his loving consolation.

OPENING PRAYER

302 After a brief period of silent prayer, the presiding minister sings or says one of the following prayers or one of those provided in nos. 398-399, p. 333.

A   A baptized child

Merciful Lord,
whose wisdom is beyond human understanding,
you adopted N. as your own in baptism
and have taken him/her to yourself
even as he/she stood on the threshold of life.
Listen to our prayers and extend to us your grace,
that one day we may share eternal life with N.,
for we firmly believe that he/she now rests with you.

We ask this through our Lord Jesus Christ, your Son,
who lives and reigns with you and the Holy Spirit,
one God, for ever and ever.

R. Amen.

B   A baptized child

Lord God,
from whom human sadness is never hidden,
you know the burden of grief
that we feel at the loss of this child.

As we mourn his/her passing from this life,
comfort us with the knowledge
that N. lives now in your loving embrace.

We make our prayer through our Lord Jesus Christ, your Son,
who lives and reigns with you and the Holy Spirit,
one God, for ever and ever.

R. Amen.

C   A child who died before baptism

O Lord, whose ways are beyond understanding,   235
listen to the prayers of your faithful people:
that those weighed down by grief
    at the loss of this [little] child
may find reassurance in your infinite goodness.

We ask this through our Lord Jesus Christ, your Son,
who lives and reigns with you and the Holy Spirit,
one God, for ever and ever.

R. Amen.

D   A child who died before baptism

God of all consolation,   236
searcher of mind and heart,
the faith of these parents [N. and N.] is known to you.

Comfort them with the knowledge
that the child for whom they grieve
is entrusted now to your loving care.

We ask this through our Lord Jesus Christ, your Son,
who lives and reigns with you and the Holy Spirit,
one God, for ever and ever.

R. Amen.

LITURGY OF THE WORD

READINGS

303 After the introductory rites, the liturgy of the word is celebrated. Depending upon pastoral circumstances, either one or two readings may be read before the gospel reading.

HOMILY

304 A brief homily is given after the gospel reading.

GENERAL INTERCESSIONS

305 The following intercessions or those given in no. 401, p. 356, may be used or adapted to the circumstances, or new intercessions may be composed.

The presiding minister begins:

The Lord Jesus is the lover of his people and our only sure hope. Let us ask him to deepen our faith and sustain us in this dark hour.

Assisting minister:
You became a little child for our sake, sharing our human life. To you we pray:
R. Bless us and keep us, O Lord.

Assisting minister:
You grew in wisdom, age and grace, and learned obedience through suffering.
To you we pray:
R. Bless us and keep us, O Lord.

Assisting minister:
You welcomed children, promising them your kingdom.
To you we pray:
R. Bless us and keep us, O Lord.

Assisting minister:

You comforted those who mourned the loss of children and friends.
To you we pray:

R. Bless us and keep us, O Lord.

Assisting minister:

You took upon yourself the suffering and death of us all.
To you we pray:

R. Bless us and keep us, O Lord.

Assisting minister:

You promised to raise up those who believe in you, just as you were raised up in glory by the Father.
To you we pray:

R. Bless us and keep us, O Lord.

The presiding minister then concludes:

Lord God,
you entrusted N. to our care
and now you embrace him/her in your love.

Take N. into your keeping
together with all children who have died.

Comfort us, your sorrowing servants,
who seek to do your will
and to know your saving peace.

We ask this through Christ our Lord.

R. Amen.

THE LORD'S PRAYER

306 Using one of the following invitations, or in similar words, the minister invites those present to pray the Lord's Prayer.

A   Now let us pray as Christ the Lord has taught us:

B   With longing for the coming of God's kingdom, let us offer our prayer to the Father:

All say:

Our Father . . .

---

307 The celebration may include holy communion (Part V, p. 377, nos. 409-410).

---

308 If the final commendation is to be celebrated at the place of committal, the procession to the place of committal (no. 315) begins following the Lord's Prayer or the prayer after communion.

FINAL COMMENDATION

309 Following the Lord's Prayer (or the prayer after communion) the presiding minister goes to a place near the coffin. The assisting ministers carry the censer and holy water, if these are to be used.

A member or a friend of the family may speak in remembrance of the deceased child before the final commendation begins.

INVITATION TO PRAYER

310 Using one of the following invitations, or one of those provided in no. 402, p. 365, or in similar words, the presiding minister faces the people and begins the final commendation.

A   A baptized child

God in his wisdom knows the span of our days; he has chosen to call to himself this child, whom he adopted as his own in baptism. The body we must now bury will one day rise again to a new and radiant life that will never end.

Our firm belief is that N., because he/she was baptized, has already entered this new life; our firm hope is that we shall do the same. Let us ask God to comfort his/her family and friends and to increase our desire for the joys of heaven.

227

B   A baptized child

With faith in Jesus Christ, we must reverently bury the body 228 of N.

Let us pray with confidence to God, in whose sight all creation lives, that he will raise up in holiness and power the mortal body of this [little] child, for God has chosen to number his/her soul among the blessed.

C   A child who died before baptism 23?

Let us commend this child to the Lord's merciful keeping; and let us pray with all our hearts for N. and N. Even as they grieve at the loss of their [little] child, they entrust him/her to the loving embrace of God.

SILENCE

311 All pray in silence.

SIGNS OF FAREWELL

312 The coffin of a baptized child may now be sprinkled with holy water and incensed, or this may take place during or after the song of farewell. If the body was sprinkled with holy water during the rite of reception at the beginning of the funeral liturgy, the sprinkling is ordinarily omitted in the rite of final commendation.

SONG OF FAREWELL

313 The song of farewell is then sung. The following or other responsories chosen from no. 403, p. 366, may be used or some other song may be sung.

A I know that my Redeemer lives:
  on the last day I shall rise again. 1?

  R. And in my flesh I shall see God.
   Or:
  R. On the last day I shall rise again.

I shall see him myself, face to face;
and my own eyes shall behold my Savior. R.

Within my heart this hope I cherish:
that in my flesh I shall see God. R.

B   Saints of God, come to his/her aid!   47
Hasten to meet him/her, angels of the Lord!

R. Receive his/her soul and present him/her to God the
Most High.

May Christ, who called you, take you to himself;
may angels lead you to the bosom of Abraham. R.

Eternal rest grant unto him/her, O Lord,
and let perpetual light shine upon him/her. R.

PRAYER OF COMMENDATION

> 314 The presiding minister then says one of the following prayers
> or one of those provided in no. 404, p. 368.

A   A baptized child

You are the author and sustainer of our lives, O God.
You are our final home.
We commend to you N., our child.

In baptism he/she began his/her journey toward you.
Take him/her now to yourself
and give him/her the life
promised to those born again of water and the Spirit.

Turn also to us who have suffered this loss.
Strengthen the bonds of this family and our community.
Confirm us in faith, in hope, and in love,
so that we may bear your peace to one another
and one day stand together with all the saints
who praise you for your saving help.

We ask this in the name of your Son,
whom you raised from among the dead,
Jesus Christ, our Lord.

R. Amen.

B   A child who died before baptism

You are the author and sustainer of our lives, O God,
you are our final home.
We commend to you N., our child.

Trusting in your mercy
and in your all-embracing love,
we pray that you give him/her happiness for ever.

Turn also to us who have suffered this loss.
Strengthen the bonds of this family and our community.
Confirm us in faith, in hope, and in love,
so that we may bear your peace to one another
and one day stand together with all the saints
who praise you for your saving help.

We ask this in the name of your Son,
Jesus Christ, our Lord.

R. Amen.

PROCESSION TO THE
PLACE OF COMMITTAL

315 An assisting minister, or in the absence of an assisting minister, the presiding minister says:

In peace let us take N. to his/her place of rest.

If a symbol of the Christian life has been placed on the coffin,
it should be removed at this time.

The procession then begins: the presiding minister and assisting ministers precede the coffin; the family and mourners follow.

One or more of the following texts or other suitable songs may
be sung during the procession to the entrance of the church. The
singing may continue during the journey to the place of committal.

A   The following antiphon may be sung with verses from Psalm 25, p. 268, or separately. A metrical version of this text is given on p. 330, no. 396, E.

May the angels lead you into paradise;   50
may the martyrs come to welcome you
and take you to the holy city,
the new and eternal Jerusalem.

B   The following antiphon may be sung with verses from Psalm 116, p. 274, or separately.

May choirs of angels welcome you   50
and lead you to the bosom of Abraham;
and where Lazarus is poor no longer
may you find eternal rest.

C   Whoever believes in me,   166
even though that person die, shall live.

R. I am the resurrection and the life.

Whoever lives and believes in me shall never die. R.

D   The following psalms may also be used.

Psalm 118, p. 275; Psalm 42, p. 269; Psalm 93, p. 272; Psalm 25, p. 268; Psalm 119, p. 277.

RITE OF COMMITTAL

The Lord is my shepherd;
fresh and green are the pastures
where he gives me repose

RITE OF COMMITTAL

316 The rite of committal, the conclusion of the funeral rites (see nos. 204-215), is celebrated at the grave, tomb, or crematorium and may be used for burial at sea.

Three forms of the rite of committal are provided for the funeral of a child: "Rite of Committal," "Rite of Committal with Final Commendation," and "Rite of Final Commendation for an Infant."

317 The rite of committal is used when the final commendation and farewell is celebrated within the funeral liturgy. The rite of committal with final commendation is used when the final commendation is not celebrated within the funeral liturgy.

When the funeral liturgy is celebrated on a day prior to the committal or in a different community, the minister may wish to adapt the rite of committal, for example, by adding a song, a greeting, one or more readings, a psalm, and a brief homily. When no funeral liturgy precedes the rite of committal, the rite of committal with final commendation is used and should be similarly adapted.

318 The "Rite of Final Commendation for an Infant" may be used in the case of a stillborn or a newborn infant who dies shortly after birth. This short rite of prayer with the parents is celebrated to give them comfort and to commend and entrust the infant to God. This rite is a model and the minister should adapt it to the circumstances. It may be used in the hospital or place of birth or at the time of the committal of the body.

OUTLINE OF THE RITE

Invitation
Scripture Verse
Prayer over the Place of Committal

Committal
Intercessions
The Lord's Prayer
Concluding Prayer

Prayer over the People

10 RITE OF COMMITTAL

Invitation

319 When the funeral procession arrives at the place of committal, the minister says the following or a similar invitation.

The life which this child N. received from his/her parents is not destroyed by death. God has taken him/her into eternal life.

As we commit his/her body to the earth/elements, let us comfort each other in our sorrow with the assurance of our faith, that one day we will be reunited with N.

Scripture Verse

320 One of the following verses or another brief Scripture verse is read. The minister first says:

We read in sacred Scripture:

A   Matthew 25:34   119

Come, you who are blessed by my Father, says the Lord,
inherit the kingdom prepared for you from the foundation
   of the world.

B   John 6:39   121

This is the will of the one who sent me, says the Lord,
that I should not lose anything of what he gave me,
but that I should raise it on the last day.

C   Philippians 3:20   124

Our citizenship is in heaven,
and from it we also await a savior,
the Lord Jesus Christ.

D   Revelation 1:5-6   126

Jesus Christ is the firstborn of the dead;
to him be glory and power forever and ever. Amen.

Prayer over the Place of Committal

321 The minister says one of the following prayers or one of those provided in no. 405, p. 370.

A   If the place of committal is to be blessed:

O God,
by whose mercy the faithful departed find rest,
bless this grave,
and send your holy angel to watch over it.

As we bury here the body of N.,
welcome him/her into your presence,
that he/she may rejoice in you with your saints for ever.

We ask this through Christ our Lord.

R. Amen.

B   If the place of committal has already been blessed:

All praise to you, Lord of all creation.
Praise to you, holy and living God.
We praise and bless you for your mercy,
we praise and bless you for your kindness.
Blessed is the Lord, our God.

R. Blessed is the Lord, our God.

You sanctify the homes of the living
and make holy the places of the dead.
You alone open the gates of righteousness
and lead us to the dwellings of the saints.
Blessed is the Lord, our God.

R. Blessed is the Lord, our God.

We praise you, our refuge and strength.
We bless you, our God and Redeemer.
Your praise is always in our hearts and on our lips.
We remember the mighty deeds of the covenant.
Blessed is the Lord, our God.

R. Blessed is the Lord, our God.

Almighty and ever-living God,
remember the love with which you graced your child N.
in life.
Receive him/her, we pray, into the mansions of the saints.
As we make ready this resting place,
look also with favor on those who mourn
and comfort them in their loss.
Grant this through Christ our Lord.

R. Amen.

C   When the final disposition of the body is to take place at a later
     time:

Almighty and ever-living God,
in you we place our trust and hope,
in you the dead, whose bodies were temples of the Spirit,
   find everlasting peace.

As we take leave of N.,
give our hearts peace in the firm hope
that one day he/she will live
in the mansion you have prepared for him/her in heaven.

We ask this through Christ our Lord.

R. Amen.

COMMITTAL

322 The minister then says the words of committal. One of the
following formularies or one provided in no. 406, p. 372, may
be used.

A   A baptized child

Into your hands, O merciful Savior, we commend N.
Acknowledge, we humbly beseech you,
a sheep of your own fold, a lamb of your own flock.
Receive him/her into the arms of your mercy,
into the blessed rest of everlasting peace,
and into the glorious company of the saints in light.

B   A child who died before baptism

Lord God,
ever caring and gentle,
we commit to your love this little one [N.],
who brought joy to our lives for so short a time.
Enfold him/her in eternal life.

We pray for his/her parents
who are saddened by the loss of their child [baby/infant].
Give them courage
and help them in their pain and grief.
May they all meet one day
in the joy and peace of your kingdom.
We ask this through Christ our Lord.

R. Amen.

> The committal takes place at this time or at the conclusion of the rite.

INTERCESSIONS

> 323 The following intercessions or those given in no. 407, p. 374, may be used or adapted to the circumstances, or new intercessions may be composed.

> The minister begins:

Dear friends, let us turn to the Lord, the God of hope and consolation, who calls us to everlasting glory in Christ Jesus.

> Assisting minister:

For N., that he/she may now enjoy the place prepared for him/her in your great love.
We pray to the Lord.

R. Lord, hear our prayer.

> Assisting minister:

For N.'s father and mother [brother(s) and sister(s)], that they may know our love and support in their grief.
We pray to the Lord.

R. Lord, hear our prayer.

Assisting minister:

For his/her friends [and teachers], that they may love one another as you have loved us.
We pray to the Lord.

R. Lord, hear our prayer.

Assisting minister:

For this community, that we may bear one another's burdens.
We pray to the Lord.

R. Lord, hear our prayer.

Assisting minister:

For all those who mourn their children, that they may be comforted.
We pray to the Lord.

R. Lord, hear our prayer.

Assisting minister:

For all who are in need, that the fearful may find peace, the weary rest, and the oppressed freedom.
We pray to the Lord.

R. Lord, hear our prayer.

The Lord's Prayer

324 Using the following or similar words, the minister invites those present to pray the Lord's Prayer.

As sons and daughters of a loving God, we pray in the confident words of his Son:

All say:

Our Father . . .

Concluding Prayer

325 The minister says one of the following prayers or one of those provided in no. 408, p. 376.

A   A baptized child

Tender Shepherd of the flock,
N. has entered your kingdom
and now lies cradled in your love.
Soothe the hearts of his/her parents
and bring peace to their lives.
Enlighten their faith
and give hope to their hearts.

Loving God,
grant mercy to your entire family in this time of suffering.
Comfort us in the knowledge that this child [N.]
lives with you and your Son, Jesus Christ,
and the Holy Spirit,
for ever and ever.

R. Amen.

B   A baptized child

Listen, O God, to the prayers of your Church
on behalf of the faithful departed,
and grant to your child, N.,
whose funeral we have celebrated today,
the inheritance promised to all your saints.

We ask this through Christ our Lord.

R. Amen.

C   A child who died before baptism

God of mercy,
in the mystery of your wisdom
you have drawn this child [N.] to yourself.
In the midst of our pain and sorrow,
we acknowledge you as Lord of the living and the dead
and we search for our peace in your will.
In these final moments we stand together in prayer,
believing in your compassion and generous love.
Deliver this child [N.] out of death
and grant him/her a place in your kingdom of peace.

We ask this through Christ our Lord.

R. Amen.

Prayer over the People

326 The assisting minister says:

Bow your heads and pray for God's blessing.

All pray silently. The minister, with hands outstretched, prays over the people:

Merciful Lord,
you know the anguish of the sorrowful,
you are attentive to the prayers of the humble.
Hear your people
who cry out to you in their need,
and strengthen their hope in your lasting goodness.
We ask this through Christ our Lord.

R. Amen.

The minister then says the following:

Eternal rest grant unto him/her, O Lord.

R. And let perpetual light shine upon him/her.

May he/she rest in peace.

R. Amen.

May his/her soul and the souls of all the faithful departed,
through the mercy of God, rest in peace.

R. Amen.

A   *A minister who is a priest or deacon says:*

May the peace of God,
which is beyond all understanding,
keep your hearts and minds
in the knowledge and love of God
and of his Son, our Lord Jesus Christ.

R. Amen.

May almighty God bless you,
the Father, and the Son, ✠ and the Holy Spirit.

R. Amen.

B A lay minister invokes God's blessing and signs himself or herself with the sign of the cross, saying:

May the love of God and the peace of the Lord Jesus Christ
bless and console us
and gently wipe every tear from our eyes:
in the name of the Father,
and of the Son, and of the Holy Spirit.

R. Amen.

The minister then concludes:

Go in the peace of Christ.

R. Thanks be to God.

A song may conclude the rite. Where it is the custom, some sign
or gesture of leave-taking may be made.

OUTLINE OF THE RITE

Invitation
Scripture Verse
Prayer over the Place of Committal

Invitation to Prayer
Silence
[Signs of Farewell]
Song of Farewell
Prayer of Commendation
Committal

Prayer over the People

11 RITE OF COMMITTAL WITH FINAL COMMENDATION

INVITATION

327 When the funeral procession arrives at the place of committal, the minister says the following or a similar invitation.

The life which this child N. received from his/her parents is not destroyed by death. God has taken him/her into eternal life.

As we commend N. to God and commit his/her body to the earth/elements, let us express in [song and] prayer our common faith in the resurrection. As Jesus Christ was raised from the dead, we too are called to follow him through death to the glory where God will be all in all.

SCRIPTURE VERSE

328 One of the following verses or another brief Scripture verse is read. The minister first says:

We read in sacred Scripture:

A   Matthew 25:34   119

Come, you who are blessed by my Father, says the Lord, inherit the kingdom prepared for you from the foundation of the world.

B   John 6:39   121

This is the will of the one who sent me, says the Lord, that I should not lose anything of what he gave me, but that I should raise it on the last day.

C   Philippians 3:20   124

Our citizenship is in heaven, and from it we also await a savior, the Lord Jesus Christ.

D   Revelation 1:5-6   126

Jesus Christ is the firstborn of the dead; to him be glory and power forever and ever. Amen.

Prayer over the Place of Committal

329 The minister says one of the following prayers or one of those provided in no. 405, p. 370.

A   If the place of committal is to be blessed: 230

O God,
by whose mercy the faithful departed find rest,
bless this grave,
and send your holy angel to watch over it.

As we bury here the body of N.,
welcome him/her into your presence,
that he/she may rejoice in you with your saints for ever.

We ask this through Christ our Lord.

R. Amen.

B   If the place of committal has already been blessed:

All praise to you, Lord of all creation.
Praise to you, holy and living God.
We praise and bless you for your mercy,
we praise and bless you for your kindness.
Blessed is the Lord, our God.

R. Blessed is the Lord, our God.

You sanctify the homes of the living
and make holy the places of the dead.
You alone open the gates of righteousness
and lead us to the dwellings of the saints.
Blessed is the Lord, our God.

R. Blessed is the Lord, our God.

We praise you, our refuge and strength.
We bless you, our God and Redeemer.
Your praise is always in our hearts and on our lips.
We remember the mighty deeds of the covenant.
Blessed is the Lord, our God.

R. Blessed is the Lord, our God.

Almighty and ever-living God,
remember the love with which you graced your child N.
    in life.

Receive him/her, we pray, into the mansions of the saints.
As we make ready this resting place,
look also with favor on those who mourn
and comfort them in their loss.

Grant this through Christ our Lord.

R. Amen.

C   When the final disposition of the body is to take place at a later
         time:

Almighty and ever-living God,
in you we place our trust and hope,
in you the dead, whose bodies were temples of the Spirit,
    find everlasting peace.

As we take leave of N.,
give our hearts peace in the firm hope
that one day he/she will live
in the mansion you have prepared for him/her in heaven.

We ask this through Christ our Lord.

R. Amen.

INVITATION TO PRAYER

330 Using one of the following invitations, or one of those provided in no. 402, p. 365, or in similar words, the minister faces
the people and begins the final commendation.

A   A baptized child

God in his wisdom knows the span of our days; he has chosen   227
to call to himself this child, whom he adopted as his own in
baptism. The body we must now bury will one day rise again
to a new and radiant life that will never end.

Our firm belief is that N., because he/she was baptized, has
already entered this new life; our firm hope is that we shall do
the same. Let us ask God to comfort his/her family and friends
and to increase our desire for the joys of heaven.

B   A baptized child

With faith in Jesus Christ, we must reverently bury the body   228
of N.

Let us pray with confidence to God, in whose sight all creation
lives, that he will raise up in holiness and power the mortal body
of this [little] child, for God has chosen to number his/her soul
among the blessed.

C   A child who died before baptism

Let us commend this child to the Lord's merciful keeping; and   237
let us pray with all our hearts for N. and N. Even as they grieve
at the loss of their [little] child, they entrust him/her to the loving embrace of God.

Silence

331 All pray in silence.

Signs of Farewell

332 The coffin of a baptized child may now be sprinkled with
holy water and incensed, or this may take place during or after
the song of farewell.

Song of Farewell

333 The song of farewell is then sung. The following or other
responsories chosen from no. 403, p. 366, may be used or some
other song may be sung.

A   I know that my Redeemer lives: 189
on the last day I shall rise again.
R. And in my flesh I shall see God.
Or:
R. On the last day I shall rise again.

I shall see him myself, face to face;
and my own eyes shall behold my Savior. R.

Within my heart this hope I cherish:
that in my flesh I shall see God. R.

B Saints of God, come to his/her aid!   47
Hasten to meet him/her, angels of the Lord!
R. Receive his/her soul and present him/her to God the
Most High.

May Christ, who called you, take you to himself;
may angels lead you to the bosom of Abraham. R.

Eternal rest grant unto him/her, O Lord,
and let perpetual light shine upon him/her. R.

PRAYER OF COMMENDATION

334 The minister then says one of the following prayers or one
of those provided in no. 404, p. 368.

A   A baptized child

You are the author and sustainer of our lives, O God.
You are our final home.
We commend to you N., our child.

In baptism he/she began his/her journey toward you.
Take him/her now to yourself
and give him/her the life
promised to those born again of water and the Spirit.

Turn also to us who have suffered this loss.
Strengthen the bonds of this family and our community.
Confirm us in faith, in hope, and in love,
so that we may bear your peace to one another
and one day stand together with all the saints
who praise you for your saving help.

We ask this in the name of your Son,
whom you raised from among the dead,
Jesus Christ, our Lord.

R. Amen.

B A child who died before baptism

You are the author and sustainer of our lives, O God,
you are our final home.
We commend to you N., our child.

Trusting in your mercy
and in your all-embracing love,
we pray that you give him/her happiness for ever.

Turn also to us who have suffered this loss.
Strengthen the bonds of this family and our community.
Confirm us in faith, in hope, and in love,
so that we may bear your peace to one another
and one day stand together with all the saints
who praise you for your saving help.

We ask this in the name of your Son,
Jesus Christ, our Lord.

R. Amen.

COMMITTAL

335 The act of committal takes place at this time or at the conclusion of the rite.

PRAYER OVER THE PEOPLE

336 The assisting minister says:

Bow your heads and pray for God's blessing.

All pray silently. The minister, with hands extended, prays over the people:

Most merciful God,
whose wisdom is beyond our understanding,
surround the family of N. with your love,
that they may not be overwhelmed by their loss,
but have confidence in your goodness,
and strength to meet the days to come.

We ask this through Christ our Lord.

R. Amen.

The minister then says the following:

Eternal rest grant unto him/her, O Lord.

R. And let perpetual light shine upon him/her.

May he/she rest in peace.

R. Amen.

May his/her soul and the souls of all the faithful departed,
through the mercy of God, rest in peace.

R. Amen.

A   A minister who is a priest or deacon says:

May the peace of God,
which is beyond all understanding,
keep your hearts and minds
in the knowledge and love of God
and of his Son, our Lord Jesus Christ.

R. Amen.

May almighty God bless you,
the Father, and the Son, ✠ and the Holy Spirit.

R. Amen.

B   A lay minister invokes God's blessing and signs himself or herself with the sign of the cross, saying:

May the love of God and the peace of the Lord Jesus Christ
bless and console us
and gently wipe every tear from our eyes:
in the name of the Father,
and of the Son, and of the Holy Spirit.

R. Amen.

The minister then concludes:

Go in the peace of Christ.

R. Thanks be to God.

A song may conclude the rite. Where it is the custom, some sign
or gesture of leave-taking may be made.

OUTLINE OF THE RITE

Brief Address
Scripture Verse
Blessing of the Body
The Lord's Prayer
Prayer of Commendation
Blessing

12 RITE OF FINAL COMMENDATION FOR AN INFANT

BRIEF ADDRESS

337 In the following or similar words, the minister addresses those who have assembled.

Dear friends, in the face of death all human wisdom fails. Yet the Lord Jesus teaches us, by the three days he spent in the tomb, that death has no hold over us. Christ has conquered death; his dying and rising have redeemed us. Even in our sorrow for the loss of this little child, we believe that, one short sleep past, he/she will wake eternally.

SCRIPTURE VERSE

338 The minister then introduces the Scripture verse.

The Lord speaks to us now of our hope for this child in these words of consolation.

A member of the family or one of those present reads one of the following verses.

A   Romans 5:5b

The love of God has been poured out into our hearts through the holy Spirit that has been given to us.

B   1 John 3:2

Beloved, we are God's children now; what we shall be has not yet been revealed. We do know that when it is revealed we shall be like him, for we shall see him as he is.

BLESSING OF THE BODY

339 Using the following words, the minister blesses the body of
the deceased child.

Trusting in Jesus, the loving Savior,
who gathered children into his arms
and blessed the little ones,
we now commend this infant [N.]
　　to that same embrace of love,
in the hope that he/she will rejoice
and be happy in the presence of Christ.

Then all join the minister, saying:

May the angels and saints lead him/her
to the place of light and peace
where one day
we will be brought together again.

The minister continues:

Lord Jesus,
lovingly receive this little child;
bless him/her
and take him/her to your Father.
We ask this in hope,
and we pray:

Lord, have mercy.

R. Lord, have mercy.

Christ, have mercy.

R. Christ, have mercy.

Lord, have mercy.

R. Lord, have mercy.

The Lord's Prayer

340 Using the following or similar words, the minister invites those present to pray the Lord's Prayer.

When Jesus gathered his disciples around him, he taught them to pray:

All say:

Our Father . . .

Prayer of Commendation

341 The minister then says the following prayer.

Tender Shepherd of the flock,
N. now lies cradled in your love.
Soothe the hearts of his/her parents
and bring peace to their lives.
Enlighten their faith
and give hope to their hearts.

Loving God,
grant mercy to your entire family in this time of suffering.
Comfort us with the hope that this child [N.]
lives with you and your Son, Jesus Christ,
and the Holy Spirit,
for ever and ever.

R. Amen.

BLESSING

342 Using one of the following blessings, the minister blesses those present.

A   A minister who is a priest or deacon says:

May the God of all consolation
bring you comfort and peace,
in the name of the Father, ✠ and of the Son,
and of the Holy Spirit.

R. Amen.

B   A lay minister invokes God's blessing and signs himself or herself with the sign of the cross, saying:

May the God of all consolation
bring us comfort and peace,
in the name of the Father, and of the Son,
and of the Holy Spirit.

R. Amen.

PART III
TEXTS OF
SACRED SCRIPTURE

We shall not live on bread alone,
but on every word that comes from God

PART III
TEXTS OF
SACRED SCRIPTURE

343 Part III, "Texts of Sacred Scripture," contains the Scriptural readings and psalms for the celebration of the funeral. It is divided into four sections: "Funerals for Adults" (p. 207), "Funerals for Baptized Children" (p. 247), "Funerals for Children Who Died before Baptism" (p. 261), "Antiphons and Psalms" (p. 267).

344 As a general rule, all corresponding texts from sacred Scripture in the funeral rites are interchangeable. In consultation with the family and close friends, the minister chooses the texts that most closely reflect the particular circumstances and the needs of the mourners.

13 FUNERALS FOR ADULTS

OLD TESTAMENT READINGS

NEW TESTAMENT READINGS

RESPONSORIAL PSALMS

ALLELUIA VERSES AND VERSES BEFORE THE GOSPEL

GOSPEL READINGS

Old Testament Readings

1   A reading from the book of Job   19:1, 23-27   83

I know that my Redeemer lives.

Job answered and said:

Oh, would that my words were written down!
     Would that they were inscribed in a record:
That with an iron chisel and with lead
     they were cut in the rock forever!
But as for me, I know that my Vindicator lives,
     and that he will at last stand forth upon the dust;
Whom I myself shall see:
     my own eyes, not another's, shall behold him,
And from my flesh I shall see God;
     my inmost being is consumed with longing.

This is the Word of the Lord.

2   Longer form:

A reading from the book of Wisdom   3:1-9   84

He accepted them as a holocaust.

The souls of the just are in the hand of God,
     and no torment shall touch them.
They seemed, in the view of the foolish, to be dead;
     and their passing away was thought an affliction
     and their going forth from us, utter destruction.
But they are in peace.
For if before men, indeed, they be punished,
     yet is their hope full of immortality;
Chastised a little, they shall be greatly blessed,
     because God tried them
     and found them worthy of himself.
As gold in the furnace, he proved them,
     and as sacrificial offerings he took them to himself.
In the time of their visitation they shall shine,
     and shall dart about as sparks through stubble;

They shall judge nations and rule over peoples,
and the Lord shall be their King forever.
Those who trust in him shall understand truth,
and the faithful shall abide with him in love:
Because grace and mercy are with his holy ones,
and his care is with his elect.

This is the Word of the Lord.

Shorter form:

A reading from the book of Wisdom   3:1-6, 9   84

He accepted them as a holocaust.

The souls of the just are in the hand of God,
and no torment shall touch them.
They seemed, in the view of the foolish, to be dead;
and their passing away was thought an affliction
and their going forth from us, utter destruction.
But they are in peace.
For if before men, indeed, they be punished,
yet is their hope full of immortality;
Chastised a little, they shall be greatly blessed,
because God tried them
and found them worthy of himself.
As gold in the furnace, he proved them,
and as sacrificial offerings he took them to himself.
Those who trust in him shall understand truth,
and the faithful shall abide with him in love:
Because grace and mercy are with his holy ones,
and his care is with his elect.

This is the Word of the Lord.

3   A reading from the book of Wisdom   4:7-15   85

A blameless life is a ripe old age.

The just man, though he die early, shall be at rest.
For the age that is honorable comes not with the passing of time,
nor can it be measured in terms of years.
Rather, understanding is the hoary crown for men,
and an unsullied life, the attainment of old age.

He who pleased God was loved;
   he who lived among sinners was transported—
Snatched away, lest wickedness pervert his mind
   or deceit beguile his soul;
For the witchery of paltry things obscures what is right
   and the whirl of desire transforms the innocent mind.
Having become perfect in a short while, he reached
     the fullness of a long career;
   for his soul was pleasing to the Lord,
   therefore he sped him out of the midst of wickedness.
But the people saw and did not understand,
   nor did they take this into account.
Because grace and mercy are with his holy ones,
   and his care is with his elect.

This is the Word of the Lord.

4   A reading from the book of the prophet Isaiah   25:6a, 7-9 86

The Lord God will destroy death for ever.

On this mountain the Lord of hosts
   will provide for all peoples.
On this mountain he will destroy
   the veil that veils all peoples,
The web that is woven over all nations;
   he will destroy death forever.
The Lord God will wipe away
   the tears from all faces;
The reproach of his people he will remove
   from the whole earth; for the Lord has spoken.

On that day it will be said:
"Behold our God, to whom we looked to save us!
   This is the Lord for whom we looked;
   let us rejoice and be glad that he has saved us!"

This is the Word of the Lord.

5   A reading from the book of Lamentations   3:17-26   87

It is good to wait in silence for the Lord God to save.

My soul is deprived of peace,
    I have forgotten what happiness is;
I tell myself my future is lost,
    all that I hoped for from the Lord.

The thought of my homeless poverty
    is wormwood and gall;
Remembering it over and over
    leaves my soul downcast within me.
But I will call this to mind,
    as my reason to have hope:

The favors of the Lord are not exhausted,
    his mercies are not spent;
They are renewed each morning,
    so great is his faithfulness.
My portion is the Lord, says my soul;
    therefore will I hope in him.

Good is the Lord to one who waits for him,
    to the soul that seeks him;
It is good to hope in silence
    for the saving help of the Lord.   ,

This is the Word of the Lord.

6   A reading from the book of the prophet Daniel   12:1-3   88

Of those who lie sleeping in the dust of the earth many will awake.

[I, Daniel, mourned and I heard this word of the Lord:]

"At that time there shall arise
    Michael, the great prince,
    guardian of your people;
It shall be a time unsurpassed in distress
    since nations began until that time.
At that time your people shall escape,
    everyone who is found written in the book.

Many of those who sleep
in the dust of the earth shall awake;
Some shall live forever,
others shall be an everlasting horror and disgrace.
But the wise shall shine brightly
like the splendor of the firmament,
And those who lead the many to justice
shall be like the stars forever."

This is the Word of the Lord.

7   A reading from the second book of Maccabees   12:43-46   89

It is good and holy to think of the dead rising again.

Judas [the ruler of Israel] then took up a collection among all
his soldiers, amounting to two thousand silver drachmas, which
he sent to Jerusalem to provide for an expiatory sacrifice. In
doing this he acted in a very excellent and noble way, inasmuch
as he had the resurrection of the dead in view; for if he were
not expecting the fallen to rise again, it would have been use-
less and foolish to pray for them in death. But if he did this
with a view to the splendid reward that awaits those who had
gone to rest in godliness, it was a holy and pious thought. Thus
he made atonement for the dead that they might be freed from
this sin.

This is the Word of the Lord.

NEW TESTAMENT READINGS

345 During the Easter season, reading 1, 17, 18, or 19 is used as the first reading instead of a reading from the Old Testament.

1   Longer form:

A reading from the Acts of the Apostles   10:34-43   90

God has appointed Jesus to judge everyone, alive and dead.

Peter proceeded to address the people in these words:

"In truth, I see that God shows no partiality. Rather, in every nation whoever fears him and acts uprightly is acceptable to him. You know the word that he sent to the Israelites as he proclaimed peace through Jesus Christ, who is Lord of all, what has happened all over Judea, beginning in Galilee after the baptism that John preached, how God anointed Jesus of Nazareth with the holy Spirit and power. He went about doing good and healing all those oppressed by the devil, for God was with him. We are witnesses of all that he did both in the country of the Jews and in Jerusalem. They put him to death by hanging him on a tree. This man God raised on the third day and granted that he be visible, not to all the people, but to us, the witnesses chosen by God in advance, who ate and drank with him after he rose from the dead. He commissioned us to preach to the people and testify that he is the one appointed by God as judge of the living and the dead. To him all the prophets bear witness, that everyone who believes in him will receive forgiveness of sins through his name."

This is the Word of the Lord.

     Shorter form:

A reading from the Acts of the Apostles   10:34-36, 42-43   90

God has appointed Jesus to judge everyone, alive and dead.

Peter proceeded to address the people in these words:

"In truth, I see that God shows no partiality. Rather, in every nation whoever fears him and acts uprightly is acceptable to him. You know the word that he sent to the Israelites as he proclaimed peace through Jesus Christ, who is Lord of all. He commissioned us to preach to the people and testify that he is the one appointed by God as judge of the living and the dead. To him all the prophets bear witness, that everyone who believes in him will receive forgiveness of sins through his name."

This is the Word of the Lord.

2 A reading from the letter of Paul to the Romans 5:5-11 91

Having been justified by his blood, we will be saved from God's anger through him.

Hope does not disappoint, because the love of God has been poured out into our hearts through the holy Spirit that has been given to us. For Christ, while we were still helpless, yet died at the appointed time for the ungodly. Indeed, only with difficulty does one die for a just person, though perhaps for a good person one might even find courage to die. But God proves his love for us in that while we were still sinners Christ died for us. How much more then, since we are now justified by his blood, will we be saved through him from the wrath. Indeed, if, while we were enemies, we were reconciled to God through the death of his Son, how much more, once reconciled, will we be saved by his life. Not only that, but we also boast of God through our Lord Jesus Christ, through whom we have now received reconciliation.

This is the Word of the Lord.

3 A reading from the letter of Paul to the Romans 5:17-21 92

Where sin increased, there grace abounded all the more.

If, by the transgression of one person, death came to reign through that one, how much more will those who receive the abundance of grace and of the gift of justification come to reign in life through the one person Jesus Christ.

In conclusion, just as through one transgression condemnation came upon all, so through one righteous act acquittal and life came to all. For just as through the disobedience of one person the many were made sinners, so through the obedience of one the many will be made righteous. The law entered in so that transgression might increase but, where sin increased, grace overflowed all the more, so that, as sin reigned in death, grace also might reign through justification for eternal life through Jesus Christ our Lord.

This is the Word of the Lord.

4   Longer form:

A reading from the letter of Paul to the Romans   6:3-9   93

Let us walk in newness of life.

Are you unaware that we who were baptized into Christ Jesus were baptized into his death? We were indeed buried with him through baptism into death, so that, just as Christ was raised from the dead by the glory of the Father, we too might live in newness of life. For if we have grown into union with him through a death like his, we shall also be united with him in the resurrection. We know that our old self was crucified with him, so that our sinful body might be done away with, that we might no longer be in slavery to sin. For a dead person has been absolved from sin. If, then, we have died with Christ, we believe that we shall also live with him. We know that Christ, raised from the dead, dies no more; death no longer has power over him.

This is the Word of the Lord.

Shorter form:

A reading from the letter of Paul to the Romans   6:3-4, 8-9   93

Let us walk in newness of life.

Are you unaware that we who were baptized into Christ Jesus were baptized into his death? We were indeed buried with him through baptism into death, so that, just as Christ was raised from the dead by the glory of the Father, we too might live in newness of life. If, then, we have died with Christ, we believe that we shall also live with him. We know that Christ, raised from the dead, dies no more; death no longer has power over him.

This is the Word of the Lord.

5   A reading from the letter of Paul to the Romans   8:14-23   94

We groan while we wait for the redemption of our bodies.

Those who are led by the Spirit of God are children of God. For you did not receive a spirit of slavery to fall back into fear, but you received a spirit of adoption, through which we cry, *"Abba,* Father!" The Spirit itself bears witness with our spirit that we are children of God, and if children, then heirs, heirs of God and joint heirs with Christ, if only we suffer with him so that we may also be glorified with him.

I consider that the sufferings of this present time are as nothing compared with the glory to be revealed for us. For creation awaits with eager expectation the revelation of the children of God; for creation was made subject to futility, not of its own accord but because of the one who subjected it, in hope that creation itself would be set free from slavery to corruption and share in the glorious freedom of the children of God. We know that all creation is groaning in labor pains even until now; and not only that, but we ourselves, who have the firstfruits of the Spirit, we also groan within ourselves as we wait for adoption, the redemption of our bodies.

This is the Word of the Lord.

6   A reading from the letter of Paul
to the Romans   8:31b-35, 37-39   95

Who can ever come between us and the love of Christ?

If God is for us, who can be against us? He who did not spare his own Son but handed him over for us all, how will he not also give us everything else along with him? Who will bring a charge against God's chosen ones? It is God who acquits us. Who will condemn? It is Christ Jesus who died, rather, was raised, who also is at the right hand of God, who indeed intercedes for us.

What will separate us from the love of Christ? Will anguish, or distress, or persecution, or famine, or nakedness, or peril, or the sword? No, in all these things we conquer overwhelmingly through him who loved us. For I am convinced that neither death, nor life, nor angels, nor principalities, nor present things, nor future things, nor powers, nor height, nor depth, nor any other creature will be able to separate us from the love of God in Christ Jesus our Lord.

This is the Word of the Lord.

7   A reading from the letter of Paul to the Romans   14:7-9, 10b-12 96

Whether alive or dead, we belong to the Lord.

None of us lives for oneself, and no one dies for oneself. For if we live, we live for the Lord, and if we die, we die for the Lord; so then, whether we live or die, we are the Lord's. For this is why Christ died and came to life, that he might be Lord of both the dead and the living. For we shall all stand before the judgment seat of God; for it is written:

"As I live, says the Lord, every knee shall bend before me, and every tongue shall give praise to God."

So then each of us shall give an account of himself to God.

This is the Word of the Lord.

8   Longer form:

A reading from the first letter of Paul to the Corinthians   15:20-23, 24b-28   97

All people will be brought to life in Christ.

Christ has been raised from the dead, the firstfruits of those who have fallen asleep. For since death came through a human being, the resurrection of the dead came also through a human being. For just as in Adam all die, so too in Christ shall all be brought to life, but each one in proper order: Christ the first-fruits; then, at his coming, those who belong to Christ; then comes the end, when he hands over the kingdom to his God and Father. For he must reign until he has put all his enemies under his feet. The last enemy to be destroyed is death, for "he subjected everything under his feet." But when it says that everything has been subjected, it is clear that it excludes the One who subjected everything to him. When everything is subjected to him, then the Son himself will also be subjected to the One who subjected everything to him, so that God may be all in all.

This is the Word of the Lord.

Shorter form:

A reading from the first letter of Paul
to the Corinthians   15:20-23   97

All people will be brought to life in Christ.

Christ has been raised from the dead, the firstfruits of those
who have fallen asleep. For since death came through a human
being, the resurrection of the dead came also through a human
being. For just as in Adam all die, so too in Christ shall all be
brought to life, but each one in proper order: Christ the
firstfruits; then, at his coming, those who belong to Christ.

This is the Word of the Lord.

9   A reading from the first letter of Paul
       to the Corinthians   15:51-57   98

Death is swallowed up in victory.

Behold, I tell you a mystery. We shall not all fall asleep, but
we will all be changed, in an instant, in the blink of an eye,
at the last trumpet. For the trumpet will sound, the dead will
be raised incorruptible, and we shall be changed. For that which
is corruptible must clothe itself with incorruptibility, and that
which is mortal must clothe itself with immortality. And when
that which is corruptible clothes itself with incorruptibility and
that which is mortal clothes itself with immortality, then the
word that is written shall come about:

> "Death is swallowed up in victory.
> Where, O death, is your victory?
> Where, O death, is your sting?"

The sting of death is sin, and the power of sin is the law. But
thanks be to God who gives us the victory through our Lord
Jesus Christ.

This is the Word of the Lord.

10   A reading from the second letter of Paul
       to the Corinthians   4:14 — 5:1

What is seen is transitory; what is unseen is eternal.

We know that the one who raised the Lord Jesus will raise us also with Jesus and place us with you in his presence. Everything indeed is for you, so that the grace bestowed in abundance on more and more people may cause the thanksgiving to overflow for the glory of God.

Therefore, we are not discouraged; rather, although our outer self is wasting away, our inner self is being renewed day by day. For this momentary light affliction is producing for us an eternal weight of glory beyond all comparison, as we look not to what is seen but to what is unseen; for what is seen is transitory, but what is unseen is eternal.

For we know that if our earthly dwelling, a tent, should be destroyed, we have a building from God, a dwelling not made with hands, eternal in heaven.

This is the Word of the Lord.

---

11   A reading from the second letter of Paul
to the Corinthians   5:1, 6-10   99

We have an everlasting home in heaven.

We know that if our earthly dwelling, a tent, should be destroyed, we have a building from God, a dwelling not made with hands, eternal in heaven.

So we are always courageous, although we know that while we are at home in the body we are away from the Lord, for we walk by faith, not by sight. Yet we are courageous, and we would rather leave the body and go home to the Lord. Therefore, we aspire to please him, whether we are at home or away. For we must all appear before the judgment seat of Christ, so that each one may receive recompense, according to what he did in the body, whether good or evil.

This is the Word of the Lord.

---

12   A reading from the letter of Paul
to the Philippians   3:20-21   100

Jesus will transfigure these wretched bodies of ours to be like his glorious body.

Our citizenship is in heaven, and from it we also await a savior, the Lord Jesus Christ. He will change our lowly body to conform with his glorified body by the power that enables him also to bring all things into subjection to himself.

This is the Word of the Lord.

13   A reading from the first letter of Paul
to the Thessalonians   4:13-18   ₁₀₁

We shall stay with the Lord for ever.

We do not want you to be unaware, brothers [and sisters], about those who have fallen asleep, so that you may not grieve like the rest, who have no hope. For if we believe that Jesus died and rose, so too will God, through Jesus, bring with him those who have fallen asleep. Indeed, we tell you this, on the word of the Lord, that we who are alive, who are left until the coming of the Lord, will surely not precede those who have fallen asleep. For the Lord himself, with a word of command, with the voice of an archangel and with the trumpet of God, will come down from heaven, and the dead in Christ will rise first. Then we who are alive, who are left, will be caught up together with them in the clouds to meet the Lord in the air. Thus we shall always be with the Lord. Therefore, console one another with these words.

This is the Word of the Lord.

14   A reading from the second letter of Paul to Timothy   2:8-13   ₁₀₂

If we have died with him, we shall live with him.

Remember Jesus Christ, raised from the dead, a descendant of David: such is my gospel, for which I am suffering, even to the point of chains, like a criminal. But the word of God is not chained. Therefore, I bear with everything for the sake of those who are chosen, so that they too may obtain the salvation that is in Christ Jesus, together with eternal glory. This saying is trustworthy:

If we have died with him
    we shall also live with him;
if we persevere
    we shall also reign with him.

But if we deny him
    he will deny us.
If we are unfaithful
    he remains faithful,
        for he cannot deny himself.

This is the Word of the Lord.

15   A reading from the first letter of John   3:1-2   103

We shall see God as he really is.

See what love the Father has bestowed on us that we may be called the children of God. Yet so we are. The reason the world does not know us is that it did not know him. Beloved, we are God's children now; what we shall be has not yet been revealed. We do know that when it is revealed we shall be like him, for we shall see him as he is.

This is the Word of the Lord.

16   A reading from the first letter of John   3:14-16   104

We have passed from death to life, because we love our brothers and sisters.

We know that we have passed from death to life because we love our brothers [and sisters]. Whoever does not love remains in death. Everyone who hates his brother is a murderer, and you know that no murderer has eternal life remaining in him. The way we came to know love was that Jesus laid down his life for us; so we ought to lay down our lives for our brothers [and sisters].

This is the Word of the Lord.

17   A reading from the book of Revelation   14:13   105

Happy are those who die in the Lord.

I heard a voice from heaven say, "Write this: Blessed are the dead who die in the Lord from now on." "Yes," said the Spirit, "let them find rest from their labors, for their works accompany them."

This is the Word of the Lord.

18   A reading from the book of Revelation   20:11 — 21:1   106

The dead have been judged according to their works.

I saw a large white throne and the one who was sitting on it. The earth and the sky fled from his presence and there was no place for them. I saw the dead, the great and the lowly, standing before the throne, and scrolls were opened. Then another scroll was opened, the book of life. The dead were judged according to their deeds, by what was written in the scrolls. The sea gave up its dead; then Death and Hades gave up their dead. All the dead were judged according to their deeds. Then Death and Hades were thrown into the pool of fire. (This pool of fire is the second death.) Anyone whose name was not found written in the book of life was thrown into the pool of fire.

Then I saw a new heaven and a new earth. The former heaven and the former earth had passed away, and the sea was no more.

This is the Word of the Lord.

19   A reading from the book of Revelation   21:1-5a, 6b-7   107

There will be no more death.

I saw a new heaven and a new earth. The former heaven and the former earth had passed away, and the sea was no more. I also saw the holy city, a new Jerusalem, coming down out of heaven from God, prepared as a bride adorned for her husband. I heard a loud voice from the throne saying, "Behold, God's dwelling is with the human race. He will dwell with them and they will be his people and God himself will always be with them as their God. He will wipe every tear from their eyes, and there shall be no more death or mourning, wailing or pain, for the old order has passed away."

The one who sat on the throne said, "Behold, I make all things new. I am the Alpha and the Omega, the beginning and the end. To the thirsty I will give a gift from the spring of life-giving water. The victor will inherit these gifts, and I shall be his God, and he will be my son."

This is the Word of the Lord.

1   Psalm 23

R. The Lord is my shepherd; there is nothing I shall want.

Or:

R. Though I walk in the valley of darkness, I fear no evil, for
you are with me.

The Lord is my shepherd;
there is nothing I shall want.
Fresh and green are the pastures
where he gives me repose.
Near restful waters he leads me,
to revive my drooping spirit. R.

He guides me along the right path;
he is true to his name.
If I should walk in the valley of darkness
no evil would I fear.
You are there with your crook and your staff;
with these you give me comfort. R.

You have prepared a banquet for me
in the sight of my foes.
My head you have anointed with oil;
my cup is overflowing. R.

Surely goodness and kindness shall follow me
all the days of my life.
In the Lord's own house shall I dwell
for ever and ever. R.

2 Psalm 25

R. To you, O Lord, I lift my soul.

> Or:

R. No one who waits for you, O Lord, will ever be put to shame.

Remember your mercy, Lord,
and the love you have shown from of old.
Do not remember the sins of my youth.
In your love remember me. R.

Relieve the anguish of my heart
and set me free from my distress.
See my affliction and my toil
and take all my sins away. R.

Preserve my life and rescue me.
Do not disappoint me, you are my refuge.
May innocence and uprightness protect me:
for my hope is in you, O Lord. R.

3 Psalm 27

110

R. The Lord is my light and my salvation.

> Or:

R. I believe that I shall see the good things of the Lord in the land of the living.

The Lord is my light and my help;
whom shall I fear?
The Lord is the stronghold of my life;
before whom shall I shrink? R.

There is one thing I ask of the Lord,
for this I long,
to live in the house of the Lord,
all the days of my life,
to savor the sweetness of the Lord,
to behold his temple. R.

O Lord, hear my voice when I call;
have mercy and answer.
It is your face, O Lord, that I seek;
hide not your face. R.

I am sure I shall see the Lord's goodness
in the land of the living.
Hope in him, hold firm and take heart.
Hope in the Lord! R.

4 Psalm 42 and 43 111

R. My soul is thirsting for the living God: when shall I see
him face to face?

Like the deer that yearns
for running streams,
so my soul is yearning
for you, my God. R.

My soul is thirsting for God,
the God of my life;
when can I enter and see
the face of God? R.

O send forth your light and your truth;
let these be my guide.
Let them bring me to your holy mountain
to the place where you dwell. R.

And I will come to the altar of God,
the God of my joy.
My redeemer, I will thank you on the harp,
O God, my God. R.

Why are you cast down, my soul,
why groan within me?
Hope in God; I will praise him still,
my savior and my God. R.

5 Psalm 63 112

R. My soul is thirsting for you, O Lord my God.

O God, you are my God, for you I long;
for you my soul is thirsting.
My body pines for you
like a dry, weary land without water. R.

So I gaze on you in the sanctuary
to see your strength and your glory.
For your love is better than life,
my lips will speak your praise.

R. My soul is thirsting for you, O Lord my God.

So I will bless you all my life,
in your name I will lift up my hands.
My soul shall be filled as with a banquet,
my mouth shall praise you with joy. R.

You have been my help;
in the shadow of your wings I rejoice.
My soul clings to you;
your right hand holds me fast. R.

6   Psalm 103   113

R. The Lord is kind and merciful.

     Or:

R. The salvation of the just comes from the Lord.

The Lord is compassion and love,
slow to anger and rich in mercy.
He does not treat us according to our sins
nor repay us according to our faults. R.

As a father has compassion on his sons,
the Lord has pity on those who fear him;
for he knows of what we are made,
he remembers that we are dust. R.

As for man, his days are like grass;
he flowers like the flower of the field;
the wind blows and he is gone
and his place never sees him again. R.

But the love of the Lord is everlasting
upon those who hold him in fear;
his justice reaches out to children's children
when they keep his covenant in truth. R.

Psalm 116

R. I will walk in the presence of the Lord in the land of the living.

Or:

R. Alleluia.

How gracious is the Lord, and just;
our God has compassion.
The Lord protects the simple hearts;
I was helpless so he saved me. R.

I trusted, even when I said:
"I am sorely afflicted,"
and when I said in my alarm:
"No man can be trusted." R.

O precious in the eyes of the Lord
is the death of his faithful.
Your servant, Lord, your servant am I;
you have loosened my bonds. R.

Psalm 122

R. I rejoiced when I heard them say: let us go to the house of the Lord.

Or:

R. Let us go rejoicing to the house of the Lord.

I rejoiced when I heard them say:
"Let us go to God's house."
And now our feet are standing
within your gates, O Jerusalem. R.

Jerusalem is built as a city
strongly compact.
It is there that the tribes go up,
the tribes of the Lord. R.

For Israel's law it is,
there to praise the Lord's name.
There were set the thrones of judgment
of the house of David. R.

For the peace of Jerusalem pray:
"Peace be to your homes!
May peace reign in your walls,
in your palaces, peace!"

R. I rejoiced when I heard them say: let us go to the house of
the Lord.

Or:

R. Let us go rejoicing to the house of the Lord.

For love of my brethren and friends
I say: "Peace upon you!"
For love of the house of the Lord
I will ask for your good. R.

9   Psalm 130   116

R. Out of the depths, I cry to you, Lord.

Or:

R. I hope in the Lord, I trust in his word.

Out of the depths I cry to you, O Lord,
Lord, hear my voice!
O let your ears be attentive
to the voice of my pleading. R.

If you, O Lord, should mark our guilt,
Lord, who would survive?
But with you is found forgiveness:
for this we revere you. R.

My soul is waiting for the Lord,
I count on his word.
My soul is longing for the Lord
more than watchman for daybreak. R.

Because with the Lord there is mercy
and fullness of redemption,
Israel indeed he will redeem
from all its iniquity. R.

R. O Lord, hear my prayer.

Lord, listen to my prayer:
turn your ear to my appeal.
You are faithful, you are just; give answer.
Do not call your servant to judgment
for no one is just in your sight. R.

I remember the days that are past:
I ponder all your works.
I muse on what your hand has wrought
and to you I stretch out my hands.
Like a parched land my soul thirsts for you. R.

Lord, make haste and give me answer:
for my spirit fails within me.
In the morning let me know your love
for I put my trust in you. R.

Teach me to do your will
for you, O Lord, are my God.
Let your good spirit guide me
in ways that are level and smooth. R.

ALLELUIA VERSES AND VERSES BEFORE THE GOSPEL

1   See Matthew 11:25   118

Blessed are you, Father, Lord of heaven and earth;
you have revealed to little ones the mysteries of the kingdom.

2   Matthew 25:34   119

Come, you whom my Father has blessed, says the Lord;
inherit the kingdom prepared for you since the foundation
   of the world.

3   John 3:16   120

God loved the world so much, he gave us his only Son,
that all who believe in him might have eternal life.

4   John 6:39   121

This is the will of my Father, says the Lord,
that I should lose nothing of all that he has given to me,
and that I should raise it up on the last day.

5   John 6:40   122

This is the will of my Father, says the Lord,
that all who believe in the Son will have eternal life
and I will raise them to life again on the last day.

6   John 6:51a

I am the living bread from heaven, says the Lord;
whoever eats this bread will live for ever.

7   John 11:25-26   123

I am the resurrection and the life, says the Lord;
whoever believes in me will not die for ever.

8   See Philippians 3:20   124

Our true home is in heaven,
and Jesus Christ, whose return we long for,
will come from heaven to save us.

9   2 Timothy 2:11b-12a   125

If we die with Christ, we shall live with him,
and if we are faithful to the end, we shall reign with him.

10   Revelation 1:5a, 6b   126

Jesus Christ is the firstborn from the dead;
glory and kingship be his for ever and ever. Amen.

11   Revelation 14:13   127

Blessed are those who have died in the Lord;
let them rest from their labors for their good deeds go with them.

1   A reading from the holy gospel
     according to Matthew   5:1-12a   128

Rejoice and be glad, for your reward will be great in heaven.

When he saw the crowds, Jesus went up the mountain, and after he had sat down, his disciples came to him. He began to
teach them, saying:

"Blessed are the poor in spirit,
     for theirs is the kingdom of heaven.
Blessed are they who mourn,
     for they will be comforted.
Blessed are the meek,
     for they will inherit the land.
Blessed are they who hunger and thirst for righteousness,
     for they will be satisfied.
Blessed are the merciful,
     for they will be shown mercy.
Blessed are the clean of heart,
     for they will see God.
Blessed are the peacemakers,
     for they will be called children of God.
Blessed are they who are persecuted for the sake
          of righteousness,
     for theirs is the kingdom of heaven.
Blessed are you when they insult you and persecute you and
utter every kind of evil against you falsely because of me. Re-
joice and be glad, for your reward will be great in heaven."

This is the Gospel of the Lord.

2   A reading from the holy gospel
    according to Matthew   11:25-30   129

Come to me . . . and I will give you rest.

On one occasion Jesus spoke thus: "I give praise to you, Father,
Lord of heaven and earth, for although you have hidden these
things from the wise and the learned you have revealed them
to the childlike. Yes, Father, such has been your gracious will.
All things have been handed over to me by my Father. No one
knows the Son except the Father, and no one knows the Father
except the Son and anyone to whom the Son wishes to reveal
him.

"Come to me, all you who labor and are burdened, and I will
give you rest. Take my yoke upon you and learn from me, for
I am meek and humble of heart; and you will find rest for yourselves. For my yoke is easy, and my burden light."

This is the Gospel of the Lord.

3   A reading from the holy gospel
    according to Matthew   25:1-13   130

Look, the bridegroom comes. Go out to meet him.

Jesus spoke this parable to his disciples:

"The kingdom of heaven will be like ten virgins who took their
lamps and went out to meet the bridegroom. Five of them were
foolish and five were wise. The foolish ones, when taking their
lamps, brought no oil with them, but the wise brought flasks
of oil with their lamps. Since the bridegroom was long delayed,
they all became drowsy and fell asleep. At midnight, there was
a cry, 'Behold, the bridegroom! Come out to meet him!' Then
all those virgins got up and trimmed their lamps. The foolish
ones said to the wise, 'Give us some of your oil, for our lamps
are going out.' But the wise ones replied, 'No, for there may
not be enough for us and you. Go instead to the merchants and
buy some for yourselves.' While they went off to buy it, the bridegroom came and those who were ready went into the wedding

feast with him. Then the door was locked. Afterwards the other virgins came and said, 'Lord, Lord, open the door for us!' But he said in reply, 'Amen, I say to you, I do not know you.' Therefore, stay awake, for you know neither the day nor the hour."

This is the Gospel of the Lord.

4   A reading from the holy gospel
according to Matthew   25:31-46

Come, you whom my Father has blessed.

Jesus said to his disciples:

"When the Son of Man comes in his glory, and all the angels with him, he will sit upon his glorious throne, and all the nations will be assembled before him. And he will separate them one from another, as a shepherd separates the sheep from the goats. He will place the sheep on his right and the goats on his left. Then the king will say to those on his right, 'Come, you who are blessed by my Father. Inherit the kingdom prepared for you from the foundation of the world. For I was hungry and you gave me food, I was thirsty and you gave me drink, a stranger and you welcomed me, naked and you clothed me, ill and you cared for me, in prison and you visited me.' Then the righteous will answer him and say, 'Lord, when did we see you hungry and feed you, or thirsty and give you drink? When did we see you a stranger and welcome you, or naked and clothe you? When did we see you ill or in prison, and visit you?' And the king will say to them in reply, 'Amen, I say to you, whatever you did for one of these least brothers of mine, you did for me.'

"Then he will say to those on his left, 'Depart from me, you accursed, into the eternal fire prepared for the devil and his angels. For I was hungry and you gave me no food, I was thirsty and you gave me no drink, a stranger and you gave me no welcome, naked and you gave me no clothing, ill and in prison, and you did not care for me.' Then they will answer and say, 'Lord, when did we see you hungry or thirsty or a stranger or naked or ill or in prison, and not minister to your needs?' He will answer them, 'Amen, I say to you, what you did not do for one of these least ones, you did not do for me.' And these will go off to eternal punishment, but the righteous to eternal life."

This is the Gospel of the Lord.

5   Longer form:

A reading from the holy gospel
according to Mark   15:33-39; 16:1-6   13

Jesus gave a loud cry and breathed his last.

At noon darkness came over the whole land until three in the afternoon. And at three o'clock Jesus cried out in a loud voice, "*Eloi, Eloi, lema sabachthani?*" which is translated, "My God, my God, why have you forsaken me?" Some of the bystanders who heard it said, "Look, he is calling Elijah." One of them ran, soaked a sponge with wine, put it on a reed, and gave it to him to drink, saying, "Wait, let us see if Elijah comes to take him down."

Jesus gave a loud cry and breathed his last. The veil of the sanctuary was torn in two from top to bottom. When the centurion who stood facing him saw how he breathed his last he said, "Truly this man was the Son of God!"

When the sabbath was over, Mary Magdalene, Mary, the mother of James, and Salome bought spices so that they might go and anoint him. Very early when the sun had risen, on the first day of the week, they came to the tomb. They were saying to one another, "Who will roll back the stone for us from the entrance to the tomb?" When they looked up, they saw that the stone had been rolled back; it was very large. On entering the tomb they saw a young man sitting on the right side, clothed in a white robe, and they were utterly amazed. He said to them, "Do not be amazed! You seek Jesus of Nazareth, the crucified. He has been raised; he is not here. Behold the place where they laid him."

This is the Gospel of the Lord.

Shorter form:

A reading from the holy gospel
according to Mark   15:33-39   132

Jesus gave a loud cry and breathed his last.

At noon darkness came over the whole land until three in the
afternoon. And at three o'clock Jesus cried out in a loud voice,
"*Eloi, Eloi, lema sabachthani?*" which is translated, "My God, my
God, why have you forsaken me?" Some of the bystanders who
heard it said, "Look, he is calling Elijah." One of them ran,
soaked a sponge with wine, put it on a reed, and gave it to him
to drink, saying, "Wait, let us see if Elijah comes to take him
down."

Jesus gave a loud cry and breathed his last. The veil of the sanctuary was torn in two from top to bottom. When the centurion
who stood facing him saw how he breathed his last he said,
"Truly this man was the Son of God!"

This is the Gospel of the Lord.

6   A reading from the holy gospel
according to Luke   7:11-17   133

Young man, I say to you, arise.

Jesus journeyed to a city called Nain, and his disciples and a
large crowd accompanied him. As he drew near to the gate of
the city, a man who had died was being carried out, the only
son of his mother, and she was a widow. A large crowd from
the city was with her. When the Lord saw her, he was moved
with pity for her and said to her, "Do not weep." He stepped
forward and touched the coffin; at this the bearers halted, and
he said, "Young man, I tell you, arise!" The dead man sat up
and began to speak, and Jesus gave him to his mother. Fear
seized them all, and they glorified God, exclaiming, "A great
prophet has arisen in our midst," and "God has visited his people." This report about him spread through the whole of Judea
and in all the surrounding region.

This is the Gospel of the Lord.

7   A reading from the holy gospel
     according to Luke   12:35-40   134

Be prepared.

Jesus said to his disciples:

"Gird your loins and light your lamps and be like servants who await their master's return from a wedding, ready to open immediately when he comes and knocks. Blessed are those servants whom the master finds vigilant on his arrival. Amen, I say to you, he will gird himself, have them recline at table, and proceed to wait on them. And should he come in the second or third watch and find them prepared in this way, blessed are those servants. Be sure of this: if the master of the house had known the hour when the thief was coming, he would not have let his house be broken into. You also must be prepared, for at an hour you do not expect, the Son of Man will come."

This is the Gospel of the Lord.

8   A reading from the holy gospel
     according to Luke   23:33, 39-43   13

Today you will be with me in paradise.

When they came to the place called the Skull, they crucified Jesus and the criminals there, one on his right, the other on his left.

Now one of the criminals hanging there reviled Jesus, saying, "Are you not the Messiah? Save yourself and us." The other, however, rebuking him, said in reply, "Have you no fear of God, for you are subject to the same condemnation? And indeed, we have been condemned justly, for the sentence we received corresponds to our crimes, but this man has done nothing criminal." Then he said, "Jesus, remember me when you come into your kingdom." He replied to him, "Amen, I say to you, today you will be with me in Paradise."

This is the Gospel of the Lord.

9   Longer form:

A reading from the holy gospel
according to Luke   23:44-46, 50, 52-53; 24:1-6a   136

Father, I put my life in your hands.

It was now about noon and darkness came over the whole land
until three in the afternoon because of an eclipse of the sun.
Then the veil of the temple was torn down the middle. Jesus
cried out in a loud voice, "Father, into your hands I commend
my spirit"; and when he had said this he breathed his last.

Now there was a virtuous and righteous man named Joseph
who, though he was a member of the council, he went to Pilate
and asked for the body of Jesus. After he had taken the body
down, he wrapped it in a linen cloth and laid him in a rock-
hewn tomb in which no one had yet been buried.

But at daybreak on the first day of the week the women took
the spices they had prepared and went to the tomb. They found
the stone rolled away from the tomb; but when they entered,
they did not find the body of the Lord Jesus. While they were
puzzling over this, behold, two men in dazzling garments appeared to them. They were terrified and bowed their faces to
the ground. They said to them, "Why do you seek the living
one among the dead? He is not here, but he has been raised."

This is the Gospel of the Lord.

Shorter form:

A reading from the holy gospel
according to Luke   23:44-46, 50, 52-53   136

Father, I put my life in your hands.

It was now about noon and darkness came over the whole land
until three in the afternoon because of an eclipse of the sun.
Then the veil of the temple was torn down the middle. Jesus
cried out in a loud voice, "Father, into your hands I commend
my spirit"; and when he had said this he breathed his last.

Now there was a virtuous and righteous man named Joseph
who, though he was a member of the council, he went to Pilate
and asked for the body of Jesus. After he had taken the body

down, he wrapped it in a linen cloth and laid him in a rock-hewn tomb in which no one had yet been buried.

This is the Gospel of the Lord.

10   Longer form:

A reading from the holy gospel
according to Luke   24:13-35   137

Was it not necessary that the Christ should suffer and so enter into his glory?

Now that very day the first day of the week two of the disciples were going to a village seven miles from Jerusalem called Emmaus, and they were conversing about all the things that had occurred. And it happened that while they were conversing and debating, Jesus himself drew near and walked with them, but their eyes were prevented from recognizing him. He asked them, "What are you discussing as you walk along?" They stopped, looking downcast. One of them, named Cleopas, said to him in reply, "Are you the only visitor to Jerusalem who does not know of the things that have taken place there in these days?" And he replied to them, "What sort of things?" They said to him, "The things that happened to Jesus the Nazarene, who was a prophet mighty in deed and word before God and all the people, how our chief priests and rulers both handed him over to a sentence of death and crucified him. But we were hoping that he would be the one to redeem Israel; and besides all this, it is now the third day since this took place. Some women from our group, however, have astounded us: they were at the tomb early in the morning and did not find his body; they came back and reported that they had indeed seen a vision of angels who announced that he was alive. Then some of those with us went to the tomb and found things just as the women had described, but him they did not see."

And he said to them, "Oh, how foolish you are! How slow of heart to believe all that the prophets spoke! Was it not necessary that the Messiah should suffer these things and enter into his glory?" Then beginning with Moses and all the prophets, he interpreted to them what referred to him in all the scriptures. As they approached the village to which they were going, he gave the impression that he was going on farther. But they urged him, "Stay with us, for it is nearly evening and the day is almost over." So he went in to stay with them.

And it happened that, while he was with them at table, he took bread, said the blessing, broke it, and gave it to them. With that their eyes were opened and they recognized him, but he vanished from their sight. Then they said to each other, "Were not our hearts burning within us while he spoke to us on the way and opened the scriptures to us?" So they set out at once and returned to Jerusalem where they found gathered together the eleven and those with them who were saying, "The Lord has truly been raised and has appeared to Simon!" Then the two recounted what had taken place on the way and how he was made known to them in the breaking of the bread.

This is the Gospel of the Lord.

Shorter form:

A reading from the holy gospel
according to Luke   24:13-16, 28-35   137

Was it not necessary that the Christ should suffer and so enter into his glory?

Now that very day the first day of the week two of the disciples were going to a village seven miles from Jerusalem called Emmaus, and they were conversing about all the things that had occurred. And it happened that while they were conversing and debating, Jesus himself drew near and walked with them, but their eyes were prevented from recognizing him.

As they approached the village to which they were going, he gave the impression that he was going on farther. But they urged him, "Stay with us, for it is nearly evening and the day is almost over." So he went in to stay with them.

And it happened that, while he was with them at table, he took bread, said the blessing, broke it, and gave it to them. With that their eyes were opened and they recognized him, but he vanished from their sight. Then they said to each other, "Were not our hearts burning within us while he spoke to us on the way and opened the scriptures to us?" So they set out at once and returned to Jerusalem where they found gathered together the eleven and those with them who were saying, "The Lord has truly been raised and has appeared to Simon!" Then the two recounted what had taken place on the way and how he was made known to them in the breaking of the bread.

This is the Gospel of the Lord.

11   A reading from the holy gospel
     according to John   5:24-29

Whoever hears my word and believes has passed from death to life.

Jesus said to the Jews:

"Amen, amen, I say to you, whoever hears my word and believes in the one who sent me has eternal life and will not come to condemnation, but has passed from death to life. Amen, amen, I say to you, the hour is coming and is now here when the dead will hear the voice of the Son of God, and those who hear will live. For just as the Father has life in himself, so also he gave to his Son the possession of life in himself. And he gave him power to exercise judgment, because he is the Son of Man. Do not be amazed at this, because the hour is coming in which all who are in the tombs will hear his voice and will come out, those who have done good deeds to the resurrection of life, but those who have done wicked deeds to the resurrection of condemnation."

This is the Gospel of the Lord.

12   A reading from the holy gospel
according to John   6:37-40   138

*All who believe in the Son will have eternal life and I will raise them to life
again on the last day.*

Jesus said to the crowd:

"Everything that the Father gives me will come to me, and I
will not reject anyone who comes to me, because I came down
from heaven not to do my own will but the will of the one who
sent me. And this is the will of the one who sent me, that I
should not lose anything of what he gave me, but that I should
raise it on the last day. For this is the will of my Father, that
everyone who sees the Son and believes in him may have eternal life, and I shall raise him on the last day."

This is the Gospel of the Lord.

13   A reading from the holy gospel
according to John   6:51-58   139

All who eat this bread will live for ever; and I will raise them up on the last day.

Jesus said to the crowd:

"I am the living bread that came down from heaven; whoever
eats this bread will live forever; and the bread that I will give
is my flesh for the life of the world."

The Jews quarreled among themselves, saying, "How can this
man give us his flesh to eat?" Jesus said to them, "Amen, amen,
I say to you, unless you eat the flesh of the Son of Man and
drink his blood, you do not have life within you. Whoever eats
my flesh and drinks my blood has eternal life, and I will raise
him on the last day. For my flesh is true food, and my blood
is true drink. Whoever eats my flesh and drinks my blood remains in me and I in him. Just as the living Father sent me
and I have life because of the Father, so also the one who feeds
on me will have life because of me. This is the bread that came
down from heaven. Unlike your ancestors who ate and still died,
whoever eats this bread will live forever."

This is the Gospel of the Lord.

14   Longer form:

A reading from the holy gospel
according to John   11:17-27   14

I am the resurrection and the life.

When Jesus arrived in Bethany he found that Lazarus had already been in the tomb for four days. Now Bethany was near Jerusalem, only about two miles away. And many of the Jews had come to Martha and Mary to comfort them about their brother. When Martha heard that Jesus was coming, she went to meet him; but Mary sat at home. Martha said to Jesus, "Lord, if you had been here, my brother would not have died. But even now I know that whatever you ask of God, God will give you." Jesus said to her, "Your brother will rise." Martha said to him, "I know he will rise, in the resurrection on the last day." Jesus told her, "I am the resurrection and the life; whoever believes in me, even if he dies, will live, and everyone who lives and believes in me will never die. Do you believe this?" She said to him, "Yes, Lord. I have come to believe that you are the Messiah, the Son of God, the one who is coming into the world."

This is the Gospel of the Lord.

Shorter form:

A reading from the holy gospel
according to John   11:21-27   14

I am the resurrection and the life.

Martha said to Jesus, "Lord, if you had been here, my brother would not have died. But even now I know that whatever you ask of God, God will give you." Jesus said to her, "Your brother will rise." Martha said to him, "I know he will rise, in the resurrection on the last day." Jesus told her, "I am the resurrection and the life; whoever believes in me, even if he dies, will live, and everyone who lives and believes in me will never die. Do you believe this?" She said to him, "Yes, Lord. I have come to believe that you are the Messiah, the Son of God, the one who is coming into the world."

This is the Gospel of the Lord.

---

15   A reading from the holy gospel
according to John   11:32-45   141

Lazarus, come out.

When Mary came to where Jesus was and saw him, she fell at his feet and said to him, "Lord, if you had been here, my brother would not have died." When Jesus saw her weeping and the Jews who had come with her weeping, he became perturbed and deeply troubled, and said, "Where have you laid him?" They said to him, "Sir, come and see." And Jesus wept. So the Jews said, "See how he loved him." But some of them said, "Could not the one who opened the eyes of the blind man have done something so that this man would not have died?"

So Jesus, perturbed again, came to the tomb. It was a cave, and a stone lay across it. Jesus said, "Take away the stone." Martha, the dead man's sister, said to him, "Lord, by now there will be a stench; he has been dead for four days." Jesus said to her, "Did I not tell you that if you believe you will see the glory of God?" So they took away the stone. And Jesus raised his eyes and said, "Father, I thank you for hearing me. I know that you always hear me; but because of the crowd here I have said this, that they may believe that you sent me." And when he had said this, he cried out in a loud voice, "Lazarus, come out!" The dead man came out, tied hand and foot with burial bands, and his face was wrapped in a cloth. So Jesus said to them, "Untie him and let him go."

Now many of the Jews who had come to Mary and seen what he had done began to believe in him.

This is the Gospel of the Lord.

16 Longer form:

A reading from the holy gospel
according to John   12:23-28   14?

If a grain of wheat falls on the ground and dies, it yields a rich harvest.

Jesus told his disciples:

"The hour has come for the Son of Man to be glorified. Amen, amen, I say to you, unless a grain of wheat falls to the ground and dies, it remains just a grain of wheat; but if it dies, it produces much fruit. Whoever loves his life loses it, and whoever hates his life in this world will preserve it for eternal life. Whoever serves me must follow me, and where I am, there also will my servant be. The Father will honor whoever serves me.

"I am troubled now. Yet what should I say? 'Father, save me from this hour'? But it was for this purpose that I came to this hour. Father, glorify your name." Then a voice came from heaven, "I have glorified it and will glorify it again."

This is the Gospel of the Lord.

Shorter form:

A reading from the holy gospel
according to John   12:23-26   14?

If a grain of wheat falls on the ground and dies, it yields a rich harvest.

Jesus told his disciples:

"The hour has come for the Son of Man to be glorified. Amen, amen, I say to you, unless a grain of wheat falls to the ground and dies, it remains just a grain of wheat; but if it dies, it produces much fruit. Whoever loves his life loses it, and whoever hates his life in this world will preserve it for eternal life. Whoever serves me must follow me, and where I am, there also will my servant be. The Father will honor whoever serves me."

This is the Gospel of the Lord.

17   A reading from the holy gospel
according to John   14:1-6   143

There are many rooms in my Father's house.

Jesus said to his disciples:

"Do not let your hearts be troubled. You have faith in God; have faith also in me. In my Father's house there are many dwelling places. If there were not, would I have told you that I am going to prepare a place for you? And if I go and prepare a place for you, I will come back again and take you to myself, so that where I am you also may be. Where I am going you know the way."

Thomas said to him, "Master, we do not know where you are going; how can we know the way?"

Jesus said to him, "I am the way and the truth and the life. No one comes to the Father except through me."

This is the Gospel of the Lord.

18   A reading from the holy gospel
according to John   17:24-26   144

Father, I want those you have given me to be with me where I am.

Jesus raised his eyes to heaven and said:

"Father, my disciples are your gift to me. I wish that where I am they also may be with me, that they may see my glory that you gave me, because you loved me before the foundation of the world. Righteous Father, the world also does not know you, but I know you, and they know that you sent me. I made known to them your name and I will make it known, that the love with which you loved me may be in them and I in them."

This is the Gospel of the Lord.

19 A reading from the holy gospel
according to John 19:17-18, 25-30

Jesus bowed his head and gave up his spirit.

Jesus carrying the cross himself went out to what is called the Place of the Skull, in Hebrew, Golgotha. There they crucified him, and with him two others, one on either side, with Jesus in the middle.

Standing by the cross of Jesus were his mother and his mother's sister, Mary the wife of Clopas, and Mary of Magdala. When Jesus saw his mother and the disciple there whom he loved, he said to his mother, "Woman, behold, your son." Then he said to the disciple, "Behold, your mother." And from that hour the disciple took her into his home.

After this, aware that everything was now finished, in order that the scripture might be fulfilled, Jesus said, "I thirst." There was a vessel filled with common wine. So they put a sponge soaked in wine on a sprig of hyssop and put it up to his mouth. When Jesus had taken the wine, he said, "It is finished." And bowing his head, he handed over the spirit.

This is the Gospel of the Lord.

14 FUNERALS FOR BAPTIZED CHILDREN

Old Testament Readings

1   A reading from the book of the prophet Isaiah   25:6a, 7-9   203

The Lord God will destroy death for ever.

On this mountain the Lord of hosts
    will provide for all peoples.
On this mountain he will destroy
    the veil that veils all peoples,
The web that is woven over all nations;
    he will destroy death forever.
The Lord God will wipe away
    the tears from all faces;
The reproach of his people he will remove
    from the whole earth; for the Lord has spoken.

On that day it will be said:
"Behold our God, to whom we looked to save us!
    This is the Lord for whom we looked;
    let us rejoice and be glad that he has saved us!"

This is the Word of the Lord.

2   A reading from the book of Lamentations   3:22-26   204

It is good to wait in silence for the Lord God to save.

The favors of the Lord are not exhausted,
    his mercies are not spent;
They are renewed each morning,
    so great is his faithfulness.
My portion is the Lord, says my soul;
    therefore will I hope in him.

Good is the Lord to one who waits for him,
    to the soul that seeks him;
It is good to hope in silence
    for the saving help of the Lord.

This is the Word of the Lord.

New Testament Readings

346 During the Easter season reading 6 or 7 is used as the first reading instead of a reading from the Old Testament.

1 A reading from the letter of Paul to the Romans   6:3-4, 8-9   205

We believe that we shall return to life with Christ.

Are you unaware that we who were baptized into Christ Jesus were baptized into his death? We were indeed buried with him through baptism into death, so that, just as Christ was raised from the dead by the glory of the Father, we too might live in newness of life. If, then, we have died with Christ, we believe that we shall also live with him. We know that Christ, raised from the dead, dies no more; death no longer has power over him.

This is the Word of the Lord.

2 A reading from the letter of Paul to the Romans   14:7-9   206

Whether alive or dead, we belong to the Lord.

None of us lives for oneself, and no one dies for oneself. For if we live, we live for the Lord, and if we die, we die for the Lord; so then, whether we live or die, we are the Lord's. For this is why Christ died and came to life, that he might be Lord of both the dead and the living.

This is the Word of the Lord.

3   A reading from the first letter of Paul
to the Corinthians   15:20-23   207

All people will be brought to life in Christ.

Christ has been raised from the dead, the firstfruits of those who have fallen asleep. For since death came through a human being, the resurrection of the dead came also through a human being. For just as in Adam all die, so too in Christ shall all be brought to life, but each one in proper order: Christ the firstfruits; then, at his coming, those who belong to Christ.

This is the Word of the Lord.

4   A reading from the letter of Paul to the Ephesians   1:3-5   208

The Father chose us in Christ, before the creation of the world, to be holy.

Blessed be the God and Father of our Lord Jesus Christ, who has blessed us in Christ with every spiritual blessing in the heavens, as he chose us in him, before the foundation of the world, to be holy and without blemish before him. In love he destined us for adoption to himself through Jesus Christ, in accord with the favor of his will.

This is the Word of the Lord.

5   A reading from the first letter of Paul
to the Thessalonians   4:13-14, 18   209

We shall stay with the Lord for ever.

We do not want you to be unaware, brothers [and sisters], about those who have fallen asleep, so that you may not grieve like the rest, who have no hope. For if we believe that Jesus died and rose, so too will God, through Jesus, bring with him those who have fallen asleep. Therefore, console one another with these words.

This is the Word of the Lord.

6   A reading from the book of Revelation   7:9-10, 15-17   210

God will wipe away all tears from their eyes.

After this I had a vision of a great multitude, which no one could count, from every nation, race, people, and tongue. They stood before the throne and before the Lamb, wearing white robes and holding palm branches in their hands. They cried out in a loud voice:

"Salvation comes from our God, who is seated on the throne,
and from the Lamb."

"For this reason they stand before God's throne
and worship him day and night in his temple.
The one who sits on the throne will shelter them.
They will not hunger or thirst anymore,
nor will the sun or any heat strike them.
For the Lamb who is in the center of the throne
will shepherd them
and lead them to springs of life-giving water,
and God will wipe away every tear from their eyes."

This is the Word of the Lord.

7   A reading from the book of Revelation   21:1a, 3-5a   211

There will be no more death.

I saw a new heaven and a new earth. I heard a loud voice from the throne saying, "Behold, God's dwelling is with the human race. He will dwell with them and they will be his people and God himself will always be with them as their God. He will wipe every tear from their eyes, and there shall be no more death or mourning, wailing or pain, for the old order has passed away."

The one who sat on the throne said, "Behold, I make all things new."

This is the Word of the Lord.

Responsorial Psalms

1   Psalm 23   ₂₁₂

R. The Lord is my shepherd; there is nothing I shall want.

The Lord is my shepherd;
there is nothing I shall want.
Fresh and green are the pastures
where he gives me repose.
Near restful waters he leads me,
to revive my drooping spirit. R.

He guides me along the right path;
he is true to his name.
If I should walk in the valley of darkness
no evil would I fear.
You are there with your crook and your staff;
with these you give me comfort. R.

You have prepared a banquet for me
in the sight of my foes.
My head you have anointed with oil;
my cup is overflowing. R.

Surely goodness and kindness shall follow me
all the days of my life.
In the Lord's own house shall I dwell
for ever and ever. R.

2   Psalm 25   213

R. To you, O Lord, I lift my soul.

Lord, make me know your ways.
Lord, teach me your paths.
Make me walk in your truth, and teach me:
for you are God my savior. R.

Remember your mercy, Lord,
and the love you have shown from of old.
Do not remember the sins of my youth.
In your love remember me. R.

252 14 FUNERALS FOR BAPTIZED CHILDREN

Preserve my life and rescue me.
Do not disappoint me, you are my refuge.
May innocence and uprightness protect me:
for my hope is in you, O Lord.

R. To you, O Lord, I lift my soul.

3   Psalm 42   214

R. My soul is thirsting for the living God: when shall I see him
face to face?

Like the deer that yearns
for running streams,
so my soul is yearning
for you, my God. R.

My soul is thirsting for God,
the God of my life;
when can I enter and see
the face of God? R.

These things will I remember
as I pour out my soul:
how I would lead the rejoicing crowd
into the house of God,
amid cries of gladness and thanksgiving,
the throng wild with joy. R.

O send forth your light and your truth;
let these be my guide.
Let them bring me to your holy mountain
to the place where you dwell. R.

And I will come to the altar of God,
the God of my joy.
My redeemer, I will thank you on the harp,
O God, my God. R.

Why are you cast down, my soul,
why groan within me?
Hope in God; I will praise him still,
my savior and my God. R.

R. Let all praise the name of the Lord.
Or:
R. Alleluia.

Praise the Lord from the heavens,
praise him in the heights.
Praise him, all his angels,
praise him, all his host. R.

All earth's kings and peoples,
earth's princes and rulers;
young men and maidens,
old men together with children. R.

Let them praise the name of the Lord
for he alone is exalted.
The splendor of his name
reaches beyond heaven and earth. R.

He exalts the strength of his people.
He is the praise of all his saints,
of the sons of Israel,
of the people to whom he comes close. R.

Alleluia Verses and Verses before the Gospel

1   See Matthew 11:25   216

Blessed are you, Father, Lord of heaven and earth;
you have revealed to little ones the mysteries of the kingdom.

2   John 6:39   217

This is the will of my Father, says the Lord,
that I should lose nothing of all that he has given to me,
and that I should raise it up on the last day.

3   2 Corinthians 1:3b-4a   218

Blessed be the Father of mercies and the God of all comfort,
who consoles us in all our afflictions.

1   A reading from the holy gospel
according to Matthew   11:25-30   219

You have hidden these things from the learned and the clever and revealed them to children.

At that time Jesus said in reply, "I give praise to you, Father, Lord of heaven and earth, for although you have hidden these things from the wise and the learned you have revealed them to the childlike. Yes, Father, such has been your gracious will. All things have been handed over to me by my Father. No one knows the Son except the Father, and no one knows the Father except the Son and anyone to whom the Son wishes to reveal him.

"Come to me, all you who labor and are burdened, and I will give you rest. Take my yoke upon you and learn from me, for I am meek and humble of heart; and you will find rest for yourselves. For my yoke is easy, and my burden light."

This is the Gospel of the Lord.

2   A reading from the holy gospel
according to Mark   10:13-16

The kingdom of heaven belongs to little children.

People were bringing children to Jesus that he might touch them, but the disciples rebuked them. When Jesus saw this he became indignant and said to them, "Let the children come to me; do not prevent them, for the kingdom of God belongs to such as these. Amen, I say to you, whoever does not accept the kingdom of God like a child will not enter it." Then he embraced them and blessed them, placing his hands on them.

This is the Gospel of the Lord.

3   Longer form:

A reading from the holy gospel
according to John   6:37-40   220

*This is the will of my Father, that I should lose nothing of all that he has given
to me.*

Jesus said to the crowd:

"Everything that the Father gives me will come to me, and I
will not reject anyone who comes to me, because I came down
from heaven not to do my own will but the will of the one who
sent me. And this is the will of the one who sent me, that I
should not lose anything of what he gave me, but that I should
raise it on the last day. For this is the will of my Father, that
everyone who sees the Son and believes in him may have eternal life, and I shall raise him on the last day."

This is the Gospel of the Lord.

Shorter form:

A reading from the holy gospel
according to John   6:37-39   220

*This is the will of my Father, that I should lose nothing of all that he has given
to me.*

Jesus said to the crowd:

"Everything that the Father gives me will come to me, and I
will not reject anyone who comes to me, because I came down
from heaven not to do my own will but the will of the one who
sent me. And this is the will of the one who sent me, that I
should not lose anything of what he gave me, but that I should
raise it on the last day."

This is the Gospel of the Lord.

4   A reading from the holy gospel
according to John   6:51-58   221

All who eat this bread will live for ever, and I will raise them up on the last day.

Jesus said to the crowd:

"I am the living bread that came down from heaven; whoever eats this bread will live forever; and the bread that I will give is my flesh for the life of the world."

The Jews quarreled among themselves, saying, "How can this man give us his flesh to eat?" Jesus said to them, "Amen, amen, I say to you, unless you eat the flesh of the Son of Man and drink his blood, you do not have life within you. Whoever eats my flesh and drinks my blood has eternal life, and I will raise him on the last day. For my flesh is true food, and my blood is true drink. Whoever eats my flesh and drinks my blood remains in me and I in him. Just as the living Father sent me and I have life because of the Father, so also the one who feeds on me will have life because of me. This is the bread that came down from heaven. Unlike your ancestors who ate and still died, whoever eats this bread will live forever."

This is the Gospel of the Lord.

5   A reading from the holy gospel
according to John   11:32-38, 40   222

If you believe, you will see the glory of God.

When Mary came to where Jesus was and saw him, she fell at his feet and said to him, "Lord, if you had been here, my brother would not have died." When Jesus saw her weeping and the Jews who had come with her weeping, he became perturbed and deeply troubled, and said, "Where have you laid him?" They said to him, "Sir, come and see." And Jesus wept. So the Jews said, "See how he loved him." But some of them said, "Could not the one who opened the eyes of the blind man have done something so that this man would not have died?"

So Jesus, perturbed again, came to the tomb. It was a cave, and a stone lay across it. Jesus said to Martha, "Did I not tell you that if you believe you will see the glory of God?"

This is the Gospel of the Lord.

6   A reading from the holy gospel
     according to John   19:25-30

This is your mother.

Standing by the cross of Jesus were his mother and his mother's sister, Mary the wife of Clopas, and Mary of Magdala. When Jesus saw his mother and the disciple there whom he loved, he said to his mother, "Woman, behold, your son." Then he said to the disciple, "Behold, your mother." And from that hour the disciple took her into his home.

After this, aware that everything was now finished, in order that the scripture might be fulfilled, Jesus said, "I thirst." There was a vessel filled with common wine. So they put a sponge soaked in wine on a sprig of hyssop and put it up to his mouth. When Jesus had taken the wine, he said, "It is finished." And bowing his head, he handed over the spirit.

This is the Gospel of the Lord.

15 FUNERALS FOR CHILDREN WHO DIED BEFORE BAPTISM

OLD TESTAMENT READINGS

1   A reading from the book of the prophet Isaiah   25:6a, 7-8b   231

The Lord God will destroy death for ever.

On this mountain the Lord of hosts
    will provide for all peoples.
On this mountain he will destroy
    the veil that veils all peoples,
The web that is woven over all nations;
    he will destroy death forever.
The Lord God will wipe away
    the tears from all faces.

This is the Word of the Lord.

2   A reading from the book of Lamentations   3:22-26

It is good to wait in silence for the Lord God to save.

The favors of the Lord are not exhausted,
  his mercies are not spent;
They are renewed each morning,
  so great is his faithfulness.
My portion is the Lord, says my soul;
  therefore will I hope in him.

Good is the Lord to one who waits for him,
  to the soul that seeks him;
It is good to hope in silence
  for the saving help of the Lord.

This is the Word of the Lord.

RESPONSORIAL PSALM

Psalm 25

R. To you, O Lord, I lift my soul.

Or:

R. No one who waits for you, O Lord, will ever be put to shame.

Lord, make me know your ways.
Lord, teach me your paths.
Make me walk in your truth, and teach me:
for you are God my savior. R.

Remember your mercy, Lord,
and the love you have shown from of old.
In your love remember me
because of your goodness, O Lord. R.

Relieve the anguish of my heart
and set me free from my distress.
Preserve my life and rescue me.
Do not disappoint me, you are my refuge. R.

Alleluia Verses and Verses before the Gospel

1   2 Corinthians 1:3b-4a

Blessed be the Father of mercies and the God of all comfort, who consoles us in all our afflictions.

2   Revelation 1:5a, 6b

Jesus Christ is the firstborn from the dead;
glory and kingship be his for ever and ever. Amen.

Gospel Readings

1   A reading from the holy gospel
according to Matthew   11:25-30

You have hidden these things from the learned and the clever and have revealed them to children.

At that time Jesus said in reply, "I give praise to you, Father, Lord of heaven and earth, for although you have hidden these things from the wise and the learned you have revealed them to the childlike. Yes, Father, such has been your gracious will. All things have been handed over to me by my Father. No one knows the Son except the Father, and no one knows the Father except the Son and anyone to whom the Son wishes to reveal him.

"Come to me, all you who labor and are burdened, and I will give you rest. Take my yoke upon you and learn from me, for I am meek and humble of heart; and you will find rest for yourselves. For my yoke is easy, and my burden light."

This is the Gospel of the Lord.

A reading from the holy gospel
according to Mark

Jesus gave a loud cry and breathed his last.

At noon darkness came over the whole land until three in the afternoon. And at three o'clock Jesus cried out in a loud voice, *"Eloi, Eloi, lema sabachthani?"* which is translated, "My God, my God, why have you forsaken me?" Some of the bystanders who heard it said, "Look, he is calling Elijah." One of them ran, soaked a sponge with wine, put it on a reed, and gave it to him to drink, saying, "Wait, let us see if Elijah comes to take him down."

Jesus gave a loud cry and breathed his last. The veil of the sanctuary was torn in two from top to bottom. When the centurion who stood facing him saw how he breathed his last he said, "Truly this man was the Son of God!" There were also women looking on from a distance. Among them were Mary Magdalene, Mary, the mother of the younger James and of Joses, and Salome. These women had followed him when he was in Galilee and ministered to him. There were also many other women who had come up with him to Jerusalem.

When it was already evening, since it was the day of preparation, the day before the sabbath, Joseph of Arimathea, a distinguished member of the council, who was himself awaiting the kingdom of God, came and courageously went to Pilate and asked for the body of Jesus. Pilate was amazed that he was already dead. He summoned the centurion and asked him if Jesus had already died. And when he learned of it from the centurion, he gave the body to Joseph. Having bought a linen cloth, he took him down, wrapped him in the linen cloth and laid him in a tomb that had been hewn out of the rock. Then he rolled a stone against the entrance to the tomb.

This is the Gospel of the Lord.

3   A reading from the holy gospel
    according to John   19:25-30

This is your mother.

Standing by the cross of Jesus were his mother and his mother's
sister, Mary the wife of Clopas, and Mary of Magdala. When
Jesus saw his mother and the disciple there whom he loved, he
said to his mother, "Woman, behold, your son." Then he said
to the disciple, "Behold, your mother." And from that hour the
disciple took her into his home.

After this, aware that everything was now finished, in order that
the scripture might be fulfilled, Jesus said, "I thirst." There was
a vessel filled with common wine. So they put a sponge soaked
in wine on a sprig of hyssop and put it up to his mouth. When
Jesus had taken the wine, he said, "It is finished." And bowing
his head, he handed over the spirit.

This is the Gospel of the Lord.

16 ANTIPHONS AND PSALMS

347 The following psalms with their antiphons may be chosen for use in various places within the rites.

1   Psalm 23

Ant. Remember me in your kingdom, Lord.   145

The Lord is my shepherd;
there is nothing I shall want.
Fresh and green are the pastures
where he gives me repose.
Near restful waters he leads me,
to revive my drooping spirit.

He guides me along the right path;
he is true to his name.
If I should walk in the valley of darkness
no evil would I fear.
You are there with your crook and your staff;
with these you give me comfort.

You have prepared a banquet for me
in the sight of my foes.
My head you have anointed with oil;
my cup is overflowing.

Surely goodness and kindness shall follow me
all the days of my life.
In the Lord's own house shall I dwell
for ever and ever.

2　　　Psalm 25

Ant. Look on my grief and my sorrow: forgive all my sins.　146
　　Or:

Ant. May the angels lead you into paradise; may the martyrs
come to welcome you and take you to the holy city, the new
and eternal Jerusalem.

To you, O Lord, I lift my soul.
I trust you, let me not be disappointed;
do not let my enemies triumph.
Those who hope in you shall not be disappointed,
but only those who wantonly break faith.

Lord, make me know your ways.
Lord, teach me your paths.
Make me walk in your truth, and teach me:
for you are God my savior.

In you I hope all day long
because of your goodness, O Lord.
Remember your mercy, Lord,
and the love you have shown from of old.
Do not remember the sins of my youth.
In your love remember me.

The Lord is good and upright.
He shows the path to those who stray,
he guides the humble in the right path;
he teaches his way to the poor.

His ways are faithfulness and love
for those who keep his covenant and will.
Lord, for the sake of your name
forgive my guilt; for it is great.

If anyone fears the Lord
he will show him the path he should choose.
His soul shall live in happiness
and his children shall possess the land.
The Lord's friendship is for those who revere him;
to them he reveals his covenant.

My eyes are always on the Lord;
for he rescues my feet from the snare.
Turn to me and have mercy
for I am lonely and poor.

Relieve the anguish of my heart
and set me free from my distress.
See my affliction and my toil
and take all my sins away.

See how many are my foes;
how violent their hatred for me.
Preserve my life and rescue me.
Do not disappoint me, you are my refuge.
May innocence and uprightness protect me:
for my hope is in you, O Lord.

Redeem Israel, O God, from all its distress.

3   Psalm 42

Ant. I will go to the dwelling of God, to the wonderful house   147
of my Savior.

Like the deer that yearns
for running streams,
so my soul is yearning
for you, my God.

My soul is thirsting for God,
the God of my life;
when can I enter and see
the face of God?

My tears have become my bread,
by night, by day,
as I hear it said all the day long:
"Where is your God?"

These things will I remember
as I pour out my soul:
how I would lead the rejoicing crowd
into the house of God,
amid cries of gladness and thanksgiving,
the throng wild with joy.

Why are you cast down, my soul,
why groan within me?
Hope in God; I will praise him still,
my savior and my God.

My soul is cast down within me
as I think of you,
from the country of Jordan and Mount Hermon,
from the Hill of Mizar.

Deep is calling on deep,
in the roar of waters:
your torrents and all your waves
swept over me.

By day the Lord will send
his loving kindness;
by night I will sing to him,
praise the God of my life.

I will say to God, my rock:
"Why have you forgotten me?
Why do I go mourning
oppressed by the foe?"

With cries that pierce me to the heart,
my enemies revile me,
saying to me all the day long:
"Where is your God?"

Why are you cast down, my soul,
why groan within me?
Hope in God; I will praise him still,
my savior and my God.

4   Psalm 51

Ant. Eternal rest, O Lord, and your perpetual light.   14

Or:

Ant. Caught up with Christ, rejoice with the saints in glory. 149

Or:

Ant. The bones that were broken shall leap for joy. 150

Have mercy on me, God, in your kindness.
In your compassion blot out my offense.
O wash me more and more from my guilt
and cleanse me from my sin.

My offenses truly I know them;
my sin is always before me.
Against you, you alone, have I sinned;
what is evil in your sight I have done.

That you may be justified when you give sentence
and be without reproach when you judge.
O see, in guilt I was born,
a sinner was I conceived.

Indeed you love truth in the heart;
then in the secret of my heart teach me wisdom.
O purify me, then I shall be clean;
O wash me, I shall be whiter than snow.

Make me hear rejoicing and gladness,
that the bones you have crushed may thrill.
From my sins turn away your face
and blot out all my guilt.

A pure heart create for me, O God,
put a steadfast spirit within me.
Do not cast me away from your presence,
nor deprive me of your holy spirit.

Give me again the joy of your help;
with a spirit of fervor sustain me,
that I may teach transgressors your ways
and sinners may return to you.

O rescue me, God, my helper,
and my tongue shall ring out your goodness.
O Lord, open my lips
and my mouth shall declare your praise.

For in sacrifice you take no delight,
burnt offering from me you would refuse,
my sacrifice, a contrite spirit.
A humbled, contrite heart you will not spurn.

In your goodness, show favor to Zion:
rebuild the walls of Jerusalem.
Then you will be pleased with lawful sacrifice,
holocausts offered on your altar.

5   Psalm 93

Ant. From clay you shaped me; with flesh you clothed me; 15▮
Redeemer, raise me on the last day.

The Lord is king, with majesty enrobed;
the Lord has robed himself with might,
he has girded himself with power.

The world you made firm, not to be moved;
your throne has stood firm from of old.
From all eternity, O Lord, you are.

The waters have lifted up, O Lord,
the waters have lifted up their voice,
the waters have lifted up their thunder.

Greater than the roar of mighty waters,
more glorious than the surgings of the sea,
the Lord is glorious on high.

Truly your decrees are to be trusted.
Holiness is fitting to your house,
O Lord, until the end of time.

6   Psalm 114 and 115:1-12

Ant. May Christ welcome you into paradise. 15▮

        Or:

Ant. Alleluia.

Alleluia!

When Israel came forth from Egypt,
Jacob's sons from an alien people,
Judah became the Lord's temple,
Israel became his kingdom.

The sea fled at the sight:
the Jordan turned back on its course,
the mountains leapt like rams
and the hills like yearling sheep.

Why was it, sea, that you fled,
that you turned back, Jordan, on your course?
Mountains, that you leapt like rams,
hills, like yearling sheep?

Tremble, O earth, before the Lord,
in the presence of the God of Jacob,
who turns the rock into a pool
and flint into a spring of water.

Not to us, Lord, not to us,
but to your name give the glory
for the sake of your love and your truth,
lest the heathen say: "Where is their God?"

But our God is in the heavens;
he does whatever he wills.
Their idols are silver and gold,
the work of human hands.

They have mouths but they cannot speak;
they have eyes but they cannot see;
they have ears but they cannot hear;
they have nostrils but they cannot smell.

With their hands they cannot feel;
with their feet they cannot walk.
No sound comes from their throats.
Their makers will come to be like them
and so will all who trust in them.

Sons of Israel, trust in the Lord;
he is their help and their shield.
Sons of Aaron, trust in the Lord;
he is their help and their shield.

You who fear him, trust in the Lord;
he is their help and their shield.
He remembers us, and he will bless us;
he will bless the sons of Israel.

7 Psalm 116

Ant. May choirs of angels welcome you and lead you to the bos- 15
om of Abraham. May you find eternal rest where Lazarus is
poor no longer.

Or:

Ant. I heard a voice from heaven: Blessed are those who die in 15
the Lord.

Or:

Ant. Alleluia.

Alleluia!

I love the Lord for he has heard
the cry of my appeal;
for he turned his ear to me
in the day when I called him.

They surrounded me, the snares of death,
with the anguish of the tomb;
they caught me, sorrow and distress.
I called on the Lord's name.

O Lord my God, deliver me!

How gracious is the Lord, and just;
our God has compassion.
The Lord protects the simple hearts;
I was helpless so he saved me.

Turn back, my soul, to your rest
for the Lord has been good;
he has kept my soul from death,
my eyes from tears
and my feet from stumbling.

I will walk in the presence of the Lord
in the land of the living.

I trusted, even when I said:
"I am sorely afflicted,"
and when I said in my alarm:
"No man can be trusted."

How can I repay the Lord
for his goodness to me?

The cup of salvation I will raise;
I will call on the Lord's name.

My vows to the Lord I will fulfill
before all his people.
O precious in the eyes of the Lord
is the death of his faithful.

Your servant, Lord, your servant am I;
you have loosened my bonds.
A thanksgiving sacrifice I make:
I will call on the Lord's name.

My vows to the Lord I will fulfill
before all his people,
in the courts of the house of the Lord,
in your midst, O Jerusalem.

8   Psalm 118

Ant. Open for me the holy gates; I will enter and praise the   155
Lord.

   Or:

Ant. This is the gate of the Lord: here the just shall enter.   156

Give thanks to the Lord for he is good,
for his love has no end.

Let the sons of Israel say:
"His love endures for ever."
Let the sons of Aaron say:
"His love endures for ever."
Let those who fear the Lord say:
"His love endures for ever."

I called to the Lord in my distress;
he answered and freed me.
The Lord is at my side; I do not fear.
What can man do against me?
The Lord is at my side as my helper:
I shall look down on my foes.

It is better to take refuge in the Lord
than to trust in men:
it is better to take refuge in the Lord
than to trust in princes.

The nations all encompassed me;
in the Lord's name I crushed them.
They compassed me, compassed me about;
in the Lord's name I crushed them.
They compassed me about like bees;
they blazed like a fire among thorns.
In the Lord's name I crushed them.

I was hard-pressed and was falling
but the Lord came to my help.
The Lord is my strength and my song;
he is my savior.
There are shouts of joy and victory
in the tents of the just.

The Lord's right hand has triumphed;
his right hand raised me.
The Lord's right hand has triumphed;
I shall not die, I shall live
and recount his deeds.
I was punished, I was punished by the Lord,
but not doomed to die.

Open to me the gates of holiness:
I will enter and give thanks.
This is the Lord's own gate
where the just may enter.
I will thank you for you have answered
and you are my savior.

The stone which the builders rejected
has become the cornerstone.
This is the work of the Lord,
a marvel in our eyes.
This day was made by the Lord;
we rejoice and are glad.

O Lord, grant us salvation;
O Lord, grant success.
Blessed in the name of the Lord
is he who comes.
We bless you from the house of the Lord;
the Lord God is our light.

Go forward in procession with branches
even to the altar.
You are my God, I thank you.
My God, I praise you.
Give thanks to the Lord for he is good;
for his love endures for ever.

9   Antiphon 1 may serve as the common antiphon for Psalm 119   157
or an antiphon proper to each part of Psalm 119 may be used.

Psalm 119:1-8

Ant. 1 They are happy who live by the law of God.

They are happy whose life is blameless,
who follow God's law!
They are happy who do his will,
seeking him with all their hearts,
who never do anything evil
but walk in his ways.

You have laid down your precepts
to be obeyed with care.
May my footsteps be firm
to obey your statutes.
Then I shall not be put to shame
as I heed your commands.

I will thank you with an upright heart
as I learn your decrees.
I will obey your statutes:
do not forsake me.

Psalm 119:9-16

Ant. 2 May you be for ever blessed, O Lord; teach me your holy
ways.

How shall the young remain sinless?
By obeying your word.
I have sought you with all my heart:
let me not stray from your commands.

I treasure your promise in my heart
lest I sin against you.
Blessed are you, O Lord;
teach me your statutes.

With my tongue I have recounted
the decrees of your lips.
I rejoiced to do your will
as though all riches were mine.

I will ponder all your precepts
and consider your paths.
I take delight in your statutes;
I will not forget your word.

Psalm 119:17-24

Ant. 3 Open my eyes, O Lord, that I may see the wonders of
your law.

Bless your servant and I shall live
and obey your word.
Open my eyes that I may see
the wonders of your law.

I am a pilgrim on the earth;
show me your commands.
My soul is ever consumed
as I long for your decrees.

You threaten the proud, the accursed,
who turn from your commands.
Relieve me from scorn and contempt
for I do your will.

Though princes sit plotting against me
I ponder on your rulings.
Your will is my delight;
your statutes are my counselors.

Psalm 119:25-32

Ant. 4 Lightly I run in the way you have shown, for you have
opened my heart to receive your law.

My soul lies in the dust;
by your word revive me.
I declared my ways and you answered:
teach me your statutes.

Make me grasp the way of your precepts
and I will muse on your wonders.
My soul pines away with grief;
by your word raise me up.

Keep me from the way of error
and teach me your law.
I have chosen the way of truth
with your decrees before me.

I bind myself to do your will;
Lord, do not disappoint me.
I will run the way of your commands;
you give freedom to my heart.

Psalm 119:33-40

Ant. 5 Lead me, Lord, in the path of your commands.

Teach me the demands of your precepts
and I will keep them to the end.
Train me to observe your law,
to keep it with my heart.

Guide me in the path of your commands;
for there is my delight.
Bend my heart to your will
and not to love of gain.

Keep my eyes from what is false:
by your word, give me life.
Keep the promise you have made
to the servant who fears you.

Keep me from the scorn I dread,
for your decrees are good.
See, I long for your precepts:
then in your justice, give me life.

Psalm 119:41-48

Ant. 6 Blessed are those who hear the word of God and cherish it in their hearts.

Lord, let your love come upon me,
the saving help of your promise.
And I shall answer those who taunt me
for I trust in your word.

Do not take the word of truth from my mouth
for I trust in your decrees.
I shall always keep your law
for ever and ever.

I shall walk in the path of freedom
for I seek your precepts.
I will speak of your will before kings
and not be abashed.

Your commands have been my delight;
these I have loved.
I will worship your commands and love them
and ponder your will.

Psalm 119:49-56

Ant. 7 In the land of exile I have kept your commands.

Remember your word to your servant
by which you gave me hope.
This is my comfort in sorrow
that your promise gives me life.

Though the proud may utterly deride me
I keep to your law.
I remember your decrees of old
and these, Lord, console me.

I am seized with indignation at the wicked
who forsake your law.
Your commands have become my song
in the land of exile.

I think of your name in the nighttime
and I keep your law.
This has been my blessing,
the keeping of your precepts.

Psalm 119:57-64

Ant. 8 I have pondered my ways and turned back to your
teaching.

My part, I have resolved, O Lord,
is to obey your word.
With all my heart I implore your favor;
show the mercy of your promise.

I have pondered over my ways
and returned to your will.
I made haste and did not delay
to obey your commands.

Though the nets of the wicked ensnared me
I remembered your law.
At midnight I will rise and thank you
for your just decrees.

I am a friend of all who revere you,
who obey your precepts.
Lord, your love fills the earth.
Teach me your commands.

Psalm 119:65-72

Ant. 9 More precious than silver or gold is the law you teach
us, O Lord.

Lord, you have been good to your servant
according to your word.
Teach me discernment and knowledge,
for I trust in your commands.

Before I was afflicted I strayed,
but now I keep your word.
You are good and your deeds are good;
teach me your commandments.

Though proud men smear me with lies,
yet I keep your precepts.
Their minds are closed to good
but your law is my delight.

It was good for me to be afflicted,
to learn your will.
The law from your mouth means more to me
than silver and gold.

Psalm 119:73-80

Ant. 10 Let your loyal love console me, as you promised your servant.

It was your hands that made me and shaped me:
help me to learn your commands.
Your faithful will see me and rejoice,
for I trust in your word.

Lord, I know that your decrees are right,
that you afflicted me justly.
Let your love be ready to console me
by your promise to your servant.

Let your love come and I shall live,
for your law is my delight.
Shame the proud who harm me with lies,
while I ponder your precepts.

Let your faithful turn to me,
those who know your will.
Let my heart be blameless in obeying you,
lest I be ashamed.

Psalm 119:81-88

Ant. 11 Heaven and earth will pass away, but my words will not pass away.

I yearn for your saving help;
I hope in your word.
My eyes yearn to see your promise.
When will you console me?

Though parched and exhausted with waiting,
I have not forgotten your commands.
How long must your servant suffer;
when will you judge my foes?

For me the proud have dug pitfalls,
against your law.
Your commands are all true; then help me
when lies oppress me.

They almost made an end of me on earth,
but I kept your precepts.
Because of your love give me life
and I will do your will.

Psalm 119:89-96

Ant. 12 I have sought to do your will, O Lord; for this you give
me life.

Your word, O Lord, for ever
stands firm in the heavens:
your truth lasts from age to age,
like the earth you created.

By your decree it endures to this day;
for all things serve you.
Had your law not been my delight,
I would have died in my affliction.

I will never forget your precepts,
for with them you give me life.
Save me, for I am yours,
since I seek your precepts.

Though the wicked lie in wait to destroy me,
yet I ponder on your will.
I have seen that all perfection has an end,
but your command is boundless.

Psalm 119:97-104

Ant. 13 Law finds its fulfillment in love.

Or:

Ant. How sweet your promise, richer than honey from the
comb.

Lord, how I love your law!
It is ever in my mind.
Your command makes me wiser than my foes;
for it is mine for ever.

I have more insight than all who teach me,
for I ponder your will.
I have more understanding than the old,
for I keep your precepts.

I turn my feet from evil paths
to obey your word.
I have not turned away from your decrees;
you yourself have taught me.

Your promise is sweeter to my taste
than honey in the mouth.
I gain understanding from your precepts;
I hate the ways of falsehood.

Psalm 119:105-112

Ant. 14 Whoever follows me will not walk in the dark, but will
have the light of life.

Your word is a lamp for my steps
and a light for my path.
I have sworn and have made up my mind
to obey your decrees.

Lord, I am deeply afflicted:
by your word give me life.
Accept, Lord, the homage of my lips
and teach me your decrees.

Though I carry my life in my hands,
I remember your law.
Though the wicked try to ensnare me,
I do not stray from your precepts.

Your will is my heritage for ever,
the joy of my heart.
I set myself to carry out your statutes
in fullness, for ever.

Psalm 119:113-120

Ant. 15 Receive me, Lord, as you promised, that I may live.

I have no love for halfhearted men:
my love is for your law.
You are my shelter, my shield;
I hope in your word.

Leave me, you who do evil;
I will keep God's command.
If you uphold me by your promise I shall live;
let my hopes not be in vain.

Sustain me and I shall be saved
and ever observe your commands.
You spurn all who swerve from your statutes;
their cunning is in vain.

You throw away the wicked like dross:
so I love your will.
I tremble before you in terror;
I fear your decrees.

Psalm 119:121-128

Ant. 16 Give your servant a loving welcome, O Lord.

I have done what is right and just:
let me not be oppressed.
Vouch for the welfare of your servant,
lest the proud oppress me.

My eyes yearn for your saving help
and the promise of your justice.
Treat your servant with love
and teach me your commands.

I am your servant, give me knowledge;
then I shall know your will.
It is time for the Lord to act,
for your law has been broken.

That is why I love your commands
more than finest gold,
why I rule my life by your precepts:
I hate the ways of falsehood.

Psalm 119:129-136

Ant. 17 Guide my steps according to your promise, O Lord.

Your will is wonderful indeed;
therefore I obey it.
The unfolding of your word gives light
and teaches the simple.

I open my mouth and I sigh
as I yearn for your commands.
Turn and show me your mercy;
show justice to your friends.

Let my steps be guided by your promise;
let no evil rule me.
Redeem me from man's oppression
and I will keep your precepts.

Let your face shine on your servant
and teach me your decrees.
Tears stream from my eyes
because your law is disobeyed.

Psalm 119:137-144

Ant. 18 Do the things you have learned, and you will be blessed.

Lord, you are just indeed;
your decrees are right.
You have imposed your will with justice
and with absolute truth.

I am carried away by anger,
for my foes forget your word.
Your promise is tried in the fire,
the delight of your servant.

Although I am weak and despised,
I remember your precepts.
Your justice is eternal justice
and your law is truth.

Though anguish and distress have seized me,
I delight in your commands.
The justice of your will is eternal:
if you teach me, I shall live.

Psalm 119:145-152

Ant. 19 I cry for your help, O Lord; your word is my hope.

I call with all my heart; Lord, hear me,
I will keep your commands.
I call upon you, save me
and I will do your will.

I rise before dawn and cry for help,
I hope in your word.
My eyes watch through the night
to ponder your promise.

In your love hear my voice, O Lord;
give me life by your decrees.
Those who harm me unjustly draw near:
they are far from your law.

But you, O Lord, are close:
your commands are truth.
Long have I known that your will
is established for ever.

Psalm 119:153-160

Ant. 20 If you love me, keep my commandments, says the Lord.

See my affliction and save me
for I remember your law.
Uphold my cause and defend me;
by your promise give me life.

Salvation is far from the wicked,
who are heedless of your commands.
Numberless, Lord, are your mercies;
with your decrees give me life.

Though my foes and oppressors are countless,
I have not swerved from your will.
I look at the faithless with disgust;
they ignore your promise.

See how I love your precepts;
in your mercy give me life.
Your word is founded on truth:
your decrees are eternal.

Psalm 119:161-168

Ant. 21 Great is the peace of those who keep your law, O Lord.

Though princes oppress me without cause,
I stand in awe of your word.
I take delight in your promise
like one who finds a treasure.

Lies I hate and detest,
but your law is my love.
Seven times a day I praise you,
for your just decrees.

The lovers of your law have great peace;
they never stumble.
I await your saving help, O Lord,
I fulfill your commands.

My soul obeys your will
and loves it dearly.
I obey your precepts and your will;
all that I do is before you.

Psalm 119:169-176

Ant. 22 I have chosen to do your will; may your hand be always
there to give me strength.

Lord, let my cry come before you:
teach me by your word.
Let my pleading come before you;
save me by your promise.

Let my lips proclaim your praise,
because you teach me your commands.
Let my tongue sing your promise,
for your commands are just.

Let your hand be ready to help me,
since I have chosen your precepts.
Lord, I long for your saving help
and your law is my delight.

Give life to my soul that I may praise you.
Let your decrees give me help.
I am lost like a sheep; seek your servant,
for I remember your commands.

10   Psalm 121   158

Ant. My help is from the Lord who made heaven and earth.

I lift up my eyes to the mountains:
from where shall come my help?
My help shall come from the Lord
who made heaven and earth.

May he never allow you to stumble!
Let him sleep not, your guard.
No, he sleeps not nor slumbers,
Israel's guard.

The Lord is your guard and your shade;
at your right side he stands.
By day the sun shall not smite you
nor the moon in the night.

The Lord will guard you from evil,
he will guard your soul.
The Lord will guard your going and coming
both now and for ever.

11   Psalm 122

Ant. Let us go to the house of the Lord.

    Or:

Ant. I rejoiced when I heard them say: let us go to the house
of the Lord.

I rejoiced when I heard them say:
"Let us go to God's house."
And now our feet are standing
within your gates, O Jerusalem.

Jerusalem is built as a city
strongly compact.
It is there that the tribes go up,
the tribes of the Lord.

For Israel's law it is,
there to praise the Lord's name.
There were set the thrones of judgment
of the house of David.

For the peace of Jerusalem pray:
"Peace be to your homes!
May peace reign in your walls,
in your palaces, peace!"

For love of my brethren and friends
I say: "Peace upon you!"
For love of the house of the Lord
I will ask for your good.

Ant. Our eyes are fixed on the Lord, pleading for his mercy.
Or:
Ant. To you, O Lord, I lift up my eyes.

To you have I lifted up my eyes,
you who dwell in the heavens:
my eyes, like the eyes of slaves
on the hand of their lords.

Like the eyes of a servant
on the hand of her mistress,
so our eyes are on the Lord our God
till he show us his mercy.

Have mercy on us, Lord, have mercy.
We are filled with contempt.
Indeed all too full is our soul
with the scorn of the rich,
with the proud man's disdain.

Ant. Those who sow in tears shall sing for joy when they reap.

When the Lord delivered Zion from bondage,
it seemed like a dream.
Then was our mouth filled with laughter,
on our lips there were songs.

The heathens themselves said: "What marvels
the Lord worked for them!"
What marvels the Lord worked for us!
Indeed we were glad.

Deliver us, O Lord, from our bondage
as streams in dry land.
Those who are sowing in tears
will sing when they reap.

They go out, they go out, full of tears,
carrying seed for the sowing:
they come back, they come back, full of song,
carrying their sheaves.

14   Psalm 130

Ant. I cry to you, O Lord. 162

    Or:

Ant. My soul has hoped in the Lord. 163

Out of the depths I cry to you, O Lord,
Lord, hear my voice!
O let your ears be attentive
to the voice of my pleading.

If you, O Lord, should mark our guilt,
Lord, who would survive?
But with you is found forgiveness:
for this we revere you.

My soul is waiting for the Lord,
I count on his word.
My soul is longing for the Lord
more than watchman for daybreak.
Let the watchman count on daybreak
and Israel on the Lord.

Because with the Lord there is mercy
and fullness of redemption,
Israel indeed he will redeem
from all its iniquity.

15   Psalm 132 164

Ant. Let your holy people rejoice, O Lord, as they enter your
dwelling place.

O Lord, remember David
and all the many hardships he endured,
the oath he swore to the Lord,
his vow to the Strong One of Jacob.

"I will not enter the house where I live
nor go to the bed where I rest.
I will give no sleep to my eyes,
to my eyelids I will give no slumber
till I find a place for the Lord,
a dwelling for the Strong One of Jacob."

At Ephrathah we heard of the ark;
we found it in the plains of Yearim.
"Let us go to the place of his dwelling;
let us go to kneel at his footstool."

Go up, Lord, to the place of your rest,
you and the ark of your strength.
Your priests shall be clothed with holiness:
your faithful shall ring out their joy.
For the sake of David your servant
do not reject your anointed.

The Lord swore an oath to David;
he will not go back on his word:
"A son, the fruit of your body,
will I set upon your throne.

"If they keep my covenant in truth
and my laws that I have taught them,
their sons also shall rule
on your throne from age to age."

For the Lord has chosen Zion;
he has desired it for his dwelling:
"This is my resting place for ever,
here have I chosen to live.

"I will greatly bless her produce,
I will fill her poor with bread.
I will clothe her priests with salvation
and her faithful shall ring out their joy.

"There David's stock will flower:
I will prepare a lamp for my anointed.
I will cover his enemies with shame
but on him my crown shall shine."

Ant. Bless the Lord, all you servants of the Lord.

Or:

Ant. In the stillness of the night, bless the Lord.

O come, bless the Lord,
all you who serve the Lord,
who stand in the house of the Lord,
in the courts of the house of our God.

Lift up your hands to the holy place
and bless the Lord through the night.
May the Lord bless you from Zion,
he who made both heaven and earth.

Part IV
OFFICE
FOR THE DEAD

With the Lord there is mercy
and fullness of redemption

Part IV
OFFICE
FOR THE DEAD

348 The vigil for the deceased may be celebrated in the form of some part of the office for the dead. To encourage this form of the vigil, the chief hours, "Morning Prayer" and "Evening Prayer," are provided here. When the funeral liturgy is celebrated the evening before the committal, it may be appropriate to celebrate morning prayer before the procession to the place of committal.

349 In the celebration of the office for the dead members of the Christian community gather to offer praise and thanks to God especially for the gifts of redemption and resurrection, to intercede for the dead, and to find strength in Christ's victory over death. When the community celebrates the hours, Christ the Mediator and High Priest is truly present through his Spirit in the gathered assembly, in the proclamation of God's word, and in the prayer and song of the Church.[1] The community's celebration of the hours acknowledges that spiritual bond that links the Church on earth with the Church in heaven, for it is in union with the whole Church that this prayer is offered on behalf of the deceased.

350 At morning prayer the Christian community recalls "the resurrection of the Lord Jesus, the true light enlightening all people (see John 1:9) and 'the sun of justice' (Malachi 4:2) 'rising from on high' (Luke 1:78)."[2] The celebration of morning prayer from the office for the dead relates the death of the Christian to Christ's victory over death and affirms the hope that those who have received the light of Christ at baptism will share in that victory.

351 At evening prayer the Christian community gathers to give thanks for the gifts it has received, to recall the sacrifice of Jesus Christ and the saving works of redemption, and to call upon Christ, the evening star and unconquerable light.[3] Through evening prayer from the office for the dead the community gives thanks to God for the gift of life received by the deceased and praises the Father for the redemption brought about by the sacrifice of his Son, who is the joy-giving light and the true source of hope.

---

[1] See General Instruction of the Liturgy of the Hours, no. 13.

[2] See General Instruction of the Liturgy of the Hours, no. 38.

[3] See General Instruction of the Liturgy of the Hours, no. 39.

STRUCTURE AND CONTENT OF
MORNING PRAYER AND EVENING PRAYER

352 Morning prayer and evening prayer from the office for the dead include the introduction (or the reception of the body), hymn, psalmody, reading, response to the word of God, gospel canticle, intercessions, concluding prayer, and dismissal.

INTRODUCTORY VERSE OR RECEPTION OF THE BODY

353 Morning prayer and evening prayer begin with the introductory verse, *God, come to my assistance*, except when the invitatory replaces it, or when the rite of reception of the body is celebrated, since this replaces both the introductory verse and the hymn.

HYMN

354 To set the tone for the hour, a hymn is sung.

PSALMODY

355 In praying the psalms of the office for the dead, the assembly offers God praise and intercedes for the deceased person and the mourners in the words of prayer that Jesus himself used during his life on earth. Through the psalms the assembly prays in the voice of Christ, who intercedes on its behalf before the Father. In the psalms of petition and lament it expresses its sorrow and its firm hope in the redemption won by Christ. In the psalms of praise the assembly has a foretaste of the destiny of its deceased member and its own destiny, participation in the liturgy of heaven, where every tear will be wiped away and the Lord's victory over death will be complete.

356 Since the psalms are songs, whenever possible, they should be sung. The manner of singing them may be:

1. antiphonal, that is, two groups alternate singing the stanzas; the last stanza, the doxology, is sung by both groups;
2. responsorial, that is, the antiphon is sung by all before and after each stanza and the stanzas are sung by a cantor;
3. direct, that is, the stanzas are sung without interruption by all, by a choir, or by a cantor.

The rubrics for each psalm in morning prayer and evening prayer indicate a way for singing it; other ways may be used.

357 The psalmody of morning prayer from the office for the dead consists of Psalm 51, a psalm of lament and petition, Psalm 146 or Psalm 150, a psalm of praise, and an Old Testament canticle from Isaiah.

358 The psalmody of evening prayer consists of Psalm 121 and Psalm 130, two psalms of lament and petition, and a New Testament canticle from the letter of Paul to the Philippians.

359 For pastoral reasons, psalms other than those given in the office for the dead may be chosen, provided they are appropriate for the time of day and suitable for use in the office for the dead (see, for example, antiphons and psalms in Part III, p. 267).[4]

READING

360 The reading of the word of God in the office for the dead proclaims the paschal mystery and conveys the hope of being gathered together again in God's kingdom. The short reading in place in the hour or a longer Scripture reading from Part III, p. 207, may be used.[5] For pastoral reasons and if circumstances allow, a nonbiblical reading may be included at morning or evening prayer in addition to the reading from Scripture, as is the practice in the office of readings.

RESPONSE TO THE WORD OF GOD

361 A period of silence may follow the reading, then a brief homily based on the reading. After the homily the short responsory or another responsorial song (see, for example, no. 403) may be sung or recited.

GOSPEL CANTICLE

362 After the response to the word of God, the Canticle of Zechariah is sung at morning prayer and the Canticle of Mary at evening prayer as an expression of praise and thanksgiving for redemption.[6]

363 During the singing of the gospel canticle, the altar, then the presiding minister and the congregation may be incensed.

INTERCESSIONS

364 In the intercessions of the office for the dead, the assembly prays that the deceased and all who die marked with the sign of faith may rise again together in glory with Christ. The intercessions provided in the hour may be used or adapted to the circumstances, or new intercessions may be composed.

---

[4] See General Instruction of the Liturgy of the Hours, no. 252.

[5] See General Instruction of the Liturgy of the Hours, no. 46.

[6] See General Instruction of the Liturgy of the Hours, no. 50.

The presiding minister introduces the intercessions. An assisting minister sings or says the intentions. In keeping with the form of the intentions in the liturgy of the hours, the assembly responds with either the second part of the intention or the response. After a brief introduction by the presiding minister the assembly sings or says the Lord's Prayer.

CONCLUDING PRAYER AND DISMISSAL

365 The concluding prayer, proclaimed by the presiding minister, completes the hour.

366 After the concluding prayer and before the dismissal a member of the family or a friend of the deceased may be invited to speak in remembrance of the deceased.

367 When the funeral liturgy is celebrated the evening before the committal, it may be appropriate to celebrate morning prayer before the procession to the place of committal. In such an instance the dismissal is omitted and the rite continues with the procession to the place of committal.

MINISTRY AND PARTICIPATION

368 The celebration of the office for the dead requires careful preparation, especially in the case of communities that may not be familiar with the liturgy of the hours. Pastors and other ministers should provide catechesis on the place and significance of the liturgy of the hours in the life of the Church and the purpose of the celebration of the office for the dead. They should also encourage members of the parish community to participate in the celebration as an effective means of prayer for the deceased, as a sign of their concern and support for the family and close friends, and as a sign of faith and hope in the paschal mystery. This catechesis will help to ensure the full and active participation of the assembly in the celebration of the office for the dead.

369 The office for the dead may be celebrated in the funeral home, parlor, chapel of rest, or in the church. In special circumstances, when the office is combined with the funeral liturgy, care should be taken that the celebration not be too lengthy.[7]

370 The place in which the celebration occurs will often suggest adaptations. A celebration in the home of the deceased, for example, may be simplified or shortened.

---

[7] See General Instruction of the Liturgy of the Hours, nos. 93-97.

371 A priest or deacon should normally preside whenever the office for the dead is celebrated with a congregation; other ministers (a reader, a cantor, an acolyte) should exercise their proper ministries. In the absence of a priest or deacon, a layperson presides.

Whenever possible, ministers should involve the family of the deceased in the planning of the hour and in the designation of ministers.

The minister vests according to local custom. If morning prayer or evening prayer is celebrated in the church, a priest or a deacon who presides wears an alb or surplice with stole (a cope may also be worn).

372 The sung celebration of the liturgy of the hours "is more in keeping with the nature of this prayer, and a mark of both higher solemnity and closer union of hearts in offering praise to God."[8] Whenever possible, therefore, singing at morning or evening prayer should be encouraged.

In the choice of music preference should be given to the singing of the hymn, the psalmody, and the gospel canticle. The introductory verse, the responsory, the intercessions, the Lord's Prayer, and the dismissal may also be sung.

An organist or other instrumentalist and a cantor should assist the assembly in singing the hymn, psalms, and responses. The parish community should also prepare booklets or participation aids that contain an outline of the hour, the texts and music belonging to the people, and directions for posture, gesture, and movement.

---

[8] Congregation of Rites, Introduction *Musicam Sacram*, 5 March 1967, no. 37: AAS 59 (1967), 310; DOL 508, no. 4158.

OUTLINE OF THE RITE

Introductory Verse
Hymn
Psalmody
Reading
Responsory
Canticle of Zechariah
Intercessions
The Lord's Prayer
Concluding Prayer
Dismissal
[Procession to the Place of Committal]

17 MORNING PRAYER

373 When the celebration begins with the rite of reception of the body at the church (nos. 82-86, p. 37), the introductory verse (no. 374) and the hymn (no. 375) are omitted and the celebration continues with the psalmody (no. 376).

When the hour begins with the invitatory, the introductory verse (no. 374) is omitted.

INTRODUCTORY VERSE

374 All stand and make the sign of the cross as the minister says:

God, come to my assistance.
R. Lord, make haste to help me.

Glory to the Father, and to the Son, and to the Holy Spirit:
R. As it was in the beginning, is now, and will be for ever.
Amen [alleluia].

HYMN

375 The celebration continues with the following hymn, one of those provided in no. 396, p. 327, or another suitable hymn.

I know that my Redeemer lives,
And on that final day of days,
His voice shall bid me rise again:
Unending joy, unceasing praise!

This hope I cherish in my heart:
To stand on earth, my flesh restored,
And, not a stranger but a friend,
Behold my Savior and my Lord.

Tune: Duke Street L.M.
Music: Attr. to John Hatton, c. 1710-1793

PSALMODY

376 During the psalms and canticle,[1] all may sit or stand, according to custom.

FIRST PSALM—The cantor sings the antiphon and all repeat it. Two groups alternate singing the stanzas of the psalm; the last stanza, the doxology, is sung by all. The antiphon may be repeated by all after the doxology.

Psalm 51

Ant. The bones that were crushed shall leap for joy before the Lord.

Group 1:

Have mercy on me, God, in your kindness.
In your compassion blot out my offense.
O wash me more and more from my guilt
and cleanse me from my sin.

Group 2:

My offenses truly I know them;
my sin is always before me.
Against you, you alone, have I sinned;
what is evil in your sight I have done.

Group 1:

That you may be justified when you give sentence
and be without reproach when you judge,
O see, in guilt I was born,
a sinner was I conceived.

Group 2:

Indeed you love truth in the heart;
then in the secret of my heart teach me wisdom.
O purify me, then I shall be clean;
O wash me, I shall be whiter than snow.

---

[1] The method for singing each psalm and canticle as presented here is one way that may be used; other ways may also be used.

Group 1:

Make me hear rejoicing and gladness,
that the bones you have crushed may revive.
From my sins turn away your face
and blot out all my guilt.

Group 2:

A pure heart create for me, O God,
put a steadfast spirit within me.
Do not cast me away from your presence,
nor deprive me of your holy spirit.

Group 1:

Give me again the joy of your help;
with a spirit of fervor sustain me,
that I may teach transgressors your ways
and sinners may return to you.

Group 2:

O rescue me, God, my helper,
and my tongue shall ring out your goodness.
O Lord, open my lips
and my mouth shall declare your praise.

Group 1:

For in sacrifice you take no delight,
burnt offering from me you would refuse,
my sacrifice, a contrite spirit.
A humbled, contrite heart you will not spurn.

Group 2:

In your goodness, show favor to Zion:
rebuild the walls of Jerusalem.
Then you will be pleased with lawful sacrifice,
holocausts offered on your altar.

All:

Glory to the Father, and to the Son,
and to the Holy Spirit:
as it was in the beginning,
is now, and will be for ever. Amen. Ant.

CANTICLE—The cantor sings the antiphon and all repeat it; the cantor then sings the stanzas of the canticle and all repeat the antiphon after each stanza.

Isaiah 38:10-14, 17-20

Ant. At the very threshold of death, rescue me, Lord.

Cantor:

Once I said,
"In the noontime of life I must depart!
To the gates of the nether world I shall be consigned
for the rest of my years." Ant.

Cantor:

I said, "I shall see the Lord no more
in the land of the living.
No longer shall I behold my fellow men
among those who dwell in the world." Ant.

Cantor:

My dwelling, like a shepherd's tent,
is struck down and borne away from me;
you have folded up my life, like a weaver
who severs the last thread. Ant.

Cantor:

Day and night you give me over to torment;
I cry out until the dawn.
Like a lion he breaks all my bones;
day and night you give me over to torment. Ant.

Cantor:

Like a swallow I utter shrill cries;
I moan like a dove.
My eyes grow weak, gazing heaven-ward:
O Lord, I am in straits; be my surety. Ant.

Cantor:

You have preserved my life
from the pit of destruction,
when you cast behind your back
all my sins. Ant.

Cantor:

For it is not the nether world that gives you thanks,
nor death that praises you;
neither do those who go down into the pit
await your kindness. Ant.

Cantor:

The living, the living give you thanks,
as I do today.
Fathers declare to their sons,
O God, your faithfulness. Ant.

Cantor:

The Lord is our savior;
we shall sing to stringed instruments
in the house of the Lord
all the days of our life. Ant.

Cantor:

Glory to the Father, and to the Son,
and to the Holy Spirit:
as it was in the beginning,
is now, and will be for ever. Amen. Ant.

SECOND PSALM—One of the following psalms is said.

A   Psalm 146: The cantor sings the antiphon and all repeat it; the
cantor then sings the stanzas of the psalm and all repeat the antiphon after each stanza.

Ant. I will praise my God all the days of my life.

Cantor:

My soul, give praise to the Lord;
I will praise the Lord all my days,
make music to my God while I live. Ant.

Cantor:

Put no trust in princes,
in mortal men in whom there is no help.
Take their breath, they return to clay
and their plans that day come to nothing. Ant.

Cantor:

He is happy who is helped by Jacob's God,
whose hope is in the Lord his God,
who alone made heaven and earth,
the seas and all they contain. Ant.

Cantor:

It is he who keeps faith for ever,
who is just to those who are oppressed.
It is he who gives bread to the hungry,
the Lord, who sets prisoners free, Ant.

Cantor:

the Lord, who gives sight to the blind,
who raises up those who are bowed down,
the Lord, who protects the stranger
and upholds the widow and orphan. Ant.

Cantor:

It is the Lord who loves the just
but thwarts the path of the wicked.
The Lord will reign for ever,
Zion's God, from age to age. Ant.

Cantor:

Glory to the Father, and to the Son,
and to the Holy Spirit:
as it was in the beginning,
is now, and will be for ever. Amen. Ant.

B   Psalm 150: The cantor sings the antiphon and all repeat it; all
        sing the stanzas of the psalm and repeat the antiphon after the
        last stanza.

Ant. Let everything that breathes give praise to the Lord.

All:

Praise God in his holy place,
praise him in his mighty heavens.
Praise him for his powerful deeds,
praise his surpassing greatness.

O praise him with sound of trumpet,
praise him with lute and harp.
Praise him with timbrel and dance,
praise him with strings and pipes.

O praise him with resounding cymbals,
praise him with clashing of cymbals.
Let everything that lives and that breathes
give praise to the Lord.

Glory to the Father, and to the Son,
and to the Holy Spirit:
as it was in the beginning,
is now, and will be for ever. Amen. Ant.

READING

377 All are seated during the reading. The following reading
or one of those provided in Part III, p. 207, may be proclaimed
by the reader.

1 Thessalonians 4:14

If we believe that Jesus died and rose, so too will God, through
Jesus, bring with him those who have fallen asleep.

After the reading a period of silence may be observed; this may
be followed by a brief homily.

RESPONSORY

378 The responsory is then said. The cantor sings or the reader
says:

I will praise you, Lord, for you have rescued me.
R. I will praise you, Lord, for you have rescued me.

Cantor or reader:
You turned my sorrow into joy,
R. for you have rescued me.

Cantor or reader:
Glory to the Father, and to the Son, and to the Holy Spirit.
R. I will praise you, Lord, for you have rescued me.

CANTICLE OF ZECHARIAH

379 If morning prayer is celebrated in the church, the altar may be incensed during the canticle, then the minister and the congregation. All stand as one of the following antiphons is sung by the cantor and then repeated by all.

Outside the Easter season:

Ant. I am the resurrection, I am the life; to believe in me means life, in spite of death, and all who believe and live in me shall never die.

Or:

During the Easter season:

Ant. The splendor of Christ risen from the dead has shone on the people redeemed by his blood, alleluia.

All then make the sign of the cross as the canticle begins. The stanzas of the canticle are sung by all and the antiphon is repeated after the last stanza.

Luke 1:68-79

All:

Blessed be the Lord, the God of Israel;
he has come to his people and set them free.

He has raised up for us a mighty savior,
born of the house of his servant David.

Through his holy prophets he promised of old
that he would save us from our enemies,
from the hands of all who hate us.

He promised to show mercy to our fathers
and to remember his holy covenant.

This was the oath he swore to our father Abraham:
to set us free from the hands of our enemies,
free to worship him without fear,
holy and righteous in his sight all the days of our life.

You, my child, shall be called the prophet of the Most High;
for you will go before the Lord to prepare his way,
to give his people knowledge of salvation
by the forgiveness of their sins.

In the tender compassion of our God
the dawn from on high shall break upon us,
to shine on those who dwell in darkness and the shadow of death,
and to guide our feet into the way of peace.

Glory to the Father, and to the Son,
and to the Holy Spirit:
as it was in the beginning,
is now, and will be for ever. Amen. Ant.

INTERCESSIONS

380 The intercessions are then said. The following may be used
or adapted to the circumstances, or new intercessions may be
composed.

The minister says:

Let us pray to the all-powerful Father who raised Jesus from
the dead and gives new life to our mortal bodies, and say to him:

R. Lord, give us new life in Christ.

Assisting minister:

Father, through baptism we have been buried with your Son
and have risen with him in his resurrection; grant that we may
walk in newness of life so that when we die, we may live with
Christ for ever.

R. Lord, give us new life in Christ.

Assisting minister:

Provident Father, you have given us the living bread that has
come down from heaven and which should always be eaten worthily; grant that we may eat this bread worthily and be raised
up to eternal life on the last day.

R. Lord, give us new life in Christ.

Assisting minister:

Lord, you sent an angel to comfort your Son in his agony; give
us the hope of your consolation when death draws near.

R. Lord, give us new life in Christ.

Assisting minister:

You delivered the three youths from the fiery furnace; free your faithful ones from the punishment they suffer for their sins.

R. Lord, give us new life in Christ.

Assisting minister:

God of the living and the dead, you raised Jesus from the dead; raise up those who have died and grant that we may share eternal glory with them.

R. Lord, give us new life in Christ.

The Lord's Prayer

381 In the following or similar words, the minister introduces the Lord's Prayer:

With God there is mercy and fullness of redemption; let us pray as Jesus taught us:

All:

Our Father . . .

Concluding Prayer

382 The minister says one of the following prayers or one of those provided in no. 398, p. 333.

A   God of loving kindness, 173
listen favorably to our prayers:
strengthen our belief that your Son has risen from the dead
and our hope that your servant N. will also rise again.

We ask this through our Lord Jesus Christ, your Son,
who lives and reigns with you and the Holy Spirit,
one God, for ever and ever.

R. Amen.

B   O God, 171
glory of believers and life of the just,
by the death and resurrection of your Son, we are redeemed:

have mercy on your servant N.,
and make him/her worthy to share the joys of paradise,
for he/she believed in the resurrection of the dead.

We ask this through our Lord Jesus Christ, your Son,
who lives and reigns with you and the Holy Spirit,
one God, for ever and ever.

R. Amen.

C   During the Easter season:

Lord, in our grief we turn to you.   33
Are you not the God of love
who open your ears to all?

Listen to our prayers for your servant N.,
whom you have numbered among your own people:
lead him/her to your kingdom of light and peace
and count him/her among the saints in glory.

We ask this through our Lord Jesus Christ, your Son,
who lives and reigns with you and the Holy Spirit,
one God, for ever and ever.

R. Amen.

A member of the family or a friend of the deceased may speak
in remembrance of the deceased.

If the procession to the place of committal is to follow morning
prayer, the dismissal is omitted.

DISMISSAL

383 The minister then blesses the people.

A   A minister who is a priest or deacon says the following or another form of blessing, as at Mass.

The Lord be with you.

R. And also with you.

May almighty God bless you,
the Father, ✠ and the Son, and the Holy Spirit.

R. Amen.

B   A lay minister invokes God's blessing and signs himself or herself with the sign of the cross, saying:

May the Lord bless us,
protect us from all evil
and bring us to everlasting life.

R. Amen.

The minister then dismisses the people:

Go in peace.

R. Thanks be to God.

PROCESSION TO THE PLACE OF COMMITTAL

384 The deacon, or in the absence of a deacon, the minister says:

In peace let us take our brother/sister to his/her place of rest.

If a symbol of the Christian life has been placed on the coffin, it should be removed at this time.

The procession then begins: the minister and assisting ministers precede the coffin; the family and mourners follow.

One or more of the following texts or other suitable songs may be sung during the procession to the entrance of the church. The singing may continue during the journey to the place of committal.

A   The following antiphon may be sung with verses from Psalm 25, p. 268, or separately. A metrical version of this text is given on p. 330, no. 396, E.

May the angels lead you into paradise;
may the martyrs come to welcome you
and take you to the holy city,
the new and eternal Jerusalem.

B   The following antiphon may be sung with verses from Psalm 116, p. 274, or separately.

May choirs of angels welcome you
and lead you to the bosom of Abraham;
and where Lazarus is poor no longer
may you find eternal rest.

C   Whoever believes in me,
even though that person die, shall live.

R. I am the resurrection and the life.

Whoever lives and believes in me shall never die. R.

D   The following psalms may also be used.

Psalm 118, p. 275; Psalm 42, p. 269; Psalm 93, p. 272; Psalm 25, p. 268; Psalm 119, p. 277.

OUTLINE OF THE RITE

Introductory Verse
Hymn
Psalmody
Reading
Responsory
Canticle of Mary
Intercessions
The Lord's Prayer
Concluding Prayer
Dismissal

18 EVENING PRAYER

385 When the celebration begins with the rite of reception of
the body at the church (nos. 82-86, p. 37) the introductory verse
(no. 386) and the hymn (no. 387) are omitted and the celebration continues with the psalmody (no. 388).

INTRODUCTORY VERSE

386 All stand and make the sign of the cross as the minister says:

God, come to my assistance.
R. Lord, make haste to help me.

Glory to the Father, and to the Son, and to the Holy Spirit:
R. As it was in the beginning, is now, and will be for ever.
Amen [alleluia].

HYMN

387 The celebration continues with the following hymn, one of
those provided in no. 396, p. 327, or another suitable hymn.

For all the saints who from their labors rest,
Who thee by faith before the world confessed,
Thy name, O Jesus, be for ever blest:
Alleluia, alleluia!

Thou wast their rock, their fortress and their might;
Thou, Lord, their captain in the well-fought fight;
Thou in the darkness drear their one true light:
Alleluia, alleluia!

O blest communion, fellowship divine!
We feebly struggle, they in glory shine;
Yet all are one in thee, for all are thine:
Alleluia, alleluia!

But, lo, there breaks a yet more glorious day;
The saints triumphant rise in bright array:
The King of glory passes on his way:
Alleluia, alleluia!

Text: William W. How, 1823-1897
Tune: Sine Nomine 10.10.10 with Alleluias
Music: R. Vaughan Williams, 1872-1958

PSALMODY

388 During the psalms and canticle,[1] all may sit or stand, according to custom.

FIRST PSALM—The cantor sings the antiphon and all repeat it; the cantor then sings the stanzas of the psalm and all repeat the antiphon after each stanza.

Psalm 121

Ant. The Lord will keep you from all evil. He will guard your soul.

Cantor:

I lift up my eyes to the mountains:
from where shall come my help?
My help shall come from the Lord
who made heaven and earth. Ant.

Cantor:

May he never allow you to stumble!
Let him sleep not, your guard.
No, he sleeps not nor slumbers,
Israel's guard. Ant.

Cantor:

The Lord is your guard and your shade;
at your right side he stands.
By day the sun shall not smite you
nor the moon in the night. Ant.

Cantor:

The Lord will guard you from evil,
he will guard your soul.
The Lord will guard your going and coming
both now and for ever. Ant.

Cantor:

Glory to the Father, and to the Son,
and to the Holy Spirit:
as it was in the beginning,
is now, and will be for ever. Amen. Ant.

---

[1] The method for singing each psalm and canticle as presented here is one way that may be used; other ways may also be used.

SECOND PSALM—The cantor sings the antiphon and all repeat it. Two groups alternate singing the stanzas of the psalm; the last stanza, the doxology, is sung by all. The antiphon may be repeated by all after the doxology.

Psalm 130

Ant. If you kept a record of our sins, Lord, who could escape condemnation?

Group 1:

Out of the depths I cry to you, O Lord,
Lord, hear my voice!
O let your ears be attentive
to the voice of my pleading.

Group 2:

If you, O Lord, should mark our guilt,
Lord, who would survive?
But with you is found forgiveness:
for this we revere you.

Group 1:

My soul is waiting for the Lord,
I count on his word.
My soul is longing for the Lord
more than watchman for daybreak.
Let the watchman count on daybreak
and Israel on the Lord.

Group 2:

Because with the Lord there is mercy
and fullness of redemption,
Israel indeed he will redeem
from all its iniquity.

All:

Glory to the Father, and to the Son,
and to the Holy Spirit:
as it was in the beginning,
is now, and will be for ever. Amen. Ant.

CANTICLE—The cantor sings the antiphon and all repeat it; the cantor then sings the stanzas of the canticle and all repeat the antiphon after each stanza.

Philippians 2:6-11

Ant. As the Father raises the dead and gives them life, so the Son gives life to whom he wills.

Cantor:

Though he was in the form of God,
Jesus did not deem equality with God
something to be grasped at. Ant.

Cantor:

Rather, he emptied himself
and took the form of a slave,
being born in the likeness of men. Ant.

Cantor:

He was known to be of human estate,
and it was thus that he humbled himself,
obediently accepting even death,
death on a cross! Ant.

Cantor:

Because of this,
God highly exalted him
and bestowed on him the name
above every other name, Ant.

Cantor:

so that at Jesus' name
every knee must bend
in the heavens, on the earth
and under the earth,
and every tongue proclaim
to the glory of God the Father:
JESUS CHRIST IS LORD! Ant.

Cantor:

Glory to the Father, and to the Son,
and to the Holy Spirit:
as it was in the beginning,
is now, and will be for ever. Amen. Ant.

READING

389 All are seated during the reading. The following reading or one of those provided in Part III, p. 207, may be proclaimed by the reader.

1 Corinthians 15:55-57

"Where, O death, is your victory?
Where, O death, is your sting?"

The sting of death is sin, and the power of sin is the law. But thanks be to God who gives us the victory through our Lord Jesus Christ.

After the reading a period of silence may be observed; this may be followed by a brief homily.

RESPONSORY

390 One of the following responsories is then said.

A Cantor or reader:

In you, Lord, is our hope. We shall never hope in vain.
R. In you, Lord, is our hope. We shall never hope in vain.

Cantor or reader:

We shall be glad and rejoice in your mercy.
R. We shall never hope in vain.

Cantor or reader:

Glory to the Father, and to the Son, and to the Holy Spirit.
R. In you, Lord, is our hope. We shall never hope in vain.

B Cantor or reader:

Lord, in your steadfast love, give them eternal rest.
R. Lord, in your steadfast love, give them eternal rest.

Cantor or reader:

You will come to judge the living and the dead.
R. Give them eternal rest.

Cantor or reader:

Glory to the Father, and to the Son, and to the Holy Spirit.
R. Lord, in your steadfast love, give them eternal rest.

CANTICLE OF MARY

391 If evening prayer is celebrated in the church, the altar may be incensed during the canticle, then the minister and the congregation. All stand as one of the following antiphons is sung by the cantor and then repeated by all.

Outside the Easter season:

Ant. All that the Father gives me will come to me, and whoever comes to me I shall not turn away.

Or:

During the Easter season:

Ant. Our crucified and risen Lord has redeemed us, alleluia.

All then make the sign of the cross as the canticle begins. The stanzas of the canticle are sung by all and the antiphon is repeated after the last stanza.

Luke 1:46-55

All:

My soul proclaims the greatness of the Lord,
my spirit rejoices in God my Savior;
for he has looked with favor on his lowly servant.

From this day all generations will call me blessed:
the Almighty has done great things for me,
and holy is his Name.

He has mercy on those who fear him
in every generation.

He has shown the strength of his arm,
he has scattered the proud in their conceit.

He has cast down the mighty from their thrones,
and has lifted up the lowly.

He has filled the hungry with good things,
and the rich he has sent away empty.

He has come to the help of his servant Israel
for he has remembered his promise of mercy,
the promise he made to our fathers,
to Abraham and his children for ever.

Glory to the Father, and to the Son,
and to the Holy Spirit:
as it was in the beginning,
is now, and will be for ever. Amen. Ant.

INTERCESSIONS

392 The intercessions are then said. The following may be used
or adapted to the circumstances, or new intercessions may be
composed.

The minister says:

We acknowledge Christ the Lord through whom we hope that
our lowly bodies will be made like his in glory, and we say:

R. Lord, you are our life and resurrection.

Assisting minister:

Christ, Son of the living God, who raised up Lazarus, your
friend, from the dead: raise up to life and glory the dead whom
you have redeemed by your precious blood.

R. Lord, you are our life and resurrection.

Assisting minister:

Christ, consoler of those who mourn, you dried the tears of the
family of Lazarus, of the widow's son, and of the daughter of
Jairus; comfort those who mourn for the dead.

R. Lord, you are our life and resurrection.

Assisting minister:

Christ, Savior, destroy the reign of sin in our earthly bodies,
so that just as through sin we deserved punishment, so through
you we may gain eternal life.

R. Lord, you are our life and resurrection.

Assisting minister:

Christ, Redeemer, look on those who have no hope because they
do not know you; may they receive faith in the resurrection and
in the life of the world to come.

R. Lord, you are our life and resurrection.

You revealed yourself to the blind man who begged for the light of his eyes; show your face to the dead who are still deprived of your light.

R. Lord, you are our life and resurrection.

Assisting minister:
When at last our earthly home is dissolved, give us a home, not of earthly making, but built of eternity in heaven.

R. Lord, you are our life and resurrection.

THE LORD'S PRAYER

393 In the following or similar words, the minister introduces the Lord's Prayer:

With God there is mercy and fullness of redemption; let us pray as Jesus taught us:

All:
Our Father . . .

CONCLUDING PRAYER

394 The minister says one of the following prayers or one of those provided in no. 398, p. 333.

A God of loving kindness,
listen favorably to our prayers:
strengthen our belief that your Son has risen from the dead
and our hope that your servant N. will also rise again.

We ask this through our Lord Jesus Christ, your Son,
who lives and reigns with you and the Holy Spirit,
one God, for ever and ever.

R. Amen.

B   O God, 171
glory of believers and life of the just,
by the death and resurrection of your Son, we are redeemed:
have mercy on your servant N.,
and make him/her worthy to share the joys of paradise,
for he/she believed in the resurrection of the dead.

We ask this through our Lord Jesus Christ, your Son,
who lives and reigns with you and the Holy Spirit,
one God, for ever and ever.

R. Amen.

C   During the Easter season:

Lord, in our grief we turn to you. 33
Are you not the God of love
who open your ears to all?

Listen to our prayers for your servant N.,
whom you have numbered among your own people:
lead him/her to your kingdom of light and peace
and count him/her among the saints in glory.

We ask this through our Lord Jesus Christ, your Son,
who lives and reigns with you and the Holy Spirit,
one God, for ever and ever.

R. Amen.

A member of the family or a friend of the deceased may speak
in remembrance of the deceased.

DISMISSAL

395 The minister then blesses the people.

A   A minister who is a priest or deacon says the following or another form of blessing, as at Mass.

The Lord be with you.
R. And also with you.

May almighty God bless you,
the Father, ✠ and the Son, and the Holy Spirit.

R. Amen.

B   A lay minister invokes God's blessing and signs himself or herself with the sign of the cross, saying:

May the Lord bless us,
protect us from all evil
and bring us to everlasting life.

R. Amen.

       The minister then dismisses the people:

Go in peace.

R. Thanks be to God.

19 ADDITIONAL HYMNS

396 The following or other suitable hymns may be used for the celebration of the office for the dead.

A 1. I know that my Redeemer lives!
What joy the blest assurance gives!
He lives, he lives, who once was dead;
He lives, my ever-living head!

2. He lives triumphant from the grave;
He lives eternally to save;
He lives in majesty above;
He lives to guide his Church in love.

3. He lives to grant me rich supply;
He lives to guide me with his eye;
He lives to comfort me when faint;
He lives to hear my soul's complaint.

4. He lives to silence all my fears;
He lives to wipe away my tears;
He lives to calm my troubled heart;
He lives all blessings to impart.

5. He lives to bless me with his love;
He lives to plead for me above;
He lives my hungry soul to feed;
He lives to help in time of need.

6. He lives, my kind, wise, heav'nly friend;
He lives and loves me to the end;
He lives, and while he lives, I'll sing;
He lives, my Prophet, Priest, and King!

7. He lives and grants me daily breath;
He lives, and I shall conquer death;
He lives my mansion to prepare;
He lives to bring me safely there.

8. He lives, all glory to his name!
He lives, my Savior, still the same;
What joy this blest assurance gives:
I know that my Redeemer lives!

Text: Based on Job 19:25 by Samuel Medley, 1738-1799, alt.
Tune: Duke Street L.M.
Music: Attr. to John Hatton, c. 1710-1793

B 1. O God, our help in ages past,
Our hope for years to come,
Our shelter from the stormy blast,
And our eternal home;

2. Beneath the shadow of your throne
Your saints have dwelt secure;
Sufficient is your arm alone,
And our defense is sure.

3. Before the hills in order stood,
Or earth received her frame,
From everlasting you are God,
To endless years the same.

4. A thousand ages in your sight
Are like an evening gone,
Short as the watch that ends the night
Before the rising sun.

5. Time, like an ever rolling stream,
Bears all our lives away;
They fly forgotten, as a dream
Dies at the op'ning day.

6. O God, our help in ages past,
Our hope for years to come,
Be now our guard while troubles last,
And our eternal home.

Text: Based on Psalm 90, Isaac Watts, 1674-1748, alt.
Tune: St. Anne C.M.
Music: Attr. to William Croft, 1678-1727

C 1. Blest be the everlasting God,
The Father of our Lord;
Be his abounding mercy praised,
His majesty adored.

2. When from the dead he raised his Son,
To dwell with him on high,
He gave our souls a lively hope
That they should never die.

3. There's an inheritance divine
   Reserved against that day,
   Which uncorrupted, undefiled,
   Can never waste away.

4. Saints by the pow'r of God are kept,
   Till their salvation come:
   We walk by faith as strangers here,
   But Christ shall call us home.

Text: Isaac Watts, 1674-1748, alt.
Tune: St. Peter C.M.
Music: Alexander Robert Reingale, 1799-1877

D   Refrain:
Alleluia! Alleluia! Alleluia!

Verses:

1. The strife is o'er, the battle done.
   The victory of life is won;
   The song of triumph has begun:
   Alleluia!

2. The pow'rs of death have done their worst,
   But Christ their legions has dispersed:
   Let shouts of praise and joy outburst:
   Alleluia!

3. On the third morn he rose again
   Glorious in majesty to reign;
   O let us swell the joyful strain:
   Alleluia!

4. He closed the yawning gates of hell,
   The bars from heav'n's high portals fell;
   Let hymns of praise his triumphs tell:
   Alleluia!

5. Lord, by your death on Calvary,
   From death's dread sting your people free,
   That we may live eternally:
   Alleluia!

Text: *Finita iam sunt praelia*, tr. by Francis Pott, 1832-1909, alt.
Tune: Victory 888 with alleluias
Music: Giovanni Pierluigi da Palestrina, c. 1525-1594, adapted
with "Alleluias" by William Henry Monk, 1823-1889

E 1. May saints and angels lead you on,
Escorting you where Christ has gone.
Now he has called you, come to him
Who sits above the seraphim.

2. Come to the peace of Abraham
And to the supper of the Lamb:
Come to the glory of the blessed,
And to perpetual light and rest.

Text: Based on *In Paradisum*
Tune: Tallis' Canon L.M.
Music: Thomas Tallis, c. 1510-1585

Part V
ADDITIONAL TEXTS

The one who raised Christ Jesus from the dead
will give your mortal bodies
life through his Spirit living in you

20 PRAYERS AND TEXTS
IN PARTICULAR CIRCUMSTANCES

397 The following prayers for the dead and prayers for the mourners are for use in the various rites of Parts I, II, and IV.

The prayers are grouped as follows:

Prayers for the Dead

398 The following prayers for the dead may be used in the various rites of Parts I and II and in Part IV. The prayers should be chosen taking the character of the text into account as well as the place in the rite where it will occur. All of the prayers in this section end with the shorter conclusion. When a prayer is used as the opening prayer at the funeral liturgy, the longer conclusion is used.

1   General

God of faithfulness,
in your wisdom you have called your servant N.
   out of this world;
release him/her from the bonds of sin,
and welcome him/her into your presence,
so that he/she may enjoy eternal light and peace
and be raised up in glory with all your saints.

We ask this through Christ our Lord.

R. Amen.

2   General

Lord, in our grief we turn to you.
Are you not the God of love
who open your ears to all?

Listen to our prayers for your servant N.,
whom you have called out of this world:
lead him/her to your kingdom of light and peace
and count him/her among the saints in glory.

We ask this through Christ our Lord.

R. Amen.

3   General

Holy Lord, almighty and eternal God,
hear our prayers for your servant N.,
whom you have summoned out of this world.
Forgive his/her sins and failings
and grant him/her a place of refreshment, light,
   and peace.

Let him/her pass unharmed through the gates of death
to dwell with the blessed in light,
as you promised to Abraham and his children for ever.
Accept N. into your safekeeping
and on the great day of judgment
raise him/her up with all the saints
to inherit your eternal kingdom.

We ask this through Christ our Lord.

R. Amen.

4   General

Into your hands, O Lord,   168
we humbly entrust our brother/sister N.
In this life you embraced him/her with your tender love;
deliver him/her now from every evil
and bid him/her enter eternal rest.

The old order has passed away:
welcome him/her then into paradise,
where there will be no sorrow, no weeping nor pain,
but the fullness of peace and joy
with your Son and the Holy Spirit
for ever and ever.

R. Amen.

5   General

Almighty God and Father,   170
it is our certain faith
that your Son, who died on the cross, was raised from the dead,
the firstfruits of all who have fallen asleep.
Grant that through this mystery
your servant N., who has gone to his/her rest in Christ,
may share in the joy of his resurrection.

We ask this through Christ our Lord.

R. Amen.

O God,   171
glory of believers and life of the just,
by the death and resurrection of your Son, we are redeemed:
have mercy on your servant N.,
and make him/her worthy to share the joys of paradise,
for he/she believed in the resurrection of the dead.

We ask this through Christ our Lord.

R. Amen.

Almighty God and Father,   172
by the mystery of the cross, you have made us strong;
by the sacrament of the resurrection
you have sealed us as your own.
Look kindly upon your servant N.,
now freed from the bonds of mortality,
and count him/her among your saints in heaven.

We ask this through Christ our Lord.

R. Amen.

God of loving kindness,   173
listen favorably to our prayers:
strengthen our belief that your Son has risen from the dead
and our hope that your servant N. will also rise again.

We ask this through Christ our Lord.

R. Amen.

To you, O God, the dead do not die,   174
and in death our life is changed, not ended.
Hear our prayers
and command the soul of your servant N.
to dwell with Abraham, your friend,
and be raised at last on the great day of judgment.

In your mercy cleanse him/her of any sin
which he/she may have committed through human frailty.

We ask this through Christ our Lord.

R. Amen.

10   General

Lord God, in whom all find refuge,   175
we appeal to your boundless mercy:
grant to the soul of your servant N.
a kindly welcome,
cleansing of sin,
release from the chains of death,
and entry into everlasting life.

We ask this through Christ our Lord.

R. Amen.

11   General

God of all consolation,   176
open our hearts to your word,
so that, listening to it, we may comfort one another,
finding light in time of darkness
and faith in time of doubt.

We ask this through Christ our Lord.

R. Amen.

12   General

O God,
to whom mercy and forgiveness belong,
hear our prayers on behalf of your servant N.,
whom you have called out of this world;
and because he/she put his/her hope and trust in you,
command that he/she be carried safely home to heaven
and come to enjoy your eternal reward.

We ask this through Christ our Lord.

R. Amen.

13   General

O God,
in whom sinners find mercy and the saints find joy,
we pray to you for our brother/sister N.,
whose body we honor with Christian burial,
that he/she may be delivered from the bonds of death.
Admit him/her to the joyful company of your saints
and raise him/her on the last day
to rejoice in your presence for ever.
We ask this through Christ our Lord.

R. Amen.

14   A pope

O God,
from whom the just receive an unfailing reward,
grant that your servant N., our Pope,
whom you made vicar of Peter and shepherd of your Church,
may rejoice for ever in the vision of your glory,
for he was a faithful steward here on earth
of the mysteries of your forgiveness and grace.
We ask this through Christ our Lord.

R. Amen.

15   A diocesan bishop

Almighty and merciful God,
eternal Shepherd of your people,
listen to our prayers
and grant that your servant, N., our bishop,
to whom you entrusted the care of this Church,
may enter the joy of his eternal Master,
there to receive the rich reward of his labors.
We ask this through Christ our Lord.

R. Amen.

16   Another bishop

O God,
from the ranks of your priests
you chose your servant N.
to fulfill the office of bishop.

Grant that he may share
in the eternal fellowship of those priests
who, faithful to the teachings of the apostles,
dwell in your heavenly kingdom.

We ask this through Christ our Lord.

R. Amen.

17   A priest

God of mercy and love,
grant to N., your servant and priest,
a glorious place at your heavenly table,
for you made him here on earth
a faithful minister of your word and sacrament.

We ask this through Christ our Lord.

R. Amen.

18   A priest

O God,
listen favorably to our prayers
offered on behalf of your servant and priest,
and grant that N.,
who committed himself zealously to the service of your name,
may rejoice for ever in the company of your saints.

We ask this through Christ our Lord.

R. Amen.

19   A priest

Lord God,
you chose our brother N. to serve your people as a priest
and to share the joys and burdens of their lives.

Look with mercy on him
and give him the reward of his labors,
the fullness of life promised to those who preach your
    holy Gospel.

We ask this through Christ our Lord.

R. Amen.

20   A deacon

God of mercy,
as once you chose seven men of honest repute
to serve your Church,
so also you chose N. as your servant and deacon.
Grant that he may rejoice in your eternal fellowship
with all the heralds of your Gospel,
for he was untiring in his ministry here on earth.

We ask this through Christ our Lord.

R. Amen.

21   A deacon

Lord God,
you sent your Son into the world
to preach the Good News of salvation
and to pour out his Spirit of grace upon your Church.

Look with kindness on your servant N.
As a deacon in the Church
he was strengthened by the gift of the Spirit
to preach the Good News,
to minister in your assembly,
and to do the works of charity.

Give him the reward promised
to those who show their love of you
by service to their neighbor.

We ask this through Christ our Lord.

R. Amen.

22   A religious

All-powerful God,
we pray for our brother/sister N.,
who responded to the call of Christ
and pursued wholeheartedly the ways of perfect love.
Grant that he/she may rejoice
on that day when your glory will be revealed
and in company with all his/her brothers and sisters
share for ever the happiness of your kingdom.

We ask this through Christ our Lord.

R. Amen.

23   A religious

God of blessings,
source of all holiness,
the voice of your Spirit has drawn countless men and women
to follow Jesus Christ
and to bind themselves to you
with ready will and loving heart.

Look with mercy on N.
who sought to fulfill his/her vows to you,
and grant him/her the reward promised to all good and
    faithful servants.

May he/she rejoice in the company of the saints
and with them praise you for ever.

We ask this through Christ our Lord.

R. Amen.

24   One who worked in the service of the Gospel

Faithful God,   178
we humbly ask your mercy for your servant N.,
who worked so generously to spread the Good News:
grant him/her the reward of his/her labors
and bring him/her safely to your promised land.

We ask this through Christ our Lord.

R. Amen.

25   A baptized child

Lord, in our grief we call upon your mercy: 223
open your ears to our prayers,
and one day unite us again with N.,
who, we firmly trust,
already enjoys eternal life in your kingdom.

We ask this through Christ our Lord.

R. Amen.

26   A baptized child

224

To you, O Lord,
we humbly entrust this child,
so precious in your sight.
Take him/her into your arms
and welcome him/her into paradise,
where there will be no sorrow, no weeping nor pain,
but the fullness of peace and joy
with your Son and the Holy Spirit
for ever and ever.

R. Amen.

27   A young person

177

Lord,
your wisdom governs the length of our days.
We mourn the loss of N.,
whose life has passed so quickly,
and we entrust him/her to your mercy.
Welcome him/her into your heavenly dwelling
and grant him/her the happiness of everlasting youth.

We ask this through Christ our Lord.

R. Amen.

28   A young person

Lord God,
source and destiny of our lives,
in your loving providence
you gave us N.
to grow in wisdom, age, and grace.
Now you have called him/her to yourself.

As we grieve the loss of one so young,
we seek to understand your purpose.

Draw him/her to yourself
and give him/her full stature in Christ.
May he/she stand with all the angels and saints,
who know your love and praise your saving will.

We ask this through Christ our Lord.

R. Amen.

29   Parents

Lord God, who commanded us to honor father and mother,   ₁₈₁
look kindly upon your servants N. and N.,
have mercy upon them
and let us see them again in eternal light.

We ask this through Christ our Lord.

R. Amen.

30   A parent

God of our ancestors in faith,
by the covenant made on Mount Sinai
you taught your people to strengthen the bonds of family
through faith, honor, and love.
Look kindly upon N.,
a father/mother who sought to bind his/her children to you.
Bring him/her one day to our heavenly home
where the saints dwell in blessedness and peace.

We ask this through Christ our Lord.

R. Amen.

31   A married couple

Lord God, whose covenant is everlasting,   ₁₈₂
have mercy upon the sins of your servants N. and N.;
as their love for each other united them on earth,
so let your love join them together in heaven.

We ask this through Christ our Lord.

R. Amen.

32   A married couple

Eternal Father,
in the beginning you established the love of man and woman
as a sign of creation.
Your own Son loves the Church as a spouse.
Grant mercy and peace to N. and N. who,
by their love for each other,
were signs of the creative love
which binds the Church to Christ.

We ask this in the name of Jesus the Lord.

R. Amen.

33   A married couple

Lord God,
giver of all that is true and lovely and gracious,
you created in marriage a sign of your covenant.
Look with mercy upon N. and N.
You blessed them in their companionship,
and in their joys and sorrows you bound them together.
Lead them into eternal peace,
and bring them to the table
where the saints feast together in your heavenly home.
We ask this through Christ our Lord.

R. Amen.

34   A wife

Eternal God,
you made the union of man and woman
a sign of the bond between Christ and the Church.

Grant mercy and peace to N.,
who was united in love with her husband.
May the care and devotion of her life on earth
find a lasting reward in heaven.
Look kindly on her husband and family/children
as now they turn to your compassion and love.
Strengthen their faith and lighten their loss.
We ask this through Christ our Lord.

R. Amen.

35   A husband

Eternal God,
you made the union of man and woman
a sign of the bond between Christ and the Church.

Grant mercy and peace to N.,
who was united in love with his wife.
May the care and devotion of his life on earth
find a lasting reward in heaven.
Look kindly on his wife and family/children
as now they turn to your compassion and love.
Strengthen their faith and lighten their loss.
We ask this through Christ our Lord.

R. Amen.

36   A deceased non-Christian married to a Catholic

Almighty and faithful Creator,
all things are of your making,
all people are shaped in your image.
We now entrust the soul of N. to your goodness.
In your infinite wisdom and power,
work in him/her your merciful purpose,
known to you alone from the beginning of time.
Console the hearts of those who love him/her
in the hope that all who trust in you
will find peace and rest in your kingdom.
We ask this in the name of Jesus the Lord.

R. Amen.

37   An elderly person

God of endless ages,
from one generation to the next
you have been our refuge and strength.
Before the mountains were born
or the earth came to be,
you are God.
Have mercy now on your servant N.
whose long life was spent in your service.
Give him/her a place in your kingdom,
where hope is firm for all who love
and rest is sure for all who serve.
We ask this through Christ our Lord.

R. Amen.

38   An elderly person

God of mercy,
look kindly on your servant N.
who has set down the burden of his/her years.
As he/she served you faithfully throughout his/her life,
may you give him/her the fullness of your peace and joy.
We give thanks for the long life of N.,
now caught up in your eternal love.
We make our prayer in the name of Jesus who is our risen Lord
now and for ever.

R. Amen.

39   One who died after a long illness

God of deliverance,   179
you called our brother/sister N.
to serve you in weakness and pain,
and gave him/her the grace of sharing the cross of your Son.
Reward his/her patience and forbearance,
and grant him/her the fullness of Christ's victory.
We ask this through Christ our Lord.
R. Amen.

40   One who died after a long illness

Most faithful God,
lively is the courage of those who hope in you.
Your servant N. suffered greatly
but placed his/her trust in your mercy.
Confident that the petition of those who mourn
pierces the clouds and finds an answer,
we beg you, give rest to N.
Do not remember his/her sins
but look upon his/her sufferings
and grant him/her refreshment, light, and peace.
We ask this through Christ our Lord.
R. Amen.

41   One who died after a long illness

O God,
you are water for our thirst
and manna in our desert.
We praise you for the life of N.
and bless your mercy
that has brought his/her suffering to an end.
Now we beg that same endless mercy
to raise him/her to new life.
Nourished by the food and drink of heaven,
may he/she rest for ever
in the joy of Christ our Lord.
R. Amen.

42   One who died suddenly

Lord,
as we mourn the sudden death of our brother/sister,
show us the immense power of your goodness
and strengthen our belief
that N. has entered into your presence.

We ask this through Christ our Lord.

R. Amen.

43   One who died accidentally or violently

Lord our God,
you are always faithful and quick to show mercy.
Our brother/sister N.
was suddenly [and violently] taken from us.
Come swiftly to his/her aid,
have mercy on him/her,
and comfort his/her family and friends
by the power and protection of the cross.

We ask this through Christ our Lord.

R. Amen.

44   One who died by suicide

God, lover of souls,
you hold dear what you have made
and spare all things, for they are yours.
Look gently on your servant N.,
and by the blood of the cross
forgive his/her sins and failings.

Remember the faith of those who mourn
and satisfy their longing for that day
when all will be made new again
in Christ, our risen Lord,
who lives and reigns with you for ever and ever.

R. Amen.

45   One who died by suicide

Almighty God and Father of all,
you strengthen us by the mystery of the cross
and with the sacrament of your Son's resurrection.
Have mercy on our brother/sister N.
Forgive all his/her sins and grant him/her peace.
May we who mourn this sudden death be comforted
    and consoled by your power and protection.

We ask this through Christ our Lord.

R. Amen.

46   Several persons

O Lord,
you gave new life to N. and N.
in the waters of baptism;
show mercy to them now,
and bring them to the happiness of life in your kingdom.

We ask this through Christ our Lord.

R. Amen.

47   Several persons

All-powerful God,
whose mercy is never withheld
from those who call upon you in hope,
look kindly on your servants N. and N.,
who departed this life confessing your name,
and number them among your saints for evermore.

We ask this through Christ our Lord.

R. Amen.

Prayers for the Mourners

399 The following prayers for the mourners may be used in the
various rites of Parts I and II. The prayers should be chosen taking
the character of the text into account as well as the place in the
rite where it will occur.

1   General

Father of mercies and God of all consolation,   34
you pursue us with untiring love
and dispel the shadow of death
with the bright dawn of life.

[Comfort your family in their loss and sorrow.
Be our refuge and our strength, O Lord,
and lift us from the depths of grief
into the peace and light of your presence.]

Your Son, our Lord Jesus Christ,
by dying has destroyed our death,
and by rising, restored our life.
Enable us therefore to press on toward him,
so that, after our earthly course is run,
he may reunite us with those we love,
when every tear will be wiped away.

We ask this through Christ our Lord.

R. Amen.

2   General

Lord Jesus, our Redeemer,   169
you willingly gave yourself up to death,
so that all might be saved and pass from death to life.
We humbly ask you to comfort your servants in their grief
and to receive N. into the arms of your mercy.
You alone are the Holy One,
you are mercy itself;
by dying you unlocked the gates of life
    for those who believe in you.
Forgive N. his/her sins,
and grant him/her a place of happiness, light, and peace
in the kingdom of your glory for ever and ever.

R. Amen.

3   General

God, all-compassionate,
ruler of the living and the dead,
you know beforehand
those whose faithful lives reveal them as your own.
We pray for those who belong to this present world
and for those who have passed to the world to come:
grant them pardon for all their sins.
We ask you graciously to hear our prayer
through the intercession of all the saints
and for your mercy's sake.

For you are God, for ever and ever.

R. Amen.

4   General

Lord our God,
the death of our brother/sister N.
recalls our human condition
and the brevity of our lives on earth.
But for those who believe in your love
death is not the end,
nor does it destroy the bonds
that you forge in our lives.
We share the faith of your Son's disciples
and the hope of the children of God.
Bring the light of Christ's resurrection
to this time of testing and pain
as we pray for N. and for those who love him/her,
through Christ our Lord.

R. Amen.

5   General

Lord God,
you are attentive to the voice of our pleading.
Let us find in your Son
comfort in our sadness,
certainty in our doubt,
and courage to live through this hour.
Make our faith strong
through Christ our Lord.

R. Amen.

6 General

Lord,
N. is gone now from this earthly dwelling
and has left behind those who mourn his/her absence.
Grant that as we grieve for our brother/sister
we may hold his/her memory dear
and live in hope of the eternal kingdom
where you will bring us together again.
We ask this through Christ our Lord.
R. Amen.

7 General

Most merciful God,
whose wisdom is beyond our understanding,
surround the family of N. with your love,
that they may not be overwhelmed by their loss,
but have confidence in your goodness,
and strength to meet the days to come.
We ask this through Christ our Lord.
R. Amen.

8 A baptized child

Lord of all gentleness, 225
surround us with your care
and comfort us in our sorrow,
for we grieve at the loss of this [little] child.

As you washed N. in the waters of baptism
and welcomed him/her into the life of heaven,
so call us one day
to be united with him/her
and share for ever the joy of your kingdom.
We ask this through Christ our Lord.
R. Amen.

9   A baptized child

Eternal Father,
through the intercession of Mary,
who bore your Son and stood by the cross as he died,
grant to these parents in their grief
the assistance of her presence,
the comfort of her faith,
and the reward of her prayers.

We ask this through Christ our Lord.

R. Amen.

10   A baptized child

Lord God,
source and destiny of our lives,
in your loving providence
you gave us N.
to grow in wisdom, age, and grace.
Now you have called him/her to yourself.

We grieve over the loss of one so young
and struggle to understand your purpose.

Draw him/her to yourself
and give him/her full stature in Christ.
May he/she stand with all the angels and saints,
who know your love and praise your saving will.

We ask this through Jesus Christ, our Lord.

R. Amen.

11   A baptized child

Merciful Lord,
whose wisdom is beyond human understanding,
you adopted N. as your own in baptism
and have taken him/her to yourself
even as he/she stood on the threshold of life.
Listen to our prayers and extend to us your grace,
that one day we may share eternal life with N.,
for we firmly believe that he/she now rests with you.

We ask this through Christ our Lord.

R. Amen.

12   A baptized child

Lord God,
from whom human sadness is never hidden,
you know the burden of grief
that we feel at the loss of this child.

As we mourn his/her passing from this life,
comfort us with the knowledge
that N. lives now in your loving embrace.

We ask this through Christ our Lord.

R. Amen.

13   A child who died before baptism

O Lord, whose ways are beyond understanding,   235
listen to the prayers of your faithful people:
that those weighed down by grief
at the loss of this [little] child
may find reassurance in your infinite goodness.

We ask this through Christ our Lord.

R. Amen.

14   A child who died before baptism

God of all consolation,   236
searcher of mind and heart,
the faith of these parents [N. and N.] is known to you.

Comfort them with the knowledge
that the child for whom they grieve
is entrusted now to your loving care.

We ask this through Christ our Lord.

R. Amen.

15   A stillborn child

Lord God,
ever caring and gentle,
we commit to your love this little one,
quickened to life for so short a time.
Enfold him/her in eternal life.

We pray for his/her parents
who are saddened by the loss of their child.
Give them courage
and help them in their pain and grief.
May they all meet one day
in the joy and peace of your kingdom.

We ask this through Christ our Lord.

R. Amen.

Placing of Christian Symbols

400 The following texts may be used during the "Reception at the Church" when placing Christian symbols on the coffin. Nos. 1 and 2 are for deceased persons who were baptized; no. 3 is for a child who died before baptism.

1 Book of the Gospels or Bible—While the Book of the Gospels or Bible is placed on the coffin, the minister says in these or similar words:

In life N. cherished the Gospel of Christ.
May Christ now greet him/her with these words of eternal life:
Come, blessed of my Father!

2 Cross—While a cross is placed on the coffin, the minister says in these or similar words:

In baptism N. received the sign of the cross.
May he/she now share
in Christ's victory over sin and death.

3 Cross—During the presentation of a cross in the case of a child who died before baptism, the minister says in these or similar words:

The cross we have brought here today was carried by the Lord Jesus in the hour of his suffering.

We place it now on [near] this coffin as a sign of our hope for N.

As the cross is placed on (or near) the coffin, the minister says:

Lord Jesus Christ,
you loved us unto death.
Let this cross be a sign of your love for N.
and for the people you have gathered here today.

General Intercessions and Litanies

401 The following intercessions and litanies may be used during a liturgy of the word or at Mass and should be adapted according to the circumstances.

1   God, the almighty Father, raised Christ his Son from the dead; 200
with confidence we ask him to save all his people, living and dead:

For N. who in baptism was given the pledge of eternal life, that he/she now be admitted to the company of the saints.
We pray to the Lord.

R. Lord, hear our prayer.

[For a layperson: For our brother/sister who ate the body of Christ, the bread of life, that he/she may be raised up on the last day.
We pray to the Lord.

R. Lord, hear our prayer.]

[For a deacon: For our brother N., who proclaimed the Good News of Jesus Christ and served the needs of the poor, that he may be welcomed into the sanctuary of heaven.
We pray to the Lord.

R. Lord, hear our prayer.]

[For a bishop or priest: For our brother N., who served the Church as a bishop/priest, that he may be given a place in the liturgy of heaven.
We pray to the Lord.

R. Lord, hear our prayer.]

[For the mourners: For the family and friends of our brother/sister N., that they may be consoled in their grief by the Lord who wept at the death of his friend Lazarus.
We pray to the Lord.

R. Lord, hear our prayer.]

For our deceased relatives and friends and for all who have helped us, that they may have the reward of their goodness.
We pray to the Lord.

R. Lord, hear our prayer.

For those who have fallen asleep in the hope of rising again,
that they may see God face to face.
We pray to the Lord.

R. Lord, hear our prayer.

For all of us assembled here to worship in faith, that we may
be gathered together again in God's kingdom.
We pray to the Lord.

R. Lord, hear our prayer.

God, our shelter and our strength,
you listen in love to the cry of your people:
hear the prayers we offer for our departed brothers and sisters.
Cleanse them of their sins
and grant them the fullness of redemption.
We ask this through Christ our Lord.

R. Amen.

2   My dear friends, let us join with one another in praying to God,   ₂₀₁
not only for our departed brother/sister, but also for the Church,
for peace in the world, and for ourselves.

That the bishops and priests of the Church, and all who preach
the Gospel, may be given the strength to express in action the
word they proclaim.
We pray to the Lord:

R. Lord, hear our prayer.

That those in public office may promote justice and peace.
We pray to the Lord:

R. Lord, hear our prayer.

That those who bear the cross of pain in mind or body may
never feel forsaken by God.
We pray to the Lord:

R. Lord, hear our prayer.

That God may deliver the soul of his servant N. from punishment and from the powers of darkness.
We pray to the Lord:

R. Lord, hear our prayer.

That God in his mercy may blot out all his/her offenses.
We pray to the Lord:

R. Lord, hear our prayer.

That God may establish him/her in light and peace.
We pray to the Lord:

R. Lord, hear our prayer.

That God may call him/her to happiness in the company of all the saints. We pray to the Lord:

R. Lord, hear our prayer.

That God may welcome into his glory those of our family and friends who have departed this life.
We pray to the Lord:

R. Lord, hear our prayer.

That God may give a place in the kingdom of heaven to all the faithful departed.
We pray to the Lord:

R. Lord, hear our prayer.

O God,
Creator and Redeemer of all the faithful,
grant to the souls of your departed servants
release from all their sins.
Hear our prayers for those we love
and give them the pardon they have always desired.
We ask this through Christ our Lord.

R. Amen.

3   Brothers and sisters, Jesus Christ is risen from the dead and sits at the right hand of the Father where he intercedes for his Church. Confident that God hears the voices of those who trust in the Lord Jesus, we join our prayers to his:

In baptism N. received the light of Christ. Scatter the darkness now and lead him/her over the waters of death.
Lord, in your mercy:

R. Hear our prayer.

Our brother/sister N. was nourished at the table of the Savior. Welcome him/her into the halls of the heavenly banquet.
Lord, in your mercy:

R. Hear our prayer.

[For a religious: Our brother/sister N. spent his/her life following Jesus, poor, chaste, and obedient. Count him/her among all holy men and women who sing in your courts.
Lord, in your mercy:

R. Hear our prayer.]

[For a bishop or priest: Our brother N. shared in the priesthood of Jesus Christ, leading God's people in prayer and worship. Bring him into your presence where he will take his place in the heavenly liturgy.
Lord, in your mercy:

R. Hear our prayer.]

[For a deacon: Our brother N. served God's people as a deacon of the Church. Prepare a place for him in the kingdom whose coming he proclaimed.
Lord, in your mercy:

R. Hear our prayer.]

Many friends and members of our families have gone before us and await the kingdom. Grant them an everlasting home with your Son.
Lord, in your mercy:

R. Hear our prayer.

Many people die by violence, war, and famine each day. Show your mercy to those who suffer so unjustly these sins against your love, and gather them to the eternal kingdom of peace.
Lord, in your mercy:

R. Hear our prayer.

Those who trusted in the Lord now sleep in the Lord. Give refreshment, rest, and peace to all whose faith is known to you alone.
Lord, in your mercy:

R. Hear our prayer.

[For the mourners: The family and friends of N. seek comfort and consolation. Heal their pain and dispel the darkness and doubt that come from grief.
Lord, in your mercy:

R. Hear our prayer.]

We are assembled here in faith and confidence to pray for our brother/sister N. Strengthen our hope so that we may live in the expectation of your Son's coming.
Lord, in your mercy:

R. Hear our prayer.

Lord God,
giver of peace and healer of souls,
hear the prayers of the Redeemer, Jesus Christ,
and the voices of your people,
whose lives were purchased by the blood of the Lamb.
Forgive the sins of all who sleep in Christ
and grant them a place in the kingdom.

We ask this through Christ our Lord.

R. Amen.

4   Let us turn to Christ Jesus with confidence and faith in the power of his cross and resurrection:

Risen Lord, pattern of our life for ever:
Lord, have mercy.

R. Lord, have mercy.

Promise and image of what we shall be:
Lord, have mercy.

R. Lord, have mercy.

Son of God who came to destroy sin and death:
Lord, have mercy.

R. Lord, have mercy.

Word of God who delivered us from the fear of death:
Lord, have mercy.

R. Lord, have mercy.

Crucified Lord, forsaken in death, raised in glory:
Lord, have mercy.

R. Lord, have mercy.

Lord Jesus, gentle Shepherd who bring rest to our souls, give
peace to N. for ever:
Lord, have mercy.

R. Lord, have mercy.

Lord Jesus, you bless those who mourn and are in pain. Bless
N.'s family and friends who gather around him/her today:
Lord, have mercy.

R. Lord, have mercy.

5   A baptized child

Jesus is the Son of God and the pattern for our own creation.
His promise is that one day we shall truly be like him. With
our hope founded on that promise, we pray:

That God will receive our praise and thanksgiving for the life
of N.:
Let us pray to the Lord.

R. Lord, have mercy.

That God will bring to completion N.'s baptism into Christ:
Let us pray to the Lord.

R. Lord, have mercy.

That God will lead N. from death to life:
Let us pray to the Lord.

R. Lord, have mercy.

That all of us, N.'s family and friends, may be comforted in
our grief:
Let us pray to the Lord.

R. Lord, have mercy.

That God will grant release to those who suffer:
Let us pray to the Lord.

R. Lord, have mercy.

That God will grant peace to all who have died in the faith of
Christ:
Let us pray to the Lord.

R. Lord, have mercy.

That one day we may all share in the banquet of the Lord, praising God for victory over death:
Let us pray to the Lord.

R. Lord, have mercy.

6   A baptized child

The Lord Jesus is the lover of his people and our only sure hope.
Let us ask him to deepen our faith and sustain us in this dark
hour.

You became a little child for our sake, sharing our human life.
To you we pray:

R. Bless us and keep us, O Lord.

You grew in wisdom, age, and grace, and learned obedience
through suffering.
To you we pray:

R. Bless us and keep us, O Lord.

You welcomed children, promising them your kingdom.
To you we pray:

R. Bless us and keep us, O Lord.

You comforted those who mourned the loss of children and
friends.
To you we pray:

R. Bless us and keep us, O Lord.

You took upon yourself the suffering and death of us all.
To you we pray:

R. Bless us and keep us, O Lord.

You promised to raise up those who believe in you just as you
were raised up in glory by the Father.
To you we pray:

R. Bless us and keep us, O Lord.

Lord God,
you entrusted N. to our care
and now you embrace him/her in your love.

Take N. into your keeping
together with all children who have died.

Comfort us, your sorrowing servants,
who seek to do your will
and to know your saving peace.

We ask this through Christ our Lord.

R. Amen.

7   A deceased child

Let us pray for N., his/her family and friends, and for all God's people.

For N., child of God [and heir to the kingdom], that he/she be held securely in God's loving embrace now and for all eternity.
We pray to the Lord.

R. Lord, hear our prayer.

For N.'s family, especially his/her mother and father, [his/her brother(s) and sister(s)], that they feel the healing power of Christ in the midst of their pain and grief.
We pray to the Lord.

R. Lord, hear our prayer.

For N.'s friends, those who played with him/her and those who cared for him/her, that they be consoled in their loss and strengthened in their love for one another.
We pray to the Lord.

R. Lord, hear our prayer.

For all parents who grieve over the death of their children, that they be comforted in the knowledge that their children dwell with God.
We pray to the Lord.

R. Lord, hear our prayer.

For children who have died of hunger and disease, that these little ones be seated close to the Lord at his heavenly table. We pray to the Lord.

R. Lord, hear our prayer.

For the whole Church, that we prepare worthily for the hour of our death, when God will call us by name to pass from this world to the next.
We pray to the Lord.

R. Lord, hear our prayer.

Lord God,
you entrusted N. to our care
and now you embrace him/her in your love.

Take N. into your keeping
together with all children who have died.

Comfort us, your sorrowing servants,
who seek to do your will
and to know your saving peace.

We ask this through Christ our Lord.

R. Amen.

FINAL COMMENDATION AND FAREWELL

Invitation to Prayer

402 The following are alternatives to the invitation to prayer.

1 With faith in Jesus Christ, we must reverently bury the body of our brother/sister.

46
65

Let us pray with confidence to God, in whose sight all creation lives, that he will raise up in holiness and power the mortal body of our brother/sister and command his/her soul to be numbered among the blessed.

May God grant him/her a merciful judgment, deliverance from death, and pardon of sin. May Christ the Good Shepherd carry him/her home to be at peace with the Father. May he/she rejoice for ever in the presence of the eternal King and in the company of all the saints.

2 Our brother/sister N. has fallen asleep in Christ. Confident in our hope of eternal life, let us commend him/her to the loving mercy of our Father and let our prayers go with him/her. He/she was adopted as God's son/daughter in baptism and was nourished at the table of the Lord; may he/she now inherit the promise of eternal life and take his/her place at the table of God's children in heaven.

183

Let us pray also on our own behalf, that we who now mourn and are saddened may one day go forth with our brother/sister to meet the Lord of life when he appears in glory.

3 Because God has chosen to call our brother/sister N.
    from this life to himself,
we commit his/her body to the earth,
for we are dust and unto dust we shall return.

184

But the Lord Jesus Christ will change our mortal bodies
    to be like his in glory,
for he is risen, the firstborn from the dead.

So let us commend our brother/sister to the Lord,
that the Lord may embrace him/her in peace
and raise up his/her body on the last day.

4   Before we go our separate ways, let us take leave of our brother/ 18
     sister. May our farewell express our affection for him/her; may
     it ease our sadness and strengthen our hope. One day we shall
     joyfully greet him/her again when the love of Christ, which con-
     quers all things, destroys even death itself.

5   Trusting in God, we have prayed together for N. and now we 18
     come to the last farewell. There is sadness in parting, but we
     take comfort in the hope that one day we shall see N. again
     and enjoy his/her friendship. Although this congregation will
     disperse in sorrow, the mercy of God will gather us together
     again in the joy of his kingdom. Therefore let us console one
     another in the faith of Jesus Christ.

SONG OF FAREWELL

> 403 The following may be used as alternatives for the song of
> farewell. These responsories may also be used during the entrance
> procession in the celebration of the funeral liturgy.

1   Saints of God, come to his/her aid! 4
6
     Hasten to meet him/her, angels of the Lord!
     R. Receive his/her soul and present him/her to God the
     Most High.

     May Christ, who called you, take you to himself;
     may angels lead you to the bosom of Abraham. R.

     Eternal rest grant unto him/her, O Lord,
     and let perpetual light shine upon him/her. R.

2   Lord our God, receive your servant,
     for whom you shed your blood.
     R. Remember, Lord, that we are dust: like grass, like a
     flower of the field.

     Merciful Lord, I tremble before you,
     ashamed of the things I have done. R.

3   You knew me, Lord, before I was born.
     You shaped me into your image and likeness.
     R. I breathe forth my spirit to you, my Creator.

Merciful Lord, I tremble before you:
I am ashamed of the things I have done;
do not condemn me when you come in judgment. R.

4   I know that my Redeemer lives: 189
    on the last day I shall rise again.
    R. And in my flesh I shall see God.
       Or:
    R. On the last day I shall rise again.

    I shall see him myself, face to face;
    and my own eyes shall behold my Savior.

    Within my heart this hope I cherish:
    that in my flesh I shall see God. R.

5   I know that my Redeemer lives,   189
    And on that final day of days,
    His voice shall bid me rise again:
    Unending joy, unceasing praise!

    This hope I cherish in my heart:
    To stand on earth, my flesh restored,
    And, not a stranger but a friend,
    Behold my Savior and my Lord.

6   Lazarus you raised, O Lord, from the decay of the tomb.   190
    R. Grant your servant rest, a haven of pardon and peace.

    Eternal rest, O Lord,
    and your perpetual light. R.

7   You shattered the gates of bronze   191
    and preached to the spirits in prison.
    R. Deliver me, Lord, from the streets of darkness.

    A light and a revelation
    to those confined in darkness. R.

    "Redeemer, you have come,"
    they cried, the prisoners of silence. R.

    Eternal rest, O Lord,
    and your perpetual light. R.

Prayer of Commendation

404 The following prayers may be used as alternative forms of the prayer of commendation.

1   A baptized person

Into your hands, Father of mercies,
we commend our brother/sister N.
in the sure and certain hope
that, together with all who have died in Christ,
he/she will rise with him on the last day.

[We give you thanks for the blessings
which you bestowed upon N. in this life:
they are signs to us of your goodness
and of our fellowship with the saints in Christ.]

Merciful Lord,
turn toward us and listen to our prayers:
open the gates of paradise to your servant
and help us who remain
to comfort one another with assurances of faith,
until we all meet in Christ
and are with you and with our brother/sister for ever.

We ask this through Christ our Lord.

R. Amen.

2   A baptized child

Lord Jesus,
like a shepherd who gathers the lambs
to protect them from all harm,
you led N. to the waters of baptism
and shielded him/her in innocence.

Now carry this little one
on the path to your kingdom of light
where he/she will find happiness
and every tear will be wiped away.

To you be glory, now and for ever.

R. Amen.

3   A baptized child

Into your gentle keeping, O Lord,
we commend this child [N.].
Though our hearts are troubled,
we hope in your loving kindness.

By the sign of the cross
he/she was claimed for Christ,
and in the waters of baptism
he/she died with Christ to live in him for ever.

May the angels, our guardians,
lead N. now to paradise
where your saints will welcome him/her
and every tear will be wiped away.
There we shall join in songs of praise for ever.

We ask this through Christ our Lord.

R. Amen.

RITE OF COMMITTAL

Prayer over the Place of Committal

405 One of the following may be used to bless the tomb or grave.

1 Lord Jesus Christ, 71
by your own three days in the tomb,
you hallowed the graves of all who believe in you
and so made the grave a sign of hope
that promises resurrection
even as it claims our mortal bodies.

Grant that our brother/sister may sleep here in peace
until you awaken him/her to glory,
for you are the resurrection and the life.
Then he/she will see you face to face
and in your light will see light
and know the splendor of God,
for you live and reign for ever and ever.

R. Amen.

2 O God, 19?
by whose mercy the faithful departed find rest,
bless this grave,
and send your holy angel to watch over it.

As we bury here the body of our brother/sister,
deliver his/her soul from every bond of sin,
that he/she may rejoice in you with your saints for ever.

We ask this through Christ our Lord.

R. Amen.

3   Almighty God, 194
    you created the earth and shaped the vault of heaven;
    you fixed the stars in their places.
    When we were caught in the snares of death
    you set us free through baptism;
    in obedience to your will
    our Lord Jesus Christ
    broke the fetters of hell and rose to life,
    bringing deliverance and resurrection
    to those who are his by faith.
    In your mercy look upon this grave,
    so that your servant may sleep here in peace;
    and on the day of judgment raise him/her up
    to dwell with your saints in paradise.
    We ask this through Christ our Lord.
    R. Amen.

4   God of endless ages, 195
    through disobedience to your law
    we fell from grace
    and death entered the world;
    but through the obedience and resurrection of your Son
    you revealed to us a new life.
    You granted Abraham, our father in faith,
    a burial place in the promised land;
    you prompted Joseph of Arimathea
    to offer his own tomb for the burial of the Lord.
    In a spirit of repentance
    we earnestly ask you
    to look upon this grave and bless it,
    so that, while we commit to the earth the body of your servant N.
    his/her soul may be taken into paradise.
    We ask this through Christ our Lord.
    R. Amen.

COMMITTAL

406 The following are alternative forms of the committal.

1   General

Because God has chosen to call our brother/sister N.   55
    from this life to himself,   72
we commit his/her body to the earth
    [or the deep or the elements or its resting place],
for we are dust and unto dust we shall return.

But the Lord Jesus Christ will change our mortal bodies
    to be like his in glory,
for he is risen, the firstborn from the dead.

So let us commend our brother/sister to the Lord,
that the Lord may embrace him/her in peace
and raise up his/her body on the last day.

2   General

In sure and certain hope of the resurrection to eternal life
    through our Lord Jesus Christ,
we commend to Almighty God
    our brother/sister N. [N., our child],
and we commit his/her body to the ground
    [or the deep or the elements or its resting place]:
earth to earth, ashes to ashes, dust to dust.

The Lord bless him/her and keep him/her,
the Lord make his face to shine upon him/her
    and be gracious to him/her,
the Lord lift up his countenance upon him/her
    and give him/her peace.

3   For ashes

My friends,
as we prepare to bury [entomb]
    the ashes of our brother/sister,
we recall that our bodies bear the imprint of the first creation
    when they were fashioned from dust;

but in faith we remember, too, that by the new creation
we also bear the image of Jesus who was raised to glory.

In confident hope that one day God will raise us and transform
our mortal bodies, let us pray.

Pause for silent prayer.

Faithful God,
Lord of all creation,
you desire that nothing redeemed by your Son
will ever be lost,
and that the just will be raised up on the last day.

Comfort us today with the word of your promise
as we return the ashes of our brother/sister to the earth.

Grant N. a place of rest and peace
where the world of dust and ashes has no dominion.
Confirm us in our hope that he/she will be created anew
on the day when you will raise him/her up in glory
to live with you and all the saints
for ever and ever.

R. Amen.

4   For burial at sea

Lord God,
by the power of your Word
you stilled the chaos of the primeval seas,
you made the raging waters of the Flood subside,
and calmed the storm on the sea of Galilee.
As we commit the body of our brother/sister N. to the deep,
grant him/her peace and tranquility
until that day when he/she and all who believe in you
will be raised to the glory of new life
promised in the waters of baptism.

We ask this through Christ our Lord.

R. Amen.

INTERCESSIONS

407 The following may be used as an alternative form of the
intercessions.

1   For our brother/sister, N., let us pray to our Lord Jesus Christ,   56
who said, "I am the resurrection and the life. Whoever believes   75
in me shall live even in death and whoever lives and believes
in me shall never die."

Lord, you consoled Martha and Mary in their distress; draw
near to us who mourn for N., and dry the tears of those who
weep.
We pray to the Lord.

R. Lord, have mercy.

You wept at the grave of Lazarus, your friend; comfort us in
our sorrow.
We pray to the Lord.

R. Lord, have mercy.

You raised the dead to life; give to our brother/sister eternal life.
We pray to the Lord.

R. Lord, have mercy.

You promised paradise to the repentant thief; bring N. to the
joys of heaven.
We pray to the Lord:

R. Lord, have mercy.

Our brother/sister was washed in baptism and anointed with
the Holy Spirit; give him/her fellowship with all your saints.
We pray to the Lord.

R. Lord, have mercy.

He/she was nourished with your body and blood; grant him/her
a place at the table in your heavenly kingdom.
We pray to the Lord.

R. Lord, have mercy.

Comfort us in our sorrow at the death of N.; let our faith be
our consolation, and eternal life our hope.
We pray to the Lord.

R. Lord, have mercy.

God of holiness and power,
accept our prayers on behalf of your servant N.;
do not count his/her deeds against him/her,
for in his/her heart he/she desired to do your will.
As his/her faith united him/her to your people on earth,
so may your mercy join him/her to the angels in heaven.

We ask this through Christ our Lord.

R. Amen.

2   Dear friends, our Lord comes to raise the dead and comforts
     us with the solace of his love. Let us praise the Lord Jesus Christ.

Word of God, Creator of the earth to which N. now returns:
in baptism you called him/her to eternal life to praise your
Father for ever:
Lord, have mercy.

R. Lord, have mercy.

Son of God, you raise up the just and clothe them with the glory
of your kingdom:
Lord, have mercy.

R. Lord, have mercy.

Crucified Lord, you protect the soul of N. by the power of your
cross, and on the day of your coming you will show mercy to
all the faithful departed:
Lord, have mercy.

R. Lord, have mercy.

Judge of the living and the dead, at your voice the tombs will
open and all the just who sleep in your peace will rise and sing
the glory of God:
Lord, have mercy.

R. Lord, have mercy.

All praise to you, Jesus our Savior, death is in your hands and
all the living depend on you alone:
Lord, have mercy.

R. Lord, have mercy.

Concluding Prayer

408 One of the following may be used as an alternative to the concluding prayer.

1   Listen, O God, to the prayers of your Church
    on behalf of the faithful departed,
    and grant to your servant N.,
    whose funeral we have celebrated today,
    the inheritance promised to all your saints.
    We ask this through Christ our Lord.
    R. Amen.

2   Loving God, from whom all life proceeds
    and by whose hand the dead are raised again,
    though we are sinners, you wish always to hear us.
    Accept the prayers we offer in sadness for your servant N.:
    deliver his/her soul from death,
    number him/her among your saints
    and clothe him/her with the robe of salvation
    to enjoy for ever the delights of your kingdom.
    We ask this through Christ our Lord.
    R. Amen.

3   Lord God,
    whose days are without end
    and whose mercies beyond counting,
    keep us mindful
    that life is short and the hour of death unknown.
    Let your Spirit guide our days on earth
    in the ways of holiness and justice,
    that we may serve you
    in union with the whole Church,
    sure in faith, strong in hope, perfected in love.
    And when our earthly journey is ended,
    lead us rejoicing into your kingdom,
    where you live for ever and ever.
    R. Amen.

21 HOLY COMMUNION OUTSIDE MASS

INVITATION TO COMMUNION

409 If there is to be communion, the minister shows the eucharistic bread to those present, saying:

This is the Lamb of God
who takes away the sins of the world.
Happy are those who are called to his supper.

All then respond:

Lord, I am not worthy to receive you,
but only say the word and I shall be healed.

Those present then receive communion in the usual way.

PRAYER AFTER COMMUNION

410 When all have received communion, the minister then says one of the following prayers after communion:

Let us pray.

All pray in silence for a brief period.

A   Outside the Easter season

Lord God,
your Son Jesus Christ gave us
the sacrament of his body and blood
to guide us on our pilgrim way to your kingdom.
May our brother/sister N., who shared in the eucharist,
come to the banquet of life Christ has prepared for us.

We ask this through Christ our Lord.

R. Amen.

B   Outside the Easter season

Father, all-powerful God,
we pray for our brother/sister N.
whom you have called from this world.
May this eucharist cleanse him/her,
forgive his/her sins,
and raise him/her up to eternal joy in your presence.

We ask this through Christ our Lord.

R. Amen.

C   During the Easter season
Lord God,
may the death and resurrection of Christ
which we celebrate in this eucharist
bring our brother/sister N. the peace of your eternal home.

We ask this in the name of Jesus the Lord.

R. Amen.

D   A baptized child
Lord,
hear the prayers of those who share in the body and blood
    of your Son.
Comfort those who mourn for this child
and sustain them with the hope of eternal life.

We ask this through Christ our Lord.

R. Amen.

E   A baptized child
Lord,
you feed us with the gift of your eucharist.
May we rejoice with this child
at the feast of eternal life in your kingdom.

We ask this through Christ our Lord.

R. Amen.

F   A child who died before baptism
Lord,
hear the prayers of those who share in the body and blood
    of your Son.
By these sacred mysteries
you have filled them with hope of eternal life.
May they be comforted in the sorrows of this present life.

We ask this in the name of Jesus the Lord.

R. Amen.

ORDO EXSEQUIARUM, 1969, INTRODUCTION*

1 At the funerals of its children the Church confidently celebrates Christ's paschal mystery. Its intention is that those who by baptism were made one body with the dead and risen Christ may with him pass from death to life. In soul they are to be cleansed and taken up into heaven with the saints and elect; in body they await the blessed hope of Christ's coming and the resurrection of the dead.

The Church, therefore, offers the eucharistic sacrifice of Christ's Passover for the dead and pours forth prayers and petitions for them. Because of the communion of all Christ's members with each other, all of this brings spiritual aid to the dead and the consolation of hope to the living.

2 As they celebrate the funerals of their brothers and sisters, Christians should be intent on affirming their hope for eternal life. They should not, however, give the impression of either disregard or contempt for the attitudes or practices of their own time and place. In such matters as family traditions, local customs, burial societies, Christians should willingly acknowledge whatever they perceive to be good and try to transform whatever seems alien to the Gospel. Then the funeral ceremonies for Christians will both manifest paschal faith and be true examples of the spirit of the Gospel.

3 Although any form of empty display must be excluded, it is right to show respect for the bodies of the faithful departed, which in life were the temple of the Holy Spirit. This is why it is worthwhile that there be an expression of faith in eternal life and the offering of prayers for the deceased, at least at the more significant times between death and burial.

Depending on local custom, such special moments include the vigil at the home of the deceased, the laying out of the body, and the carrying of the body to the place of burial. They should be marked by the gathering of family and friends and, if possible, of the whole community to receive in the liturgy of the word the consolation of hope, to offer together the eucharistic sacrifice, and to pay last respects to the deceased by a final farewell.

4 To take into account in some degree conditions in all parts of the world, the present rite of funerals is arranged on the basis of three models:

1. The first envisions three stations, namely, at the home of the deceased, at the church, and at the cemetery.
2. The second covers only two stations, at the church and at the cemetery.
3. The third involves only one station, which is at the home of the deceased.

5 The first model for a funeral is practically the same as the former rite in the Roman Ritual. It includes as a rule, at least in country places, three stations, namely, at the home of the deceased, at the church, and at the cemetery, with two processions in between. Especially in large cities, however, processions are seldom held or are inconvenient for various reasons. As for the stations at home and at the cemetery, priests sometimes are unable to lead them because of a shortage of clergy or the distance of the cemetery from the church. In view of these considerations, the faithful must be urged to recite the usual psalms and prayers themselves when there is no deacon or priest present. If that is impossible, the home and cemetery stations are to be omitted.

6 In this first model the station at the church consists as a rule in the celebration of the funeral Mass; this is forbidden only during the Easter triduum, on solemnities, and on the Sundays of Advent, Lent, and the Easter season. Pastoral reasons may on occasion require that a funeral be celebrated in the church without a Mass (which in all cases must, if possible, be celebrated on another day within a reasonable time); in that case a liturgy of the word is prescribed absolutely. Therefore, the station at the church always includes a liturgy of the word, with or without a Mass, and the rite hitherto called "absolution" of the

---

* As emended by the Congregation for the Sacraments and Divine Worship, 12 September 1983.

dead and henceforth to be called "the final commendation and farewell."

7 The second funeral plan consists of only two stations, namely, at the cemetery, that is, at the cemetery chapel, and at the grave. This plan does not envision a eucharistic celebration, but one is to take place, without the body present, before the actual funeral or after the funeral.

8 A funeral rite, following the third model, to be celebrated in the deceased's home may perhaps in some places be regarded as pointless. Yet in certain parts of the world it seems needed. In view of the many diversities, the model purposefully does not go into details. At the same time it seemed advisable at least to set out guidelines so that this plan might share certain elements with the other two, for example, the liturgy of the word and the rite of final commendation or farewell. The detailed directives will be left to the conferences of bishops to settle.

9 In the future preparation of particular rituals conformed to the Roman Ritual, it will be up to the conference of bishops either to keep the three models or to change their arrangement or to omit one or other of them. For it is quite possible that in any particular country one model, for example, the first with its three stations, is the only one in use and as such the one to be kept. Elsewhere all three may be needed. The conference of bishops will make the arrangements appropriate to what particular needs require.

10 After the funeral Mass the rite of final commendation and farewell is celebrated.

The meaning of the rite does not signify a kind of purification of the deceased; that is what the eucharistic sacrifice accomplishes. Rather it stands as a farewell by which the Christian community together pays respect to one of its members before the body is removed or buried. Death, of course, always has involved an element of separation, but Christians as Christ's members are one in him and not even death can part them from each other.[1]

The priest's opening words are to introduce and explain this rite, a few moments

of silence are to follow, then the sprinkling with holy water and the incensation, then a song of farewell. Not only is it useful for all to sing this song, composed of a pertinent text set to a suitable melody, but all should have the sense of its being the high point of the entire rite.

Also to be seen as signs of farewell are the sprinkling with holy water, a reminder that through baptism the person was marked for eternal life, and the incensation, signifying respect for the body as the temple of the Holy Spirit.

The rite of final commendation and farewell may only be held during an actual funeral service, that is, when the body is present.

11 In any celebration for the deceased, whether a funeral or not, the rite attaches great importance to the readings from the word of God. These proclaim the paschal mystery, they convey the hope of being gathered together again in God's kingdom, they teach remembrance of the dead, and throughout they encourage the witness of a Christian life.

12 In its good offices on behalf of the dead, the Church turns again and again especially to the prayer of the psalms as an expression of grief and a sure source of trust. Pastors are, therefore, to make an earnest effort through an effective catechesis to lead their communities to a clearer and deeper grasp of at least some of the psalms provided for the funeral liturgy. With regard to other chants that the rite frequently assigns on pastoral grounds, they are also to seek to instill a "warm and living love of Scripture"[2] and a sense of its meaning in the liturgy.

13 In its prayers the Christian community confesses its faith and makes compassionate intercession for deceased adults that they may reach their final happiness with God. The community's belief is that deceased children whom through baptism God has adopted as his own have already attained that blessedness. But the commu-

---

[1] See Simeon of Thessalonica, *De ordine sepulturae*: PG 155, 685 B.

[2] Vatican Council II, Constitution on the Liturgy *Sacrosanctum Concilium*, art. 24.

nity pours forth its prayers on behalf of their parents, as well as for all the loved ones of the dead, so that in their grief they will experience the comfort of faith.

14 The practice of reciting the office of the dead on the occasion of funerals or at other times is based in some places on particular law, on an endowment for this purpose, or on custom. The practice may be continued, provided the office is celebrated becomingly and devoutly. But in view of the circumstances of contemporary life and for pastoral considerations, a Bible vigil or celebration of God's word may be substituted.

14bis Funeral rites are to be celebrated for catechumens. In keeping with the provisions of CIC, can. 1183, celebration of funeral rites may also be granted to:

1. children whose baptism was intended by their parents but who died before being baptized;
2. baptized members of another Church or non-Catholic Ecclesial Community at the discretion of the local Ordinary, but not if it is known that they did not wish this nor if a minister of their own is available.

15 Funeral rites are to be granted to those who have chosen cremation, unless there is evidence that their choice was dictated by anti-Christian motives.

The funeral is to be celebrated according to the model in use in the region. It should be carried out in a way, however, that clearly expresses the Church's preference for the custom of burying the dead, after the example of Christ's own will to be buried, and that forestalls any danger of scandalizing or shocking the faithful.

The rites usually held in the cemetery chapel or at the grave may in this case take place within the confines of the crematorium and, for want of any other suitable place, even in the crematorium room. Every precaution is to be taken against the danger of scandal or religious indifferentism.

Offices and Ministries toward the Dead

16 In the celebration of a funeral all the members of the people of God must re-

member that to each one a role and an office is entrusted: to relatives and friends, funeral directors, the Christian community as such, finally, the priest, who as the teacher of faith and the minister of comfort presides at the liturgical rites and celebrates the eucharist.

17 All should also be mindful, and priests especially, that as they commend the deceased to God at a funeral, they have a responsibility as well to raise the hopes of those present and to build up their faith in the paschal mystery and the resurrection of the dead. They should do so in such a way, however, that as bearers of the tenderness of the Church and the comfort of faith, they console those who believe without offending those who grieve.

18 In preparing and planning a funeral, priests are to keep in mind with delicate sensitivity not only the identity of the deceased and the circumstances of the death, but also the grief of the bereaved and their needs for a Christian life. Priests are to be particularly mindful of those who attend the liturgical celebration or hear the Gospel because of the funeral, but are either non-Catholics or Catholics who never or seldom take part in the eucharist or have apparently lost the faith. Priests are, after all, the servants of Christ's Gospel on behalf of all.

19 Except for the Mass, a deacon may conduct all the funeral rites. As pastoral needs require, the conference of bishops, with the Apostolic See's permission, may even depute a layperson for this.

When there is no priest or deacon, it is recommended that in funerals according to the first model laypersons carry out the stations at the home and cemetery; the same applies generally to all vigils for the dead.

20 Apart from the marks of distinction arising from a person's liturgical function or holy orders and those honors due to civil authorities according to liturgical law,[3] no special honors are to be paid in the cele-

---

[3] See Vatican Council II, Constitution on the Liturgy *Sacrosanctum Concilium*, art. 32.

bration of a funeral to any private persons or classes of persons.

Adaptations Belonging to the Conferences of Bishops

21 In virtue of the Constitution on the Liturgy (art. 63 b), the conferences of bishops have the right to prepare a section in particular rituals corresponding to the present section of the Roman Ritual and adapted to the needs of the different parts of the world. This section is for use in the regions concerned, once the *acta* of the conferences have been reviewed by the Apostolic See.

In making such adaptations it shall be up to the conferences of bishops:

1. to decide on the adaptations, within the limits laid down in the present section of the Roman Ritual;
2. to weigh carefully and prudently which elements from the traditions and culture of individual peoples may be appropriately admitted and accordingly to propose to the Apostolic See further adaptations considered to be useful or necessary that will be introduced into the liturgy with its consent;
3. to retain elements of particular rituals that may now exist, provided they are compatible with the Constitution on the Liturgy and contemporary needs, or to adapt such elements;
4. to prepare translations of the texts that are truly suited to the genius of the different languages and cultures and, whenever appropriate, to add suitable melodies for singing;
5. to adapt and enlarge this Introduction in the Roman Ritual in such a way that the ministers will fully grasp and carry out the meaning of the rites;
6. in editions of the liturgical books to be prepared under the direction of the conferences of bishops, to arrange the material in a format deemed to be best suited to pastoral practice; this is to be done in such a way, however, that none of the contents of this *editio typica* are omitted.

When added rubrics or texts are judged useful, these are to be set off by some typographical symbol or mark from the rubrics and texts of the Roman Ritual.

22 In drawing up particular rituals for funerals, it shall be up to the conferences of bishops:

1. to give the rite an arrangement patterned on one or more of the models, in the way indicated in no. 9;
2. to replace the formularies given in the basic rite with others taken from those in Chapter VI, should this seem advantageous;
3. to add different formularies of the same type whenever the Roman Ritual provides optional formularies (following the rule given in no. 21, 6);
4. to decide whether laypersons should be deputed to celebrate funerals (see no. 19);
5. to decree, whenever pastoral considerations dictate, omission of the sprinkling with holy water and the incensation or to substitute another rite for them;
6. to decree for funerals the liturgical color that fits in with the culture of peoples, that is not offensive to human grief, and that is an expression of Christian hope in the light of the paschal mystery.

Function of the Priest in Preparing and Planning the Celebration

23 The priest is to make willing use of the options allowed in the rite, taking into consideration the many different situations and the wishes of the family and the community.

24 The rite provided for each model is drawn up in such a way that it can be carried out with simplicity; nevertheless the rite supplies a wide selection of texts to fit various contingencies. Thus, for example:

1. As a general rule all texts are interchangeable, in order to achieve, with the help of the community or the family, a closer reflection of the actual circumstances of each celebration.
2. Some elements are not assigned as obligatory, but are left as optional additions, as, for example, the prayer for

the mourners at the home of the deceased.

3. In keeping with liturgical tradition, a wide freedom of choice is given regarding the texts provided for processions.

4. When a psalm listed or suggested for a liturgical reason may present a pastoral problem, another psalm may be substituted. Even within the psalms a verse or verses that seem to be unsuitable from a pastoral standpoint may be omitted.

5. The texts of prayers are always written in the singular, that is, for one deceased male. Accordingly, in any particular case the text is to be modified as to gender and number.

6. In prayers the lines within parentheses may be omitted.

25 Like the entire ministry of the priest to the dead, celebration of the funeral liturgy with meaning and dignity presupposes a view of the priestly office in its inner relationship with the Christian mystery.

Among the priest's responsibilities are:

1. to be at the side of the sick and dying, as is indicated in the proper section of the Roman Ritual;

2. to impart catechesis on the meaning of Christian death;

3. to comfort the family of the deceased, to sustain them amid the anguish of their grief, to be as kind and helpful as possible, and, through the use of the resources provided and allowed in the ritual, to prepare with them a funeral celebration that has meaning for them;

4. finally, to fit the liturgy for the dead into the total setting of the liturgical life of the parish and his own pastoral ministry.

BIBLICAL INDEX